For Alan Neuman —

Whose philosophy is beautifully expressed on pages 11-13.

Walter H. Uphoff

Mary Jo Uphoff —

Other books by Walter and Mary Jo Uphoff:
   New Psychic Frontiers: Your Key to New Worlds (3 editions)

   Neuland der Psyche—der Schuessel zu neuen Welten der PSIForschung (Wilhelm Heyne Verlag Munich)

   Group Health Plan: An American Success Story of Prepaid Health Care

by Walter H. Uphoff:

   The Kohler Strike: Its Socio-Economic Causes and Effects

   Kohler on Strike: Thirty Years of Conflict

This book also distributed by:

SAMUEL WEISER, INC., 740 Broadway, New York, NY 10003

and

WESTWOOD PUBLISHING CO., 312 Riverdale Drive, Glendale, CA 91204

MIND over MATTER

Implications of Masuaki Kiyota's PK Feats with Metal and Film

For: Healing
Physics
Psychiatry
War & Peace
Et cetera

Walter and Mary Jo Uphoff

foreword by Berthold E. Schwarz, M.D.

Published in the U.S. by:
NEW FRONTIERS CENTER
Oregon, Wisconsin 53575

and simultaneously in Great Britain by:
COLIN SMYTHE Ltd.
Gerrards Cross, Bucks

First Edition published in the
United States of America, October 1980
by New Frontiers Center
Oregon, Wisconsin 53575

and simultaneously in Great Britain
by Colin Smythe Ltd.
  Gerrards Cross, Bucks, England

© Walter and Mary Jo Uphoff
  Oregon, Wisconsin 53575

Library of Congress Catalog Card No. 80-81495
ISBN 0-86140-062-3

Produced in the United States of America

Printed by Bolger Publications, Inc.
Minneapolis, MN 55414

Hard cover ISBN 0-86140-079-8

DEDICATION

Dedicated to all who have the courage to examine the evidence for things that may seem to be outside of generally accepted belief systems, and the ability to defer judgement, both "pro" and "con," until enough evidence has accumulated to warrant even a tentative conclusion, and the integrity and flexibility of mind to modify their conclusions if the evidence strongly suggests they are in error.

(This includes the authors.)

CONTENTS

symbolism role in PK — strong psychics influence electrical components, resistors, diodes, magnetic tapes, bits of wire, etc.

FOREWORD

Beginning as skeptics, the Uphoffs have studied psychic phenomena for more than forty years. During the last four years, since Prof. Uphoff took early retirement from the University of Colorado, they have given a good deal of their attention, energies, affection and resources to their search of psi, possibly the ultimate reality. Earlier, their *New Psychic Frontiers,* an innovative parapsychology text, aroused wide interest by exploring psychic areas often ignored by others. Now, in *Mind Over Matter,* they present new and challenging material on psychokinesis. For example, they tell about two Japanese youths, principally Masuaki Kiyota, and to a lesser extent, Hiroto Yamashita, who have demonstrated extraordinary abilities in metal bending, thoughtography and telepathy. The Uphoffs observed the young men in many mind-boggling experiments in Japan and at their Wisconsin farm where these young psychics had their light moments and also participated in workshops directed by Prof. John Hasted and participated in by leading scientists.

Their American visit also included an all-too-brief stint at the Mayo Clinic. The Uphoffs have interviewed physicists, physicians and other experts in the pure and behavioral sciences who subjected the boys to ingenious tests. In addition to describing the technical criteria, including various devices and gadgets, the Uphoffs, by caring and giving of themselves, demonstrated a singular ability to establish a most necessary prerequisite for successful experiments—warm rapport with the youths.

Mrs. Uphoff's notes describe the interplay between some of the paranormal feats and the personalities of the boys. Although purists might object that anedcotal information should not be included, I strongly disagree. These sidelights are worthwhile and may be helpful in penetrating the mystery of psychokinesis. The Uphoffs give revealing glimpses into Masuaki's and Hiroto's characters, whimsicalities, and other emotional traits, some pertaining to the universality of youth, and some with specific cultural and familial aspects. The highly adaptable youths and the equally flexible Uphoffs graciously adjusted to these conditions, be they at the Kiyota home and restaurant in Japan, TV studios, or in the United States. Many of the reported items point the way for future experimentation and speculation. For instance, there are detailed clues in Masuaki's family history and in his mention of the cryptic Zenefu: "a life" without a body.

Mind Over Matter gives the reader a wide-angle, and at times, a highly personal perspective to psychokinesis by citing studies of other leading "mediums" like Uri Geller, Matthew Manning and Silvio. Supporting comments and articles by leading parapsychologists, East as well as West, do much to enhance the value of the book. There is a lively section on the role of the professional debunkers of psychokinesis and the influence of this on future research. Prof. Uphoff does not pull his punches and the reader, if not amused, might become incensed at reports of some of the chicanery and grossness perpetrated by the so-called "exposures." But he can read for himself and decide.

There is discussion about psychokinesis and the influence of training, the role of the group, and the significance of frustrating situations. The Uphoffs delve into the theoretical and possible practical applications of these unique abilities. For example, in medicine there are possible psychokinetic factors in such age-old questions as 1) why people get sick, and 2) how they get well. Related to this is also the fondly cherished hope that by studying psychokinesis in relation to interdependent psychic and psychodynamics, we human beings might better learn how to live with each other, as well as with ourselves.

In reference to military applications, Prof. Uphoff does not mince words about any theoretically possible destructive use of psychokinesis and the categorical need to come to grips with the menace of war to our shrinking world with its ever increasing population.

Mind Over Matter is a practical compendium that will be of interest to all who are curious about the nature of psychokinetic talent. Some may discover that they have hidden or latent abilities of their own. It is hoped that from this, gifted new experimenters and subjects will step forth and make discoveries which will push forward the frontiers of knowledge and advance an understanding of how these processes work. On the up-beat side, the Uphoffs have prepared a reasoned and expanded account of the near-limitless potential of a human being; and they present this intricate and complex subject matter in a straightforward way that is brave in outlook, measured in in-look, and something that will challenge thoughtful readers and serve as a model for future investigations.

Berthold E. Schwarz, M.D.
Montclair, New Jersey

PREFACE

In this book, we hope to pull aside the curtain on some areas of human capability and experience which have too frequently been ignored, denied or unexplored. It has long been known that we use only a small part of the mind's potential. Perhaps the greatest deterrent to making greater use of the untapped power of the mind is the culturally-supported, erroneous belief about what is possible or impossible. How can we be sure unless we try?

In one sense there is "nothing new under the sun." But in many ways mankind has gained insights through experience and experimentation that have broadened horizons and understanding. Many things which were regarded as "science fiction" or "impossible" only a few decades ago are now an accepted part of our day-to-day living. Electronic technology for example, which is now used for such things as airline travel reservations, in meteorology and satellite communications, in data processing, and in audio and video communications, has made possible things which our ancestors could not have imagined.

These things became possible only after one or more minds imagined it might be possible and proceeded to add to previous knowledge, new concepts to construct the first telephone, the first airplane, the first radio, etc. These were followed by the newer and improved inventions and designs and the end is not in sight.

This book deals with phenomena related to the power of the mind over matter. One book could not possibly cover the entire spectrum of phenomena or the range of psychokinesis and the explanations which have been advanced for it. It does present factual first-hand evidence and illustrations, as well as viewpoints of others, to give readers, both new and experienced in this field, additional information that can provide clues or insights into the nature and the power of the mind.

The material presented may well raise more questions than it answers, but that is a natural step in the learning process. We need to look at the evidence before we even make tentative judgements about the validity, significance, and meaning of the words and pictures contained in this book.

- What is the relationship of the mind to the brain?
- What is the role of the subconscious?
- What can hypnosis tell us about the role of the mind?

- Is the mind confined to our physical body or can it go on trips?
- What about such concepts as Jung's "collective unconscious"?
- What about "cosmic consciousness"?
- What evidence is there for an interconnectedness of all life at some seldom or dimly recognized level?
- Is psycho-kinetic ability present to some degree in everyone, but more fully developed in some individuals, just as certain abilities are more pronounced in some artists, musicians and inventors?
- What about the artists and inventors who report a sense of receiving inspiration or help from some force or intelligence outside themselves? (Chester F. Carlson, inventor of the xerox process, felt he owed much to "the other side" and left a generous bequest for the pursuit of psychic research. Artists, authors and composers like Yeats, Shelley, Mozart, Beethoven and Chopin experienced "frenzies of creativity" as they sought to record flashes of full-blown impressions which they felt came from outside themselves.)
- What can be done to help raise the level of consciousness so that humanity will have a better chance of living free from the threat of nuclear annihilation?
- When will heads of state and their military establishments mature to the point where differences and conflicts are resolved in non-military ways? (Chapter XIII)
- If Masuaki Kiyota can return exposed film to an unexposed state "through inverse energy" as postulated by Dr. T. Miyauchi (Chapter XIII), do we not have to modify our concepts of the mind?
- If the 26.7 and 34.5 megaherz frequencies emitted from the left frontal lobe of the two young psychics' brains, as reported by Prof. M. Suzuki and reported by Nippon TV Network, can light a flourescent tube, what else might be possible? (Chapters VI and XI)
- Was it coincidence, or did the radio frequencies emitted by Yamashita and Kiyota have something to do with an electronically-controlled garage door at the Hubbard home in Milwaukee opening "by itself" only on the one night the young men slept there? (Chapter VIII)

These are some of the questions the readers may want to ponder in the perusal of this book. The conditions under which the information and evidence were obtained are clearly stated so there should be no difficulty in distinguishing between first-hand evidence, anecdotal reports, and opinions and judgements.

Walter H. Uphoff
Mary Jo Uphoff
September 1980

ACKNOWLEDGEMENTS

How does one begin to acknowledge all the contributions made by others when writing a book? If Professor Walter Wier, director of the honors programs at the University of Colorado had not approved Walter's proposal to teach a survey course in parapsychology in 1970, we might not have been invited to write a book on the subject for Colin Smythe and Peter Bander, Gerrards Cross, England. Through Colin and Peter we met Matthew Manning of Linton/Cambridge whose paranormal talents in some ways are similar to those of Uri Geller whom we met later at the Book Fair in Frankfurt, Germany where our book was one of those publicized by the Colin Smythe publishing firm. Later we were to meet Geller again at Harold Sherman's Mind/Body/Spirit Workshop in St. Louis in June 1976.

Had we not written the book, *New Psychic Frontiers: Your Key to New Worlds,* Alan Neuman, a Hollywood producer, most likely would not have invited Walter to accompany him to the Philippines and Japan in the fall of 1976 to help locate psychic talent for filming the 90-minute special program, "Exploring the Unknown," (narrated by Burt Lancaster) presented on NBC-TV October 30, 1977.

If we had not known Harold Sherman and read his book, *Wonder Healers of the Philippines,* we would not have known about Dr. Hiroshi Motoyama and his research center in Tokyo. There Rande Brown, a young American who worked for Dr. Motoyama, arranged for Toshiaki Harada, Ph.D., a physicist working for Dr. Motoyama, to go with Walter to Dr. Tsutomu Miyauchi, the managing director of the Japan Nengraphy Association, to discuss possible subjects for the Neuman film. Dr. Miyauchi and Dr. Harada both accompanied him and Neuman to the Yoshinori Kiyota family home in Northeast Tokyo to meet their young son Masuaki who had already shown remarkable abilities in metal bending and nengraphy (thoughtography). Those who saw the NBC program may recall the scene of this young Japanese boy concentrating on a polaroid camera and producing a recognizable image of the Tokyo Tower.

This visit led to a continuing correspondence with the Kiyota father and son, a visit to them in Tokyo in March 1979, and an invitation to Masuaki and his friend Hiroto Yamashita to come to the U.S. during their school vacation in July and August 1979 to participate in further investigation of their exceptional psychic abilities. Scientists and investigators from various parts of the country participated in workshops in Madison, San Francisco and at our home where the two teenagers bent and twisted metal by PK and produced paranormal effects on film.

The report which we had planned for workshop attenders and others interested in psychokinesis (PK)—the phenomenon of producing observable effects with "mind power"—outgrew the form of a monograph and has become this book—so much data and material having accumulated concerning the feats of these boys and other persons who possess PK abilities in varying degrees.

We wish to thank all those who shared experiences and knowledge with us. They have contributed much which we hope will further the understanding of these remarkable persons and the dimensions of reality which the PK phenomenon represents. It should be of interest, and a challenge, to those who accept the occurrence of these events as well as to skeptics.

Our special thanks to Mr. Jun-Ichi Yaoi of the Nippon Television Network (NTV) for arranging to supply us with photos, some of which appear in Chapter VI. We are grateful also to Mr. Hedeye Yamaguchi and Mr. Seido Hino and the film crew for the impressive demonstration of patience they gave us when we witnessed the initial filming at the Kiyota home for the documentary they presented in Japan later in the year.

Mr. Miyauchi gave us two beautiful books of color illustrations and plates as evidence for paranormal effects on film. Prof. Shegemi Sasaki of the Electro-Communications University supplied us with more than a dozen professional papers (with English synopses) dealing with laboratory experiments with PK effects on metal, film, bamboo, etc. Mr. Yutaka Fukuda, a professional photographer who has closely observed and studied the paranormal effects these two young Japanese can produce on film, gave us both photos and illustrated reports on nengraphy experiments.

Prof. John B. Hasted, a British physicist who has worked extensively with a number of young metal benders, interrupted his vacation plans to come to lead discussions and participate in experiments at our workshops on "Psychokinesis and its Effects on Metal and Film"—a major contribution to this project.

Naturally the friendship of the Kiyota family and the complete willingness and cooperation of Masuaki Kiyota and Hiroto Yamashita in the experiments and demonstrations was the key to the study and observations which have been made. It is not possible to adequately express appreciation for their role as subjects in these experiments.

We wish also to thank:

Dr. Berthold E. Schwarz, author of *A Psychiatrist Looks at ESP, Parent-Child Telepathy,* etc., for his suggestion that some staff members at the Mayo Clinic, Rochester, Minnesota might be interested in running tests on the two boys;

The Mayo staff members, who skeptical but open-minded, took time to run the experiments, even though paranormal events only occurred after the electrodes had been removed from the boys' heads;

The Capital Times and *The Wisconsin State Journal* for providing an interesting case study of the sociology of belief systems, and how belief, as well as peer and "superior" pressures, affects reportage;

The Sheboygan Press for good coverage, even though the wire services did not consider the effects newsworthy or believable enough to carry the story. WTMJ-TV (Milwaukee) and WISC-TV and Cable 4 (Madison) as well as radio stations WIBA and WORT which aired interviews related to our guests from Japan;

Jamie Hubbard from the Asian Studies department at the University of Wisconsin who was helpful as interpreter until Elaine Morikawa arrived from Japan, and who translated the NTV videotape commentary so that those who saw the documentary at the workshops could better understand it;

Henry S. Dakin, Jeffrey Mishlove and Jean Millay at the Washington Research Center, San Francisco who provided hospitality to all of us while the experiments were conducted at the Research Center, and together with Brendan O'Regan from the Institute of Noetic Sciences, arranged a public program for the community and for interested persons from the Parapsychological Association convention who stayed over an extra day;

William E. Cox, Rolla, Missouri, from the staff of the Foundation for Research on the Nature of Man; Prof. John B. Hasted and Mark G. Shafer, University of California/Irvine, for permission to print their papers on their research findings on PK;

Toshihiko Maruta, M.D. psychiatrist at Mayo Clinic who was helpful translating and summarizing the essential content of some research reports from Prof. Shegemi Sasaki.

In the broader areas of PK we are indebted to Dr. Hans Bender, Dr. Friedbert Karger, Prof. Werner Schiebeler, Burkhard Heim, Dr. Sigrun Seutemann, Fr. Dr. Roswitha Rees-Dietz, Dr. Konstantin Raudive and others in Germany, and Dr. Hans Naegeli, Prof. Alex Schneider and Paul and Edith Affolter in Switzerland for sharing knowledge, experiences and information with us on a number of occasions.

Others who should be mentioned include Prof. David Mack, of the metallurgy department and Prof. Richard G. Koegel in mechanical engineering at the University of Wisconsin who ran tests relevant to Masuaki's spoon bending; Laurence J. Venne, technical director of ESCO Steel Corporation, Portland, Oregon, and his two research staff members who examined the twisted cutlery and provided us information concerning the physical effects of the phenomenon; Glenn Austin, our neighbor and professional photographer; and Roger A. Severson, Professor of Educational Psychology at the University of Wisconsin and director of the Institute of Clinical Hypnosis, Madison, who as co-chairman of the New Frontiers Center planning committee, helped in countless ways to implement the PK project. The support of Richard Brostrum, Prof. Frank Meyer and Peter Rank, M.D., other members of the committee, was also much appreciated.

Articles and relevant excerpts from publications which indicate the range of viewpoints, pro and con, have been included. Our thanks to the following for illustrating the variety of views which have appeared in print: *Esotera, FATE magazine, Human Dimensions, Metals and Materials, National Enquirer, Newsweek, The Princeton Alumni Weekly, PSI-M, Psychic News, The Skeptical Inquirer,* and *TIME,* as well as to Alan Neuman for supplying the script related to Masuaki Kiyota's appearance in the program on NBC-TV.

Our thanks to Frank Farrelly, ACWS, psychotherapist, Madison, Wisconsin, and Roger A. Severson for reading sections of the manuscript while keeping an eye out for typographical errors, etc. which every author hopes will never get into print. We hope their help and our efforts have kept such errors at a minimum.

Photo credits: Glenn Austin, pages 16, 45, 54, 55; Yutaka Fukuda, pages 17, 52, 53, 55, 63, 101; Nippon TV Network, pages 59, 61 and picture on cover. David Sandell and Rich Righ of *The Capital Times* staff supplied photos for the articles on pages 117 and 122.

I. INTRODUCTION

By Walter H. Uphoff

Anyone who gathers evidence comes to realize that some findings are more specific, evidential, and compelling than others. It is, of course, desirable to go to primary sources whenever possible, and we have made it a practice to go to the original sources whenever we can.

People's experiences and philosophical outlook influence their perceptions or interpretations. As knowledge has become systematized, progress has been made on many fronts. Persons trained to do research in chemistry, physics, biology, etc. have drawn upon the accumulated knowledge in their fields to push the frontiers of learning forward with their own explorations. By and large, this has contributed enormously to the rate at which progress and technology have become part of our scientific world.

Our dictionary defines *science* as:

1. a branch of knowledge or study dealing with a body of facts or truths systematically arranged and showing the operation of general laws. 2. systematic knowledge of the physical and material world. 3. systematized knowledge of any kind. 4. any skill that reflects a precise application of facts or principles.

These definitions point to useful or practical ways to proceed in any area of knowledge, providing we do not assume that all "knowledge" or "facts" accumulated to date are final and immutable. There is a general tendency to move from doubt to possibility to probability to certainty. Since the path of scientific investigation is strewn with so much which has been modified or changed as new evidence came along, it should be obvious that it is desirable to view things as being *probable,* rather than absolutely true or false. Such an approach is more likely to enhance knowledge (although not in any absolute sense) than automatic acceptance of what those who have positions of power, influence or authority assert to be true—be it the value or limitations of x-ray treatment, chemotherapy, organic gardening, jogging, nuclear power, war, etc.

The scientific community feels more comfortable with evidence obtained in a laboratory or via a telescope, and if it is repeatable and reported by those considered experts in the field. Much is to be said for that approach if it is not pushed too far, but there are many instances where the biases and belief systems of scientific persons violate their own rules and result in judgements without adequate evidence simply because the phenomenon does, or does not fit their "real" world.

There could be more progress on many fronts if more scientists were to say: "On the basis of what I have learned and experienced to date, what you report seems quite improbable and I cannot accept it unless (or until) such impressive data is accumulated that a second look is warranted." Reports of very unusual events are difficult to deal with "scientifically." We think there is room for both the laboratory approach and the gathering of direct evidence from ordinary people, keeping in mind that memory distortion and interpretation may have a significant bearing on what finally "comes out in the wash."

Max Planck, the German Nobel prize-winning physicist said:

> New scientific truth does not triumph by convincing its opponents and making them see the light, but rather because its opponents die and a new generation grows up that is familiar with it.

We are optimistic enough to think that may be only partly true, but the history of science is replete with pioneers in astronomy, physics, biology, etc. who were shunned by their colleagues because their discoveries and theories were at variance with the dominant view of the times.

It is easier to understand phenomena which occur in our lifetime and which can be recorded on videotape or film, or observed in a laboratory setting. Interest in psychic phenomena has grown tremendously in the last decade because there has been both a "push" and a "pull" in that direction. The *push* comes from the inadequacies of presently held concepts to explain all the experiences encountered; the *pull* comes from the intriguing implications such evidence suggests about the nature of reality. This interest is obviously increased by reports of the unusual feats attributed to Uri Geller, Jean-Pierre Girard, Matthew Manning, Silvio, Ted Serios, and more recently, Yukio Ishii, Masuaki Kiyota, Hiroto Yamashita and others. Public opinion ranges all the way from rejection of these feats as fraud and trickery to acceptance of them as genuine paranormal phenomena.

In our observations of Geller, Manning, Kiyota and Yamashita we have not encountered any fraud or trickery, although that does not categorically prove that one or more of them may not, at times, or for that matter at all times, have performed feats by deception. But it is just as unscientific to allege fraud without evidence, or to generalize from one instance of what appeared to be fraud and claim that all a psychic does is trickery, as it is to assert that all reported PK phenomena are genuine. We can only speak for what we have personally observed and experienced and state why, in our judgement, we think the phenomena

Left: **Dr. Tsutomi Miyauchi gave us this picture of Masuaki taken when he was perhaps nine or ten years old. He was already doing the raised fingers gesture which appears in many photos of him.**
Right: **Masuaki with some of the twisted and contorted cutlery he had influenced at the time when his PK abilities were first discovered.**

we are familiar with are genuine.

We attended Uri Geller's lecture and demonstration at Harold Sherman's ESP Research Associates Foundation workshop in St. Louis, July 25, 1976. We witnessed about 200 persons bring watches to the stage, where after several minutes, most of them began running. The ticking was amplified by microphones placed near the pile of watches which was carefully guarded by several police so that none would be taken, since many of them were valuable.

Jeff Bergey, a jeweller in Oregon, Wisconsin, had given us a "junk" watch on which he had broken one end of the balance pivot to see what Geller could do with it. Mary Jo had this watch and did not get it to the stage before Geller requested, "Stop! That's enough! Those who still have watches, please take them to your seats and we will work on them afterward." He asked the audience to join him in commanding the watches to "Work! work! work!" and everyone participated in a lighthearted mood. The watch in Mary Jo's hand started running, although she was about fifty feet away from the stage in the Chase-Park Plaza Hotel where Geller was standing. A number of astonished people found their watches ticking away in their hands after Geller asked, "Now, let's see how many watches in the audience have started running."

At this point we have no adequate explanation for what happened, but there is no question that it did. How can Geller be accused of trickery when he was about fifty feet away and did not see or touch the watch? This watch ran for about thirteen hours and stopped the following noon, about two minutes after it was shown to David Hoy, a rival of Geller.

When we reached Bergey by phone on the morning of June 26th, he was non-plussed. The following spring, a young woman from Madison, Wisconsin, who has some psychic ability, held the watch a short time and it again started running. So long as it was wound, it ran for days. I took the watch to Dykman and to Goodman jewellers in Madison to be examined. Both repairmen said, "Why this watch shouldn't run—it's got a broken balance pivot," to which I replied, "Yes, I know. I just wanted to have it verified by an independent witness." The watch still keeps good time when wound, but only when lying flat. At first it would run in any position.

Hiroto Yamashita started a watch for Maurice Quirk in San Francisco and Masuaki Kiyota started another watch for W. E. Cox (see *Appendix:* paper by W. E. Cox "On the Recent Japanese Claims of Psychic Photography and Metal Bending.") We sent four "junk" watches supplied by Bergey, to Masuaki and Hiroto to see what they could do with them. Hiroto phoned in excitement all the way from Tokyo when he was able to start one of the watches sent to him. I have worn it for six months and it keeps accurate time. Masuaki returned two of the four watches sent to him. One keeps very good time; the second is erratic. Although we make no claims here for paranormality, we think this anecdotal evidence corroborates reports of watches and clocks starting in homes where people have watched Geller on TV. The usual argument advanced by skeptics—that the watches simply had dirty grease lodged in the gears which is warmed and liquified by heat from the hand—seems quite inadequate to explain why so many watches which were not in working order, have started and have run for years after a Geller program. Certainly a watch with a broken balance pivot is not likely to run because it was held in a warm hand.

We have learned from experiences like these and many others not to prejudge and not to use a broad brush in making claims that reported phenomena are either genuine or fraud. We have not been at all the places where Geller has appeared, so we cannot say if he cheats at times, as is so often asserted by his critics. Based on what we have witnessed, we believe that his talents are genuine. The same applies to Matthew Manning, Masuaki Kiyota and Hiroto Yamashita, Ted Serios and others whom we have observed perform psychic feats. We have no basis for concluding that they resorted to trickery on occasions when we were not present. Although deception and tricks are an essential element of a magician's performance, there is too much at stake for a psychic to risk the possibility of being caught at trickery. Once a person cheats or lies, s/he can never regain the complete confidence and respect of those who are interested in his or her work. *Wer einmal lueght, den glaubt man nicht, wenn er auch die Wahrheit spricht.* (He who lies once will not be believed, even when he tells the truth.) There are stories and rumors that Geller and others have resorted to trickery "when their powers failed" and there are those who claim that it is all trickery but we have no evidence to support that assertion in connection with our investigations of PK.*

What is Psychokinesis (PK)?

Defined in the simplest terms, it is "mind over matter." As researchers in parapsychology and other disciplines investigate what is often referred to as the physical manifestations of psychic phenomena, more sophisticated concepts and definitions will emerge. A growing number of physicists, psychiatrists and psychologists have tentative theories about energies involved when metal is bent in ways which could not normally occur if it were bent by brute force; or when images appear on film even when the shutter is not tripped; and when psychics, such as the well-known Nina Kulagina in the Soviet Union, can move objects by "the power of the mind."

Charles Panati, science writer for *Newsweek,* defines psychokinesis as "the placing of an object in motion by volition alone." Telekinesis, a term sometimes used interchangably with PK, is defined as the movement of material objects by some external force, untouched by either medium or sitters. Whether PK effects are solely the result of will power exerted by individuals, or whether there may be "help" from somewhere, is a question that does not have to be settled while getting evidence about paranormal events such as metal bending.

Students of psychic phenomena are familiar with PK events that go back as far as recorded history, including events recorded in the Bible. We are fully aware that events recorded from the past can only be considered as anecdotal and not scientifically proven, so we will not take much space to review the extensive history of PK phenomena. Only in retrospect have many of these events been interpreted as having a psychokinetic component. Since the evidence for PK has been

---

We have seen what we thought was a "phony" materialization and on another occasion took part in a skotography demonstration which did not seem genuine. We have also seen persons who have, or think they have, some psychic ability, give readings which were singularly unimpressive—perhaps a combination of a little psychically-obtained information, supplemented by a good imagination. On the other hand, we have also seen mediums like Ena Twigg, London, who get such precise information that the evidence for the claim that some can clairvoyantly or clairaudiently "tap into" other dimensions is very impressive.

frequently observed and often recorded or measured in laboratories, fraud and trickery seem totally inadequate to explain all that is reported.

The truly scientific approach considers ALL conceivable explanations for a phenomenon, putting them in a rank order from the most likely to the least likely, and leaving room for several other possible explanations which may not yet have been thought of. One should be willing to examine all the evidence, pro and con, and to modify the rank order if the evidence warrants. Any other approach is "scientific" in name only.

The first part of this book deals with the unique, although no longer rare, PK abilities of two young Japanese whom we have observed in Japan and the United States. The evidence that these lads possess such abilities, which many now believe are latent in a large number of persons, poses questions worth investigating. It is unfortunate that such persons are labelled "tricksters" by those with rigid belief systems, who have never met them or seen them demonstrate their talents. Should objective and thorough investigation someday show that the boys are merely "clever tricksters," we will certainly modify our rank order of possible explanations.

Although this book is titled *Mind Over Matter,* we do not mean to imply that such a simple dichotomy fully characterizes the area we are exploring. Those who have explored the broader areas of consciousness have often concluded that mind and matter are closely related and that we live in an interpenetrating universe with many dimensions or levels of reality. Modern technology, with its increasingly sensitive equipment, is causing many physicists to raise questions about what was at one time assumed to be a hard science.

Willis W. Harman, president of the Institute of Noetic Sciences, founded by the former astronaut, Edgar Mitchell, presented a paper at the 1979 meeting of the American Association for the Advancement of Science, entitled "The Role of Consciousness in the Physical World." The three points which he elaborated were:

1. Ordinary consciousness comprises but the most minute fraction of the total activity of the mind.
2. Mind is not brain. Mind is not limited in ways implied by models of the physical brain, even quantum-mechanical and holographical ones. The various states of consciousness and their contents are the primary data of human experience.
3. The return of spiritual experience. Scientists of an earlier generation were guilty of overclaiming when, with abundant *hubris** they dismissed religion as pre-scientific theories about matters on which scientists would eventually have the later word, if not the

---

**Excessive pride or self-confidence.*

last. To be sure, religionists were particularly vulnerable when they insisted that characteristics of the physical world, such as the relative positions of the Earth and Sun, the age of the Earth. . should be established by Holy Writ rather than empirical observation. But the scientists on the other hand, were egregiously arrogant in insisting that all the religious traditions of the world were based on illusion, since the realm of human experience they took as central was not caught in the net cast by science.

Curtis Fuller, publisher of *FATE* magazine quoted from a recent statement by the World Council of Churches:

> *One senses the prospect of a new and more comprehensive vision of reality. Both in science and in Christianity, in different ways, it is a vision of a wider truth and coherence which lies without our reach if each could find a way to free itself of the sterile conflict and protective armor of its past relationship with the other.*

Fuller reports that at its 1979 meeting there was a feeling that both science and religion have lost credibility in the eyes of the public because of the failures of each, and that each should remain open to the ideas of the other while retaining its own integrity. He concludes that their statement still falls far short of encompassing the basic conflict between religion and science because it does not deal with "the nature of reality." Rather than a mind vs. matter dualism Fuller sees the possibility of moving toward a unified concept which recognizes the two as inseparable. He quotes Gary Zukav, a Harvard psychologist and student of physics, who pointed out that "as science penetrated deeper into the subatomic world and discovered objects millions of times smaller than the nucleus of the atom, it appeared the act of observation itself had an organic impact on the object being observed, changed it from what it was."

Such concepts may bring us closer to comprehending the forces at work when gifted psychics affect metal, film, etc. A retired engineer whom we know, who never expected he could bend metal, when it happened said he merely "visualized the molecules expanding"—not a meaningful concept for metallurgists, but it worked. Do we really know to what extent we can direct, rather than disperse, the energies that come from or through the mind?

Why This Book?

It is our hope that persons actively working in the field of parapsychology may find the book of value in their work and for supplemental reading in parapsychology courses and in workshops on psychic phenomena—not as the final and complete answer, but as a compilation of specific information and illustrations which should stimulate discussion and inquiry in an area which can no longer be dismissed.

As can be seen from the Table of Contents, the Chapters II, III, IV, V, VI and VIII deal largely with the unique abilities of two young Japanese. Chapters VII, IX, XI, XII, and XIII discuss broader implications of PK. In Chapter X we discuss those who still claim there is little or no evidence for that which lies beyond the five senses, and who are embarked on a crusade to "expose" all "these charlatans" and "psychic hucksters."

Later in this book you will read about U.S. taxpayers' dollars being spent to check on young Kiyota's PK abilities, surprising as this may be for some members of the Committee for the Scientific Investigation of Claims of the Paranormal.

When the author was a student at the University of Wisconsin, he ridiculed someone who told him about some psychic experiences and was fortunate to be challenged by the question, "Do you consider yourself open-minded?" His "umbilical cord" was not so firmly attached to either the theological or scientific "establishment" that he was afraid to question, and this was the beginning of a life-long quest for whatever is true. For about thirty years he let the evidence accumulate until it became obvious to his skeptical mind that there was something worth exploring in the field of the paranormal. This interest has grown as we have come across more and more "white crows" and could not longer be satisfied with the conventional belief that all crows are black. We have also discovered that many people are more concerned with neatness than with accuracy; they want their world neatly defined and tend to rely heavily on authorities they respect—be it science, their church, or whatever, and find it difficult to live with uncertainty and ambiguity. As Prof. Roger Severson says, "a high level of 'ambiguity tolerance' is necessary when investigating the paranormal" because simple or precise answers do not readily emerge.

Some parapsychologists struggle to remain aloof from anecdotal evidence. We ourselves were also strongly indoctrinated about what is presumably possible and it has taken years to develop an attitude of letting the evidence accumulate and not being in a hurry to accept or reject.

This book is intended for those who are familiar with other psychic phenomena, those who would like to learn more about the field, as well as those who believe there is no compelling evidence for nonmaterial realities. We will let the evidence speak for itself and suggest that the reader suspend judgement, both for and against, until s/he has finished the book.

We hope this book will be read in the spirit in which it is written. Our lives have been greatly enriched by the writings of others. We recognize that on some aspects of the paranormal, there are others who would write with greater insights, but we do know that sharing our observations and experiences has contributed to understanding, provided assurance, or supported tentative conclusions which others had reached.

The evidence presented is in our files for those who are interested in additional documentation. As you read this account of a venture into what may be unfamiliar and strange territory, please keep in mind that we have honestly reported the information to which we had access. We have identified the circumstances under which we obtained the evidence, some of it in a laboratory setting and some based on personal reports and observations. The reader is free to decide how much can be integrated into his/her expanding world of reality.

Those who have read our earlier book, **New Psychic Frontiers,** or have heard us lecture, have often been eager to share some of their unusual or psychic experiences with us, once they were sure we would not laugh, or call them "crazy." With a growing interest in the paranormal, more and more people are eager to discuss experiences which they have kept to themselves or discussed only with their intimate associates because they did not want to risk ostracism or, in some cases, a promotion or their job.

Rather than wait six months or perhaps a year to get the material into print, we decided to prepare the manuscript for this book in camera-ready form so it could more quickly be available to workshop participants and others. It is being simultaneously published by Colin Smythe, Ltd. in England and New Frontiers Center, a non-profit foundation incorporated under Chapter 181 of the Wisconsin statutes, and committed to "the exploration and dissemination of evidence related to the broader dimensions of health (holistic), psychic phenomena, and survival."

As the reader may note, Mary Jo prefers the "low key" approach in writing. Each of us has written those sections in which we have had the greater interest. Walter, a professor most of his adult ife, is inclined to be more explicit, at times repetitious, for the sake of emphasis, agreeing with the saying, "Never underestimate a persons's intelligence or over-estimate his knowledge." In the author's teaching experience he found that students remember aphorisms or truisms long after they have forgotten thousands of words of prose. Some of these aphorisms and quotations which were helpful in his teaching are:

"Taint knowin' nothin' that does so much harm as knowin' too much that aint so."

"Imagination takes over when information stops."

"People are often down on things they are not up on."

"Pooling ignorance does not produce wisdom."

"It is not what a person believes, but why he believes it that reveals the quality of his thinking."

Believing also, that a picture is worth a thousand words, we have included numerous photos and photocopies in the text.

We invite readers to look at the evidence we have gathered and to speculate as to the implications. We hope that the "Et Cetera" at the end of the long sub-title will convey our impression that psychokinesis (PK) is a pervasive aspect of reality; and that mind and consciousness can and do interact with the physical dimensions of the universe in many dimly understood ways.

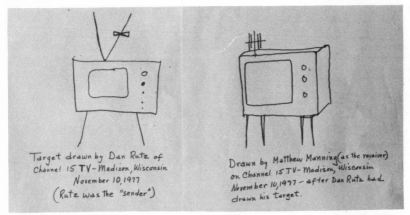

Target drawn by Dan Rutz of Channel 15 TV-Madison, Wisconsin November 10, 1977 (Rutz was the "sender")

Drawn by Matthew Manning (as the receiver) on Channel 15 TV-Madison, Wisconsin November 10, 1977 - after Dan Rutz had drawn his target.

When Matthew Manning, the young British psychic, was our guest in 1977, he was interviewed on live TV in Madison, Wisconsin. Dan Rutz, the interviewer and a skeptic, drew a target sketch *(left)* and Matthew drew his own telepathic impressions. Later Matthew said that he had received telepathically a two-dimensional impression of a television set, but thought it "too crude" so added the third dimension. He should have stopped after his impressions stopped—nevertheless an obvious "hit."

Some of the persons the reader will encounter in the book are introduced here: *(left to right)* Hiroto Yamashita, Elaine Morikawa, Masuaki Kiyota, Walter H. Uphoff, Dr. Tsutomu Miyauchi, Yutaka Fukuda, and Toru Ozaki. Photo by Mary Jo Uphoff.

II. Alan Neuman Films Masuaki

The Body/Mind/Spirit Workshops, which Harold Sherman's ESP Research Associates Foundation, Little Rock, Arkansas, sponsored annually for years, have brought together laymen, scientists and psychics of the U.S. for very worthwhile exchanges of ideas and experiences. It was at the 1976 Workshop in St. Louis where we met Alan Neuman, of Alan Neuman Productions, Inc., who had been producing and directing television programs and films, many of which had received honors and awards, including the *Wide, Wide World* series, *Meet the Press,* and many others.

Neuman was looking for psychic phenomena and psychic talent which could be dramatically and accurately portrayed for a long documentary film he had in mind and after reading our recently published book, *New Psychic Frontiers,* he concluded that because of our contacts with psychics and investigators in the U.S. and other countries, we could be of assistance. He came to spend part of several days at our home at Oregon, Wisconsin discussing his plans. His philosophy and approach were compatible with our own. In the resume he presented to us, he said:

We live in a time of great conflict. Individuals, nations, the earth itself is endangered. Violence and disease, corruption and decay, deprivation—both physical and spiritual—have become commonplace. The negative aspects of our existence are repeated in the media. The newspaper headlines blare. The radio shouts. The television sensationalizes.

We witness military excursions, gang warfare, unemployment, poverty. Media even contributes to the negative atmosphere in the way it disproportionately accents the negative in the news, favors violence and avarice in its programming elsewhere, and systematically excludes that which is positive and uplifting.

With nuclear proliferation, we no longer feel secure behind the shield of atomic weaponry. The obscenities of starvation, cancer and armed build-up still remain. Our atmosphere, physical and moral, has become polluted. We walk down the streets of any large city in any nation at any given hour and the faces mirror the dissatisfaction and disaffection of society as a whole.

All of this is particularly true in the United States. There was a time when we could look for spiritual sustenance to the Family, but the family unit is breaking down. We once looked for guidance to the Church, but the church is more often interested in its buildings and its trappings. We look to the government, to the President of the United States, to lead us, to allay our fears, our anxieties and to show us the way, and then there is [was] Watergate. So we are a world, a nation of people in trouble.

How can we effect a change? Change manifests itself in a similar manner whether for the individual or for society. First, there must be recognition that there is trouble and that we are in trouble.

Second, there must be acceptance of the idea that things can be better. Third, the wherewithal to make things better must be understood and must be in hand. Fourth, the desire—the will—must be sufficient to do what must be done to effect change.

I believe that people are aware of the dangers existing to themselves and to society as a whole. As I have indicated, the media has been all too effective in bringing this message home. It may be that we had to arrive at this moment in time, with the loss of morality, the breakdown of the family unit, the inadequacy of the church and the agony of Watergate, for the trauma to be so great that the need for change would finally be felt.

The first step is in the process of taking place—the recognition that we are unhealthy and that we might even be dying. The second step—the additional recognition that it need not be, that we can change, is also taking place. We can alter our existence so that not only do we survive but that the best that man is capable of can be brought into play and a better society, a better world can come forth.

Here, too, the media can play an important role. Just as it now exposes the emptiness and the dangers, it can also be used to demonstrate the promise and to guide.

. . .this film. . .will be part of the role that communication can offer for the New Age. When people fully understand that there is a choice, that they already possess the power to alter their existence, that there is a better place that can be made by them for them, then it all can happen.

We are involved in step two. We must provide the right information through mass communication—information about the tools that man will need to effect change once the need for change has been recognized. These tools include ideas as to how human beings can live to the maximum of their potential. Then they will discover what enormous power they possess and they will know that they can alter their destiny as well as the very face of the earth they live on. . .

I believe that if the communicators are effective in step two, then steps three and four will follow. When people understand that they have an alternative to the death of the spirit and to the destruction in which we live, then they will find sufficient strength, courage, wisdom and faith to change.

The motion picture feature that we are embarking upon will help make people become more aware:

(1) It is about so-called "psychic phenomena."

(2) It is about the exploration of the psychic in both our most primitive and most advanced societies.

(3) It is about increased potentials for all human beings in all dimensions.

(4) It is about the development of additional levels of consciousness.

(5) It is about the spirit.

Neuman intended no staged or studio production—"everything that takes place will be...real people taking part in real events." We were in complete agreement with the objectives of this project. Walter left on September 16th for three weeks in the Philippines and Japan to assist in the search for phenomena which could be effectively portrayed on film.

This was Walter's first experience with a professional film crew and he learned a lot about the logistics, mechanics and the human elements involved in producing the filmed segments which were to become part of a larger program. Since he had been asked to "identify talent" and also serve as an "advance man" for the film crew, lining up events one or two days in advance of their arrival, he got to see events from a different perspective than those who were behind the cameras. He left the Philippines for Tokyo two days ahead of the crew. There he went to Dr. Motoyama's Institute for Religion and Parapsychology, the best contact he had in Japan, to get suggestions for what might be worth filming. In his notebook he had made the following notes for himself:

What in Japan? If possible—

1. Dr. Motoyama's work
2. Croiset's (the Dutch clairvoyant) TV Experiment
3. "Geller Children" or "Response to Matthew Manning's Appearance"
4. ?? Yukio Ishii—"The New Ted Serios" Nengraphy (thoughtography)
5. Arrange to have local equipment in reserve for Tuesday shooting— possibly Tuesday to Thursday, if warranted.
6. Filming crew—Bob Collins to work with local film crew
7. Learn about the "Third Eye" of 10-year-old Sayuri Tanaka
8. ?? Hurkos
9. Contact Muramatsu

When Alan Neuman, Bob Collins, and Pamela de Maigret reached Tokyo, it was agreed that it would be difficult to visually portray the research work at Dr. Motoyama's laboratory in a five-minute segment in a meaningful way. Yukio Ishii, whose thoughtography had appeared in the German publication **Esotera** (two of his pictures were in our book), was no longer available to the media. His parents had decided that the pressures on this sensitive youth were too great for him to endure more publicity. Because of Gerard Croiset's international reputation for psychically locating lost and missing persons, a Japanese television station had flown him from Holland that May 1976 to see if he could help locate a seven-year-old girl who had been sought for four days by 750 police. This looked like an interesting event to film so Walter went to the *Japan Times* for an English version of the story.

Clairvoyant 'Finds' Missing Girl's Body

The Japan Times

Friday, May 7, 1976

A visiting Dutch clairvoyant, invited here to appear on a TV program, located the body of a school girl missing since last Thursday.

The body was found early Wednesday morning by a team of TV staffers who went to the location described by the Dutch occultist. They were ahead of the police.

The search for the body was filmed by the TV team and it was broadcast Wednesday at 7:30 p.m. by the NET station.

The 67-year-old occultist, Gerald Croiset, arrived in Tokyo on Monday at the invitation of the Tokyo TV station, to appear in the 80-minute weekly show which features occultism, and unusual personalities and events.

During the program, Croiset was shown a picture of the missing girl, Miwa Kikuchi, 7, daughter of Takeshi Kikuchi, 30, of Ichihara, Chiba Prefecture.

The second-grader did not return home after she was last seen by her friends near a national highway about 50 meters from her home Thursday afternoon last week.

A total of 750 policemen were mobilized in the subsequent search for her over the next four days.

However, no trace of the girl had been found until Croiset began "seeing" Miwa's

Gerald Croiset

whereabouts after studying her picture.

The Dutchman said that Miwa was dead "on the surface of a lake near her home and near a quay for boats near a yellow protruding structure."

After studying a map of the area, TV staffers learned that there is a reservoir about one kilometer from the girl's home.

A team of 10 staffers headed for the reservoir early Wednesday with a TV camera and searched around the lake for the girl.

One of the TV directors found her body afloat in the reservoir near a quay for row boats and a water supply tower which is painted yellow.

Astounded by what they found, the team members immediately telephoned the

police who, together with the girl's parents, rushed to the scene.

The parents identified the body as that of Miwa.

A spokesman for the special police squad formed for investigating the disappearance of the girl later said that the reservoir was one of the key places they had been searching.

One of the officers claimed that they would have found the body regardless of Croiset's clairvoyance.

He said that squad members were planning to search the reservoir in the belief that if the girl had drowned there, her body would rise to the surface sometime around Wednesday.

The apparent accuracy of the clairvoyance by the Dutchman left the viewers in the show spellbound.

Program staffers claimed that they did not give Croiset the girl's address or any other details about her.

Croiset helped police solve more than 800 cases in the Netherlands and other countries, they said.

In a press conference after the show, Croiset was asked whether he could name high officials who were bribed in the Lockheed scandal.

He replied that he did not want to get involved in politics.

It would have been very difficult to reconstruct all the details of that tragic event and luck was with us when we learned about Masuaki Kiyota. He was one of the "Geller children" whose psychic abilities had become known after Geller appeared on TV in Japan.

Rande Brown, a young American working with Dr. Motoyama, introduced Walter to Toshiaki Harada, Ph.D., a physicist on Dr. Motoyama's staff, who as a student at the University of Hawaii had acquired proficiency in English.* He offered to serve as interpreter and

---

Neuman, Collins and de Maigret had arrived on the weekend and we needed an interpreter when Dr. Harada was not available. Fortunately Walter remembered that

Section from one of many Japanese newspapers that reported Croiset's success in finding child's body.

took Walter to meet Dr. Tsutomu Miyauchi, managing director of the Japan Nengraphy Association. Miyauchi immediately thought that Masuaki Kiyota, with whom he had been working, would be a good subject for the film project and he phoned Mr. Kiyota. School children in Japan who hope to go to college are under severe academic pressures and it took some persuasion on Dr. Miyauchi's part to arrange a meeting at the Kiyota home.

*when he was on the University of Minnesota faculty, Mr. Matsumi Muramatsu who was then a representative of a Japan-U.S. trade commission in Washington, D.C. had spoken at a conference at the University. He had since returned to Tokyo and now headed SIMUL, a large translation agency for business and government visitors. A phone call to Mrs. Muramatsu was a "life-saver"; she was able to help us with arranging to have a local camera crew ready for filming. In March 1979 we again saw Mr. Muramatsu in Tokyo. He had recently written a best-selling book, **I Couldn't Speak English Either**, recounting some of his humorous experiences as an interpreter.*

The reports about what Masuaki could do in metal bending and thoughtography sounded so interesting that it was hoped he would prove to be a good subject for the film. Dr. Miyauchi and Dr. Harada accompanied the film crew to the home in the Senju district in Tokyo. Our group had brought along a Polaroid camera and film. Walter stopped at a hardware store en route to buy three heavy tablespoons of stainless steel and two teaspoons for an initial experiment.

Masuaki, then 14 years old, was handed one of the newly-purchased tablespoons. He took it, stroked the handle lightly with his fingers, then made a quick clockwise motion with his wrist and tossed the spoon in the air. When it landed on the floor it had a pronounced twist in the handle of about 180 degrees and the bowl of the spoon "drooped." (See illustration below for a top and side view of the handle.) Masuaki twisted a number of spoons for other members of the film crew before they moved upstairs for an experiment in thoughtography. Alan Neuman let Walter keep the first spoon as evidence and souvenir. Two days later Masuaki twisted another spoon for Walter, and on the evening before the crew's departure, Walter tried his best to communicate to Masuaki that he would like an *unbent* spoon to take along home for tests. Masuaki got another spoon and while he walked toward Walter, gave his wrist a quick twist and produced a third *bent* spoon instead.

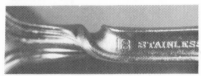 

The Nengraphy Experiment

Dr. Miyauchi had brought along a chart recorder to monitor this experiment with a Silicon-Photo Diode. Masuaki asked what hotel we were staying at, and after we told him "The Keio Plaza" he concentrated on the camera for a minute or so, emitted a loud cry that conveyed exertion and excitement, and when the film was peeled from the negative, there was the Keio Plaza hotel, clearly recognizable and produced from an aerial perspective which would normally have required a helicopter to achieve. Yet it was evening in the Kiyota home, about ten miles from the Keio Plaza. (See page 147.)

Masuaki wanted to try again and he produced the top half of the hotel with the air conditioning units visible on the roof and the lower structures surrounding the hotel appearing from an aerial perspective.

Dr. Miyauchi had conducted many experiments with Masuaki prior to our visit; this was not a new experience for him, startling as it was for us. He tore the paper from the pen-recorder he had been using and gave it to Walter as "evidence."

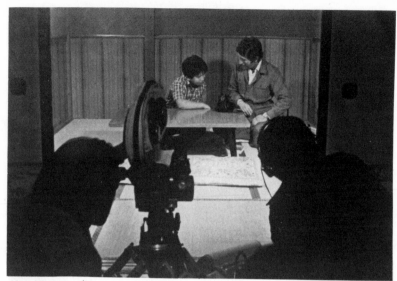

Alan Neuman talks with Masuaki Kiyota as camera crew gets ready to film.

At the next filming session, with the movie cameras set up and running, Masuaki produced images of the Tokyo Tower. This was the film segment incorporated in the 90-minute program, "Exploring the Unknown" shown by NBC-TV, October 30, 1977. The commentary narrated by Burt Lancaster described the experiment as follows:

First paranormal of tower.

Masuaki with Miyauchi and Fukuda

We are concerned with the extension of the human potential: of broadening the areas of human creativity into dimensions that hitherto have been relatively unexplored.

Any photography expert will tell you that there are a lot of things which can effect photographic film. Light exposes film of course, but heat, pressure, chemicals and various types of radiation, like x-rays will also mark films.

Many of us who have been around film labs have heard stories about people who seem to fog film just by being near it. Apparently they emit some sort of unknown radiation which ruins the film. Instead of being studied scientifically, they usually get fired.

That situation is different with a Japanese boy who seems to have some control over this energy. He seems to direct it, and what is more astounding, he appears to create pictures with it.

CU Black Box

Two Professors and
Masuaki Loading
Equipment and Showing
Inside of Box

CU Masuaki Watching
Two Professors Finish
Loading Film, Pull Out
Tape, Pull Out Control
Film, Hand Box to
Masuaki

Masuaki Holds Box,
Concentrates and
Suddenly Gestures

Two Professors and
Masuaki with Read Out
Chart and Control
Picture

CU Two Professors
and Equipment

CU Two Professors
and Masuaki Profs.
Open Up Picture and
Masuaki Reaches For It

Close Up on Picture

Alan Neuman and
Masuaki Seated
Together

Masuaki Answers
Alan Neuman Watches
as Masuaki Concentrates
on Putting Image on Film
with His Mind. They
Wait for the Film to
Develop. A.N. Strips
Off Backing to Show
Print of Tokyo Tower

With him is Professor Miyauchi, a physicist, and Mr. Fukuda a photographic expert. They believe that Masuaki is creating light energy and he can somehow project it into a sealed black metal box.

Professor Miyauchi built equipment to test this idea. The light-tight metal box has nine photoelectric cells mounted on the inside top surface. A film pack can be inserted into the box, then each film can be pulled out individually and it automatically developes immediately.

The first film in the pack is always used as a control to make sure that the box is properly closed and that no light is getting in around the edges.

Masuaki says that he needs to be able to visualize the image. Then he concentrates on the box and lets his energy or tension build up. When he feels ready, he lets go of the energy suddenly by saying the Japanese equivalent of "POW."

Each of the light sensitive photoelectric cells inside the box is attached by an electric wire to one pen on this nine channel chart recorder. As soon as Masuaki creates light inside the box, the pens on the chart recorder show the position and duration of the light strike. This is verified again when the film is pulled out and developed.

LANCASTER VOICE OVER

Masuaki can usually make streaks and even patterns on the film. At the beginning of the experiment he was asked to place a light-strike on the lower left hand side of the picture. . .and he did it.

This was our camera, and this was our film. And we brought it here for the first time and you are seeing me insert it. Now I am pulling the tab and I am handling it to the boy. The lens is capped.

(Japanese dialogue)

Tokyo Tower. All right, let's see what we have here. In thirty seconds we should know. I kinda helped on that one. . .

Alan Neuman with Real Tokyo Tower in B.G.

Towering Tokyo Tower

You are looking at the Tokyo Tower. It is a landmark. It was the Tokyo Tower that Masuaki projected for us. We thought you would like to see the real thing and compare.

LANCASTER:
When we look at a photograph, we take for granted the process that placed the picture upon the paper. . .the subject being photographed, the snap of a shutter that allows the lens to project an image upon the negative from which the print is made.

Now ponder: creating such a picture without a camera at all, using neither shutter nor lens nor negative as Masuaki has done here in this picture of the Tokyo Tower.

Masuaki claims to be able to place an image upon film simply by creating the same image in his mind—projecting what amounts to a figment of his imagination onto the tangible reality of a photograph.

Think further. . .if the mind can do this, what more can it do?

(l. to r.) **Dr. Tsutomu Miyauchi, Dr. Toshiaki Harada, Masuaki Kiyota, Alan Neuman, Pamela de Maigret, Bob Collins and members of the Japanese film crew. Walter Uphoff is seated (*back to camera*) across from Masuaki, and Masuaki's father and younger sister were seated at Dr. Miyauchi's right.**

We continue to meet persons from time to time who saw the 1977

NBC-TV program and virtually all of them remember the segment in which Masuaki projected the Tokyo Tower onto Polaroid film. Since this first appearance on film, he has received invitations from television companies in Australia and England; and in July 1979, along with Hiroto Yamashita, was the subject of two half-hour documentary programs on Nippon TV Network.

Masuaki's Mysterious Disappearance

Anyone—no matter how open-minded—who explores or experiences paranormal events, is likely at some time or other to encounter phenomena which tax his or her capacity to accept their reality. With Elaine Morikawa as our interpreter, we had a conversation with Yoshinori Kiyota, Masuaki's father, about an experience with his son which had shaken him.

This occurred when Masuaki was about twelve. He had been teasing his young sister Yukizi unmercifully, until his father threatened to punish him if he persisted. Like many a twelve-year-old, Masuaki continued his teasing and Kiyota proceeded to carry out his threat to spank him. Masuaki ran out of the restaurant into what is a narrow dead-end alley. As his father reached out to grab him, the boy disappeared into "thin air." His horrified parent yelled, "Come back here!" and a terrified Masuaki literally plopped down in front of his father. By this time, as one would expect, his intention to punish the boy had vanished.

The first, or perhaps even the tenth time, something so unbelievable occurs, it can be dismissed, but eventually self-honesty and integrity forces one to evaluate the evidence. Had we not read Uri Geller's autobiography* before hearing about Masuaki's "dematerialization," we would have had even greater difficulty comprehending the validity of the Kiyotas' experience.

In his autobiography, Geller tells how he had been jogging near First Avenue in New York City about 6 p.m. on November 9, 1973 and what seemed an instant later, crashing through the screened porch of Dr. Andrija Puharich's house at Ossining, New York, about 30 miles away. Mystified and stunned, Uri was relieved to find that he had only a sore knee and no broken bones. He had great difficulty comprehending what had happened, but there were enough persons in New York City who had been with him at 5:30 p.m. so that there was no way that his precipitious arrival in Ossining could be explained by *any known mode of travel.*

We had another "mind-boggling" experience with teleportation which we think was connected with our visit to Japan. When we were preparing to leave Manila, where we had spent nearly two weeks after leaving Tokyo, the telephoto lens for Walter's 35 mm. Canon camera could not be found. We laid out every item we had with us, emptied the suitcases and brief cases, before leaving for Colombo in Sri Lanka. We concluded that it had been stolen and reported the loss to our insurance agent in Oregon, Wisconsin, upon our arrival in Colombo.

A week later, after our flight to Zurich, we drove as far as a small town near Freiburg, Germany, where we again checked through our luggage. There, on top of everything else in the carrying case was the telephoto lens! Even now we have difficulty believing what we experienced ourselves. We can appreciate how difficult it is for others to comprehend second-hand reports of unusual, "far-out" experiences.

---

*Geller, Uri, **My Story**. Praeger Publishers, New York, 1975. pp. 210-18.*

III. Continuing Correspondence

Masuaki's feats which Walter had observed in Tokyo interested him in continuing the contact by correspondence. Airmail letters crossed the Pacific frequently, at times simultaneously in both directions. A total of 30 letters were written by Masuaki and/or his father, Yoshinori Kiyota, before we were to see them again in Tokyo in March 1979.

Walter sent some stainless steel tablespoons and a case-hardened flat file to Masuaki which he asked him to try to bend by PK. They were returned twisted, along with some bi-metal and aluminum strips that had been twisted in experiments conducted by Prof. Shegemi Sasaki at the University of Electro-Communications. Files become very brittle when case-hardened and should normally break instead of bend under pressure, yet this file and the four additional files Masuaki sent along had all been influenced by PK. One was bent into a U-shape, and several of the lighter ones apparently had broken in shipment because they were not securely packed. But the paranormal bends were still observable.

Walter had noticed Masuaki's enthusiasm for baseball, so he sent him a baseball at Christmas and a book of photos of Midwest U.S.A. Masuaki reciprocated with color photos taken of himself and his friend Toru Ozaki on a skiing holiday, as well as a number of paranormal pictures which he had made, and a super-8 movie film taken by Toru which showed Masuaki and another youngster successfully applying PK on metal objects.

The spoons which Walter had bought at the hardware store near Kiyota's home in 1976 were magnetic [type 410 ferritic stainless steel containing about 18% chromium and .2 to .25% carbon]. Before leaving Tokyo he bought 15 more stainless steel tablespoons at the Keio-Plaza department store for further experiments in the U.S. These happened to be of the non-magnetic type [austinetic stainless 304, containing about 17% chromium, .8% nickel, and about .01% carbon]. He mailed two of these to Masuaki on January 13, 1977 to see if he could also twist or bend this type of stainless steel. These came back with similar twists in the handles—a visible answer to his question. As a "bonus" Masuaki had also sent along two teaspoons, one with a tight left-right double twist in the handle, and the other with about a centimeter's distance between the reverse twists.

Masuaki's father sent Walter a special signature stamp in Japanese characters of a kind used for papers of importance for the name "Uphoff," explaining that the Japanese characters pronounced (a)(fu)(ho)(fu), meant "a man who goes his own way."

On March 24, 1977, Masuaki wrote a letter enclosing a photocopy of the certificate he received for the highest grade in Fourth Grade English Proficiency. Only 20 of his 250 classmates had received this certificate, he reported proudly, and his correspondence with us had inspired him to study harder in the subject.

These first letters began with the words: "My dear American grandfather" and "Dear new American grandfather"—an indication of respect in Japan. These letters were written on stationery decorated with stars and stripes in red and blue and signed, "Your new grandson." Later most of his letters were typewritten instead of written in his careful longhand. It is possible, although we have never asked, that the friend of his father occasionally helps transcribe letters for Masuaki. Masuaki's father who does not read or write English, has enlisted the services of a friend who translates and writes the letters to us. The improvement in Masuaki's command of English has been remarkable in the time that he has been corresponding with us.

On April 4, 1977, Mr. Kiyota wrote three letters. In the first he said:

We also believe in hereditism [heredity]. . .because my father (Masuaki's grandfather) and I can do Nengraphy when no one sees us. And my wife, Setsuko (Masuaki's mother) sometimes can see a white ghost. I can perceive my relative's death by seeing a ghost or by intuition. . .

Frankly speaking, my father and I can make others who inflict an injury on us destroy themselves. But we didn't notice it till ten years ago. And we thought that it was just a coincidence. Since then we know our power we have struggled not to have ill will against anyone, because we are sorry for them and feel bad. But men are made incomplete [imperfect] and the struggle not to have ill will toward anyone is very hard. I suppose you can understand our feelings. . .

I had a drill [bit] bended in the shape of a right angle, but I forgot the place where I kept it with care. As soon as I find it out, I'll send you its photograph.

In the second letter of the same date, he included several intriguing bits of information:

I have told you that we can make others who inflict injury on us destroy themselves. . .we have also discovered that it can be the power that makes our family and others happy. . .

Masuaki can do to bend spoons, to produce Nengraphy, to put small things into an orange without cutting the peel. . .He can make a thing appear or disappear. And he can reach to the school within 2 minutes instead of a 15 minute walk.

. . .He was born at 4:25 p.m. on April 30, 1962 in the hospital near my house. About 3 hours later my wife, Setsuko, was binded [bound] *by an unknown force and could not move herself. When she looked at her newborn baby sleeping beside her, she found him wrapped by something like a white mist, and could not see him. She said it continued for a while. and I said to her it was just an illusion. But thinking back now I wonder if it was something connected with Masuaki's psychic abilities. . .One summer night in the year Masuaki was born I saw in the sky a bright ball as large as a moon. It came flying from the North and stopped above my head and went flying to the South. At that time I thought it was a bright balloon. But I don't know yet what it was.*

Masuaki wants to take the psychological course in a college in Japan and then to go to an American college for the study of parapsychology. . .I think Masuaki could go to college because he takes a high rank in school record at present.

An explanation of Masuaki's experiences with Nengraphy came in a letter from Yoshinori Kiyota, May 4, 1977:

Masuaki sometimes takes [produces] *photographs of men. He once took a photograph of a man without face and hands. But only the sleeves of his shirt were taken and one of them had a camera. The man who took this photograph is Mr. Jiro Tunoda, a famous cartoonist in Japan. . .Mr. Tunoda is one of the members of the London Psychic Association and is much interested in physic phenomena. He also has some psychic abilities.*

Masuaki likes the photographs of buildings better than those of men. So he has taken buildings of the Nengraphy photographs. Most of all he is fond of the Empire State building and the Goddess of Liberty in New York. . .

When Masuaki bends a metal, he doesn't feel any warmth or heat.

In this letter Masuaki's father explained in some detail, experiments which Prof. Shegemi Sasaki had been conducting with his son. (See Chapter XI.) He then went on to answer a question we had put to him about something he had mentioned in a previous letter: Who is Zenefu?

Zenefu [whom] *Masuaki can see says to him, 'When you become old you have a duty but I can't tell you about it now.' Masuaki wonders 'What is it?'*

Now I will tell you about Zenefu. At first I thought Zenefu was an illusion but later I knew Zenefu was not a mere illusion. The predictions Zenefu tells Masuaki come true at the rate of 90 percent. From this fact, you will know that Zenefu is not a mere illusion. . .

It was about April 1974 when Masuaki began to contact with Zenefu.

Zenefu wears such a round hat and a gown as a clergyman wears. He is shining brightly and always smiling. But when Masuaki tries to do some wrong acts, he gets angry. . .

mark

Zenefu says, 'I am coming here by an order from the upper class [higher order?] I am not a human being nor God who is in the upper class. I cannot also see God. If a man can see God through his own eyes, he will be only able to perceive God as light. My present form is not a real one. It is only just the way to bring you around. My country is the star in the south of this earth which you can see in Australia. But I am not a creature in the star. I have not the body. And the creatures with bodies are not high-leveled ones.

. . .I am not a spirit or a creature. Though you may take me [to be] a thing like a spirit, I am not a spirit of a human being. So you had better take me 'a life' without a body. . .I haven't a name, but if I haven't a name, you will find it difficult to call me. . .So I named myself 'Zenefu'.

Though I try to hear more about Zenefu from Masuaki, he doesn't want to tell me further. . .Masuaki seems to have some promise with Zenefu.

Translation of concepts from one language to another is not easy, yet we are surprised at times how well we can understand what is said in the letters. There are instances when we have questions. In his June 29, 1977 letter, Mr. Kiyota continues his explanation about what Masuaki has learned from his teacher, Zenefu:

Zenefu seems to have been guiding Masuaki's steps in the path of righteousness. I think [he] is under the proper guidance of Zenefu and Zenefu is a good guide. By the way, the name like Zenefu is not originally used in Japan or in the Eastern countries. The image. . .that comes to my mind is the name used in some European countries. . .At the early days Zenefu said to Masuaki, 'I am surprised that some creatures on Earth make internecine struggles against one another.' If Zenefu is the spirit of a human being, he ought to know as much.

Masuaki says, 'Zenefu speaks to me many things about the microcosm but it is too difficult for me to understand. When he asks Zenefu to talk about them easier, Zenefu says, 'There is no way to explain them easier. . .' I suppose an energy in the universe appears in human shape as Zenefu and Masuaki can see [him].

Kiyota continues his discussion about Zenefu in his letter of August 15th:

Zenefu says to Masuaki, 'A substance has a physical law and a simple spiritual element. Then it becomes a living thing. A living thing has an instinct and becomes [comes] to have an emotion, according to its revolution. [evolution]. On human revolution men became to have intelligence. People think intelligence is the best thing. But there are psychic abilities above it. Men, including Masuaki, with these abilities began to appear on Earth. By and by these abilities will be more powerful and the modern civilization will be replaced by the psychic one. But before the psychic civilization is born, human spiritual structure is required to develop not to affect badly each other. Because this psychic power is a tremendous one, it is quite dangerous when it is used for wrong purposes. . .Men with these abilities have duties as the seeds of forthcoming new human beings.'

Zenefu says. . .'Your power. . .stays at the limit of projecting Nengraphical images or bending spoons. It is because your society still can't receive psychic phenomena extensively.'

But this problem will work itself out. . .

On a number of occasions, Masuaki, according to his father, has seen spirits, identified as deceased relatives whom Masuaki had not known. He also mentioned that Masuaki knew Yukio Ishii about whom we had written in our earlier book, **New Psychic Frontiers:**

. . .we don't know where he is now. He was very delicate at heart. . .he was always worried about his psychic abilities. . .Once there were about 3,000 boys and girls with psychic abilities in Japan, but they abandoned their abilities from the social pressure of contempt and derision. Fortunately Masuaki is strong-minded.

On October 13, 1977 he wrote:

Masuaki says, "Some people dare to call me a liar openly to my face instead of saying 'I can't believe it,' or 'I can't understand it well.' I feel this is equal to calling me a thief, but they cast an imputation on my character by calling me a liar. And these people wouldn't try to work with me by scientific experiments. There's no rights for psychics in this country. But I do love this country."

Masuaki has discovered at a tender age what others who have worked in the psychic field for years, either as investigators or psychics, have had to put up with—regardless of country.

As was to be expected, the media soon discovered Masuaki's unique talents and, just as with Matthew Manning in England, sought interviews for whatever sensational value they might have. Mr. Kiyota reported that **The National Enquirer** was one of the first on the scene, October 26, 1977:

*The other day we were called on by two reporters and one cameraman. They were foreign correspondents in Japan: Mr. David Tharp of **The Australian Times** and Miss Mary Mine of **Los Angeles Times**. They said to us, 'We have been told by telephone from **National Enquirer** to meet Masuaki and to see whether he can do mystical things or not.'*

The experiment ended up in success. Five Nengraphical pictures were taken: The Goddess of Liberty (2), the Washington Monument (1), Manhattan (1) and the London Tower (1). Eight spoons were twisted;

turned round from once to thrice or being broken after twist.

Professor Miyauchi's experiment was succeeded too. They were truly astonished. They said 'We don't know how to write these that we have seen [with] our own eyes. Can people in our own country believe in the article that we'll write?'. . .When the Washington monument was projected by Masuaki's Nengraphy, no Japanese including Masuaki couldn't understand [knew] what it was. Then one of the foreign reporters said it was the Washington monument so we found it out at last.

He elaborated on this report when he wrote again on December 12, 1977:

*. . . The interview of the **National Enquirer** was carried on for 3 days. Mr. Tharp and Miss Mine said they must make these psychic phenomena widely known to the world. But the witnesses selected from the **National Enquirer** seemed to think in the bottom of their hearts that Masuaki must use a trick, though they saw the phenomena in [with] their own eyes. They seemed to be against the interviewers writing articles. One of them was a prist [priest]. He seemed to have an opposite opinion because of the religious reason that no one except Christ can do wonders. Other witnesses had administrative positions in Japanese branches of American companies. Though they were good businessmen, they were quite strangers to parapsychological field. They were skeptical about our experiment, though they actually saw it with their own eyes.*

*One of the reasons was, I think, they were afraid of being thought queer, or not to be proper to administrative positions. I think that the **National Enquirer** had bad choices of witnesses. It is just to send for an engineer instead of a doctor to a patient. I believe when we do an experiment, a witness [should] be a scholar or a researcher who is keenly interested in the parapsychological field. . .*

On the experiments with the reporters, several Nengraphical pictures were projected. One of them was the Goddess of Liberty. . .

This image, double-inverted, of the Statue of Liberty is very similar to the one obtained March 23, 1979 when Yutaka Fukuda, Toru Ozaki and Mary Jo Uphoff took a polaroid camera, for which we had bought film, into the street and after waiting for 5 minutes pulled out the next picture (No. 5) and got such an image. Walter and two other witnesses stayed upstairs in the Kiyota home and held hands while Masuaki concentrated on influencing the film.

They were very astonished to see it. But I wonder how they will write about this. Probably, this may not come out as there are those who are opposed to write this. Reporters brought [took] all Masuaki's Nengraphical pictures and twisted spoons. If they don't write articles, I wish they will bring them all back to me because I want to keep them all as Masuaki's experimental record. . .

Comments about the *National Enquirer* episode continued in Kiyota's letter January 9, 1978:

*I told you before that the interviewing from the **National Enquirer** has gone on for three days. But I forgot to tell you that the reporters had planned to continue the experiment with Masuaki more than three days, and that I declined to accept their offer, saying Masuaki was too tired to go on [with] the experiment.*

*In this country's custom, it is generally considerd a very shameful act to receive money except on business. As Masuaki is a student and not a showman, so we thought it a shameful act to get money from the **National Enquirer**, and we worked together with them without pay. In such a case as this, I think they ought to show their thanks to us in some ways—the **National Enquirer** should tell us whether they will write an article or not.*

But I resigned myself to the inevitable owing to the differences between people's thinking things, though I felt very unpleasant. At the same time I felt very sorry for Masuaki who exerted all possible efforts. We say in such a case as this, 'Hone ore zon no kutibire mouke' in Japanese which means 'I gained nothing for all my efforts. . .'

*. . .most films and spoons that were used by Masuaki's experiments were brought by the **National Enquirer**. Therefore I don't know well [if] Masuaki or the **National Enquirer** has the right of ownership of the Nengraphical pictures and twisted spoons. . .[and] when the trouble has become larger by our protest, we may lost temper and get excited. And, as I told you before when we throw our energy with anger to others, something [some] unfortunate things may happen to them. If this [should] happen, we'll feel sorry for them and feel very unpleasant.*

The *National Enquirer* started out as a sensational scandal sheet and acquired a reputation for huge headlines and stories which other papers would not print. As its circulation grew, it developed a more responsible approach to journalism. We had first hand information that feature articles were checked with persons who were knowledgeable about a particular subject before the articles were printed. On a number of occasions we, ourselves, had been called for corroboration by assistant editors and reporters, so when Joe Mullins of the *Enquirer* staff phoned about another matter, shortly after we received the letter from Mr. Kiyota, Walter told him he did not see much point in continuing to talk with their reporters if nothing ever came of it. He was told about Kiyota's disappointment and discouragement that after spending three days with representatives of the *Enquirer,* all the paranormally-bent spoons and thoughtography pictures had been taken away and no one had gone to the trouble of telling the family whether anything was going to come from their efforts.

Mullins seemed concerned and said he would check into it. On

January 23rd, John Cooke, another reporter, called and said he hoped the article he planned to write about Masuaki would be accepted by the editor. It appeared in the March 14, 1978 issue of *The National Enquirer.* (See Chapter IX)

Kiyota's letter, February 3, 1978:

The other day I had a phone call from a Japanese female reporter who had been asked [to tell me] the **National Enquirer** *will write an article about Masuaki. . .I felt much relieved.*

February 25, 1978:

Mr. John Cooke called on us three times. . .

Masauki passed an entrance examination to the Senshu Senior High School which he wished to go to. This is a school affiliated with the Senshu University which has a psychology course. . .there are only 22 colleges or universities which have psychology courses, therefore I think Masuaki must be one of the lucky persons. . .

Masuaki had been advised by his teacher that he had not scholarship enough to take the entrance examination to the Senshu High School though his grades were excellent. But as Zenefu. . .said to Masuaki, 'You can surely pass the test to that school'. . .and what Zenefu said turned out to be true.

Masuaki's 16th birthday was coming up. We found a brass belt buckle with a design we thought rather typically "American" to send to him. Masuaki wrote to thank us and told about his school:

Our school has more than 40 classrooms and other rooms. . .such as a science room, a language laboratory and music room. . .Our school is a mammoth school with about 3,000 pupils and more than 40 teachers.

In our school we have many clubs—an English club, a baseball club, a basketball club, a soccer club, a Judo club, a literature club. . .and so on which anybody can belong to. I've been practicing Judo since I was 6 years old. But I don't belong to the Judo club because I like English better than Judo now. . .

My psychic abilities have surely been esclating. The other day I showed the most favorable data on Professor Sasaki's equipment. I think I can [could] do wonders if I produce PK. . .without other person's pressures. To my regret, when I get pressures, my psychic abilities are weakened. But this problem will be solved of itself. . .Zenufu promised to help me producing PK through my life. . .

I was asked to come to Australia and to make my appearance on TV. . .but I declined their offers because I must go to school. Then I said OK to go there in summer vacation. . .

I'm glad to say that I've come to take much more interest in studying English since I started correspondence with you.

On June 22, 1978 we got a letter from Masuaki—a short one. We had been asked to suggest psychics who might be able to perform feats of PK for a special program contemplated by Granada Television of Birmingham, England. We suggested Masuaki, if travel could be arranged during his school vacation.

Mr. Miyauchi, Mr. Tharp, Miss Morikawa (our friend) and I will go to London in August. . .

In his letter of September 27, 1978, Mr. Kiyota told us about the London visit:

Shooting on the film was done for four days. Masuaki succeeded in projecting seven thoughtographs as well as bending spoons. Thoughtographs were those of the guards of the Buckingham Palace, the Eiffel Tower, the statue of Admiral Nelson, a triangular shape of light and so on. But the results were not so good as Masuaki usually gets at home, what with the fatigue from his first visit to a foreign country and with the pressure from shooting.

. . .there was an unexpected unhappy trouble. Objectors were invited by Granada Television which came as quite a shock to Masuaki. The objectors said, 'Masuaki plays a trick.' Then they said to Mr. Tharp, 'You have been tricked by the Japanese.' Mr. Tharp got angry at hearing this and gave back the performance fee to Granada Television saying, 'you are very rude to this Japanese boy. Why didn't you obtain Masuaki's prior approval as to your inviting objectors before he came to London? It is very cowardly of you. We came all the way to London, not because we wanted money, but we wanted to show as many people as we could the existence of psychokinesis.'

. . .a letter from Prof. J. B. Hasted said, 'We are all quite certain of Masuaki's PK.'

Of the interview scene Masuaki said, 'I have never played any trick or don't know how to trick. A trick leads to corruption.'

(The next sentence is paraphrased for clarity:)

I feel kind of guilty if I keep the truth about the existence of psychokinesis a secret.

If Copernicus. . .held his tongue for fear of objection, the Ptolemaic theory would have been justified and the progress of science would have been far more delayed. . .I wonder whether the objectors. . .object scientifically? I think it can't be scientific to object [to] things because they can't believe them. . .Objectors are apt to decide only by their own limited knowledge or experiences. Four billion people have four billion knowledges and experiences.

In January 1979 correspondence resumed again when we wrote the Kiyota family that we were planning a trip to Japan sometime early in March. We learned that Masuaki would have more time to spend with us if we came after he had finished his annual school examinations March 20th. Yoshinori Kiyota wrote about an interesting incident in his January 27th letter:

My wife saw in a dream that you would visit us on March 18. After I heard this from her, I received your letter and we were surprised to know that you would come to Japan some time in March. She sometimes knows such a thing in a dream. As for your mother's death, she saw that dream last September [Walter's mother died on September 27th]. *We are truly astonished at this coincidence.* [So were we because we had not informed the family of Walter's mother's death until several months later.]

At present Masuaki is projecting Nengraphical photographs of landscapes of London, Paris and so on. [Masuaki had taken a week to visit Scotland and Paris en route home from London in August] *saying, 'I saw such a place.' I think this ability is so convenient; if he didn't take a camera with him, later he can take a picture of a landscape he saw before.*

Masuaki's response to the announcement of our visit to Japan was enthusiastic:

My dear American grandfather and grandmother. . .I am very very very very very pleased to hear the news you will come to Japan.

This was a three-page single-spaced typewritten letter with detailed instructions accompanied by precise drawings of the best way to get from the airport to the air terminal in downtown Tokyo. Reservations

Well, I wrote some maps which were from the hotel to the nearest station (The station name is SHIN-OCHANOMIZU.), inside Shin-Ochanomizu station, from Shin-Ochanomizu to our nearest station (KITA-SENJU), inside Kita-Senju station, and from Kita-Senju station to our house.

*From the hotel to Shin-Ochanomizu station (subway Chiyoda line)

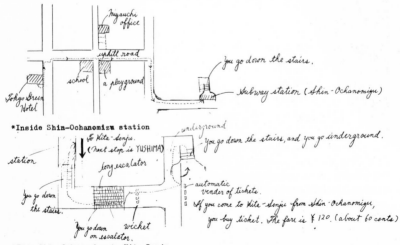

*Inside Shin-Ochanomizu station

*From Shin-Ochanomizu to Kita-Senju

30

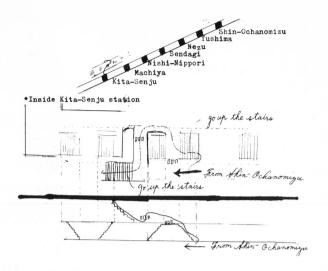

Shin-Ochanomizu
Yushima
Nezu
Sendagi
Nishi-Nippori
Machiya
Kita-Senju

*Inside Kita-Senju station

go up the stairs

From Shin-Ochanomizu

go up the stairs

From Shin-Ochanomizu

*Fron Kita-Senju station to our house

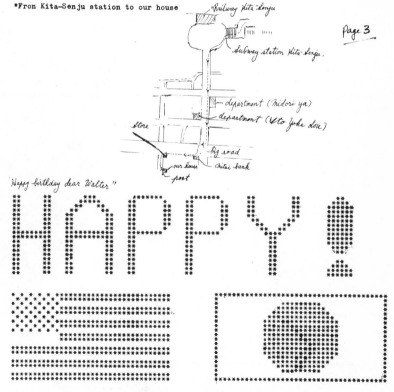

Railway Kita-Senju

Subway station Kita-Senju.

department (midori ya)

department (Eto joka dou)

store

big road

our house

mitui bank

post

Page 3

Happy birthday dear Walter"

HAPPY!

U . S . A .

J A P A N

Your birthday is February, if I remember right. I send my sincere greeting of "Happy birthday" to you. May your birthday be full of happiness, and may God bless you!!

31

had been made for us at the Tokyo-Green Hotel in Chiyoda, Tokyo and Elaine Morikawa had been engaged as interpreter for us. Using the red and black ribbon of the typewriter, he had composed a birthday greeting for Walter and the U.S. and Japanese flags side by side. They would wait for us on the second floor of the terminal at the escalator, he wrote:

We will wait for you there. You'll meet us. I'm going to have a twisted spoon and "WELCOME MR. AND MRS. UPHOFF" which is made of paper written by me. . .I have written down everything that I want to talk about. I'll write you again. Please remember me to all of your family.

Yoshinori Kiyota wrote us a letter the same day, February 16th, with information about hotel, interpreter and connections. There was one more letter before we arrived in the TCAT (air terminal) on March 20th. The Kiyotas had never seen the film made by Alan Neuman in 1976, but had heard that it was being released to theaters in Japan late in March. Could we please find out if this were true before we came to Tokyo? To our regret we could not tell them.

A collection of spoons, files and metal strips twisted by Masuaki Kiyota. Walter Uphoff witnessed the twisting of the three spoons at the left when he was at the Kiyota home, October 1976. The next tablespoon (made in Germany) was mailed to Masuaki along with a non-magnetic stainless steel tablespoon and a flat file, all of which were returned twisted or bent along with extra spoons, files and two metal strips.

IV. Tests With Twisted Spoons

By Walter H. Uphoff

Most people prefer first-hand evidence when confronted with an anomaly and in that respect we are not different from others. As mentioned in Chapter III, we now have a substantial collection of twisted cutlery and metal and have been reluctant to give any pieces to friends, even when they begged for "just one" because no one ever knows when one of these pieces might be of importance in further tests. We gladly sacrificed several for science and are willing to make some of the others available if the situation is warranted.

Our collection, one year after my 1976 visit to Japan, included three tablespoons from the Tokyo visit to the Kiyota home, numerous spoons sent later by Masauki, including two which we had mailed from here and which he returned along with additional bent spoons and metal strips. Still in our possession up to the time of the boys' visit in the summer of '79, were more than a dozen spoons, one twisted strip of aluminum, one strip of bi-metal twisted in the presence of Prof. Sasaki, and five files, one bent into a U-shape and fully intact, and four that were bent and broken. Even though we communicated frequently by letter, the translation from English to Japanese and Japanese to English was complicated enough so that I could not be certain whether the four files had been broken in experiments, or because they had been mailed in a light-weight envelope which was punctured when it arrived.

I had bought a supply of heavy stainless steel tablespoons at Keio Plaza department store before I left Tokyo because I wanted to find out how much force it would take to bend them, and also whether the same tight bends could be produced mechanically as the twists we had seen Masuaki produce. The first person to apply a torque test was our neighbor, Glenn Austin.*

Glenn put one of the unbent spoons in a vise, attached a torque wrench and turned the handle as steadily as possible. He got a reading of about 7-foot pounds of force required to produce a very wide, gentle twist, rather than the tight twist in the "Masuaki spoons." That means a force of about 84 pounds would be required at a leverage distance of one

---

Professional photographer with training in physics.

inch, instead of 12 inches and *twice that amount* if the leverage was only ½ inch. How much force would you figure it would take to twist a spoon with bare hands (or with gloves for that matter?) on contact with no leverage? We would be at least as excited to see someone produce such a tight twist with his hands, as we were to see Masuaki demonstrate his PK ability.

Next I took some of the twisted spoons to Prof. David J. Mack in the Department of Metallurgical and Mineral Engineering at the University of Wisconsin in Madison. He examined some of the spoons with a magnifying glass, was intrigued with what he saw, and agreed to run some tests at a later date.

Prof. Richard G. Koegel and two of his students agreed to make some torque tests on tablespoons I had brought back from Japan. Koegel put plywood on both sides of the bowl of the spoon before putting it into the vise so that no visible marks would be made on the spoon. Then he clamped the torque wrench on the handle at 1¼ inches above the bowl (spoon No. 17) and recorded an estimated torque of 5 foot-pounds, or 60 inch-pounds. The twist produced in the handle was a very gradual one as can be seen in the photo. Next another spoon (No. 18, the same kind as No. 17) was then put into the vise and twisted with the torque wrench applied at ¾ inches above the bowl. Again it took about 60 inch-pounds of force to twist the handle and the result was another gentle twist, a little tighter than the first one but without the droop of the bowl that so often appears in Masuaki's spoons. As can be seen in the closeup of the first spoon Masuaki twisted, there is a pronounced "droop" which suggests a momentary softening or plasticizing in the area of the bend (page 16).

To see what explanations for the Kiyota-bent spoons I might elicit, I showed the twisted spoons from Japan to several staff members in the Engineering building. The responses I got were interesting, to say the least. One suggested that it was possible that all the hardware stores in the area where the Kiyota family lives were in league with the family to perpetrate a hoax on foreigners by selling them "pre-softened" spoons.* Without inquiring how many witnesses there were, another offered the same explanation I had gotten from "non-experts"; namely, that the spoons had somehow been stuck into a keyhole or crevice while I was not looking. (Twelve persons were present when Masuaki, standing in the middle of the room, had twisted the spoon.) He did not inquire whether there had been any "keyholes" within reach, nor did he seem to consider how many pounds of force would be required to twist the spoon without leverage. Another said it must be a "gag," and just wasn't interested in looking at the spoons.

When I mentioned to one of the professors that two physicists had

---

Masuaki has just as easily twisted spoons obtained 15 and 9000 miles away.

been present when the spoons were bent, he responded, "How do I know they were not in "kahoots" with the boys? I would have to have the testimony of a Nobel Prize winner." When I told him that Dr. Brian Josephson, a Nobel prize winner in physics from Cambridge, England was one of those who investigated Matthew Manning who had bent cutlery in Toronto in June 1974, he said, "Oh well, I would have to see it myself."

Upper spoon was twisted mechanically in a vise by Prof. Koegel. Lower spoon bent by hand as described in text. Both had a gentle twist rather than the tight twists Masuaki usually gets. Prof. Mack sawed out the twisted section for tests of the two spoons in the middle — one twisted by Prof. Koegel and the other by Masuaki Kiyota.

After the testing was complete, one of Prof. Koegel's students figured out how to bend a spoon by physical force and he did a credible enough job to reinforce their beliefs that "there is no such thing as mind over matter." What he did was manually bend the handle of the spoon into a right angle near the bowl. Any man with strong hands can do that. Then he held the bowl firmly, upside down flat on the edge of a solid table and applied considerable force to turn the handle clockwise toward him about 180 degrees. Then he took the bent spoon and straightened out the 90-degree angle until the handle was approximately "straight." The spoon did then have a gentle twist of about 160 degrees in the handle. It was apparent that they were not interested in reading about laboratory tests done elsewhere, so I thanked them for their cooperation and left.

Number 18, the spoon that Prof. Koegel had bent with the torque wrench attached ¾ inch above the bowl, and a spoon bent paranormally by young Kiyota were then taken to Prof. David Mack's laboratory. He used a jeweller's saw and in each case had to saw about 10 minutes to cut through the handles near the twist as shown in the photo. He tried to break them when the saw was about halfway through the metal but could not do it with his hands. He put the two twisted pieces in a holder, filled it with bakelite compound and with heat and pressure produced a "plug" which he ground down to 600 fineness, at which level there were no significant differences when they were examined under a microscope.

I had met David Ashpole, a sales representative of ESCO Corporation on a plane trip. Later that fall (1977) when we were in Portland, Oregon, I phoned the ESCO Steel Manufacturing Corporation and discussed PK metal bending with him. He thought that their research department might be interested in hearing about the spoons which I had seen paranormally twisted. Mr. Laurence J. Venne, the technical director, invited two of his associates into his office to hear my report on the metal bending I had witnessed. Since he is on the 'firing line' in industry where it pays to be open to ideas and possibilities and not to be concerned about possibly having to rewrite some lecture notes if PK could be demonstrated in a laboratory setting, Mr. Venne and his co-workers asked a number of pertinent questions. After visually examining the spoons he estimated that they would have to be heated to 2000-2500 degrees Fahrenheit to produce a twist like the one in the spoons, and said that if heat had been used, the metal should have been discolored. The paranormally bent spoons showed no signs of discoloration whatsoever. If the bending had been done by physical force, Mr. Venne said he would expect to see striations or fractures where the bend occurred. These were also absent.

Later Mr. Venne mailed me a reprint of an article about the Geller effect from the magazine ***Metals and Materials***, October 1977, page 52. It is reproduced here for readers to see how someone was able to produce the bends which simulate the Geller effect. We suggest that you read it carefully and then decide whether you think Geller, Manning or Kiyota had the technical knowhow and access to the elaborate equipment and materials required to produce these effects.

Spoon with triple twist in handle sent by MK early in 1977.

A closeup of two tablespoons in which Masuaki said he "willed" a double twist—one with a greater distance between the two twists. The spoon in the center shows a triple twist as though the spoon was twirled while it was momentarily plastic. The bowl of the spoon broke off in the mail.

This article was reproduced with permission from the publisher of **METALS and Materials**, *Mr. R. Keith Evans, 1 Carlton House Terrace, London SW1Y 5D8, England and Dr. W. E. Duckworth, whose talk formed the basis for the article.*

The Uri Geller effect

Chilterns Metallurgical Society, January 7, 1977

In view of the publicity given to the Uri Geller effect it is surprising that there has been no serious examination of the phenomenon in the metallurgical literature. With this in mind, Dr W. E. Duckworth gave a talk on his interpretation of the subject to the Society.

Dr Duckworth began by pointing out that the bending or breaking of metal without the apparent use of external force was not a new phenomenon in metallurgy: The most recent example being that of special metals possessing the shape memory effect. He provided a dramatic illustration at the outset when a strip of beta brass, which had been straightened from its previous bent position in liquid nitrogen, was allowed to warm up with heat from the projector, and in front of the audience it bent spontaneously with no apparent external intervention. He then went on to simulate the Uri Geller effect even more closely with strips of the same metal in fork form. Their alloy composition was such that immersion in an alcohol/ice mixture performed the necessary phase transformation required in the shape-memory phenomenon. These forks had previously been bent at room temperature: after cooling in the alcohol/ice mixture they were quickly straightened and handed around the audience. When stroked by human hand, several

37

members of the audience had the satisfaction of seeing the forks bend very convincingly.

Other bending and breaking phenomenon were then demonstrated. A spoon made from Wood's metal was plunged into hot water just above its melting point at 66°C; when quickly removed it was seen to bend spontaneously and then break. Next, an aluminium strip was brushed with cotton wool soaked in mercurous nitrate, and after placing one or two drops of mercury upon the surface, the strip quickly fractured under a very light load. Finally, a steel sample under tension was surrounded by zinc, and when a sulphuric acid solution was allowed to drip between the metals hydrogen was generated. This was absorbed by the steel strip which subsequently fractured spontaneously.

The speaker claimed that the demonstrations confirmed his thesis that there were many ways by which metals could be shown to bend or break without apparent external intervention. Energy was needed however and he demonstrated this by separately fracturing brittle steel and brittle plastic. The pieces flew a considerable distance, thus illustrating that a considerable amount of energy had to be supplied.

Dr Duckworth then posed the question, how did Uri Geller supply the energy to do the bending and breaking? and went on to speculate about the processes which might be used. Through the good offices of Professor John Taylor of King's College London, a foreign stainless steel fork was shown which according to Professor Taylor, had been bent and broken by Uri Geller. Figure 1 shows the fork, and the more magnified appearance of the fracture is illustrated in Fig. 2. A stereoscan picture of the fractured surface is illustrated in Fig. 3. The rippled pattern shown on the fork surface in Fig. 2, and the appearance of the fracture in Fig. 3, suggest that failure was due to high strain fatigue.

To check this hypothesis a similar fork was flexed until it broke. To do this it had to be bent some ten times through an angle of about 50°. The appearance after fracture is shown in Fig. 4. In this, the ripples are coarser and the fracture appearance is clearly indicative of high strain fatigue. In other experiments a much smaller angle of bend, about 5°, was used, and the number of reversals to failure increased to about 100. The appearance of the fractured fork was then as shown in Fig. 5, and a stereoscan of the fracture in Fig. 6. Although the ripples are still coarser than on the Uri Geller fork, the general appearance of Figs. 5 and 6, and Figs, 2 and 3 respectively is quite similar.

On this basis, the speaker implied that one method of reproducing the Uri Geller effect would be by repeated cycling through a very small angle, possibly only one or two degrees, until fracture was imminent. It should then be possible for a skilled conjurer to be able to reproduce all the effects demonstrated in Uri Geller's public appearances.

Dr Duckworth was careful to suggest, however, that the evidence was not sufficient to assert definitely that Uri Geller did in fact perform this imminent pre-fracture operation before presenting his show. He pointed out that whatever external source of energy was used to bend or

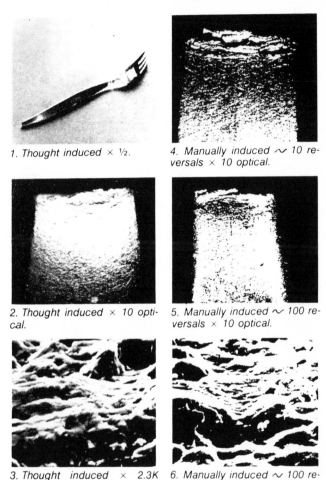

1. Thought induced × ½.

4. Manually induced ∿ 10 reversals × 10 optical.

2. Thought induced × 10 optical.

5. Manually induced ∿ 100 reversals × 10 optical.

3. Thought induced × 2.3K S.E.M.

6. Manually induced ∿ 100 reversals × 2.3K S.E.M.

break the metal, it must ultimately deform and fracture by one of the well known mechanisms he had described. The mechanism which caused the Uri Geller fork to break was clearly akin to that of high strain fatigue. But this was not to say that the actual process used by him was high strain fatigue: there may well be sources of energy other than flexing by physical means which could cause failure, and all that we witnessed at such performances was the manifestation of a high strain fatigue failure in the final product.

Dr Duckworth concluded by saying that it may never be possible to determine without dispute the source of Uri Geller's power by external examination of the actual pieces used by him. All that metallurgists could properly say is that it would be possible for a skilled conjurer to reproduce the Uri Geller effect by pre-strain flexing on the forks. Whether Uri Geller himself did that was something on which each individual would have formed his own decided views. He added that Professor John Taylor would also welcome further metallurgical examination of his bent forks, and any other laboratories should contact him for specimens if they wish.

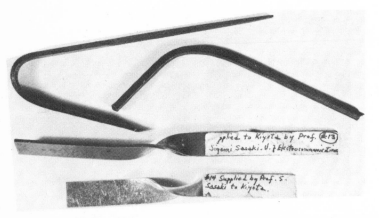

The metal in files is brittle and normally breaks instead of bending. The U-shaped file bent in the handle which is not case-hardened, suggesting that whatever energies are at work influence that part which has least resistance. Spoons and forks generally twist or bend where the metal is thinnest. The metal strips were supplied by Prof. Shegemi Sasaki of the University of Electro-Communications in Tokyo. No. 13 was a bi-metal strip—two kinds of metal fused into one, each having a different coefficient of expansion. yet this strip also twisted without signs of stress or separation where the two metals meet. No. 14 is an aluminum strip.

V. Six Days in Tokyo, March 1979

Masuaki's last letter before we left for Japan contained precise, detailed instructions for going to the Shin-Ochanomizu subway station from the Tokyo Green Hotel, a map of the six stops before the Kita-Senju station where we were to get off the train, and careful directions for the walk from the station to his home. This was much appreciated, since neither of us knew a word of Japanese.

Losing our passports in the Honolulu airport had delayed our flight to Tokyo by two hours, but courteous PanAm employees had managed to make contact with Tokyo for us and to notify the Kiyota family of the altered plans.

Excerpts from a diary Mary Jo Uphoff kept on the trip to record personal impressions may add some dimensions to the understanding of the observations and experiments which are included in other chapters. More detailed observations of the experiments we witnessed in Tokyo are described in this chapter.

Notes from our Tokyo Diairies—Mary Jo Uphoff
March 20
Late as we were, we were greeted by the "Kiyota delegation" at the air terminal—Masuaki, his parents, his two sisters, Mr. Fukuda, and Dr. Miyauchi, all of whom took our bags after a flurry of introductions, escorted us in two cabs to our hotel and then dined with us at the hotel dining room. . .everyone very hungry after the long wait. After struggling valiantly with chopsticks and conversation, we said good-night. Our hotel room is small but has good beds and all the amenities plus slippers of plastic and neatly folded kimonos!

March 21
. . .Went down at 11 to meet Elaine Morikawa who is to be our interpreter. She is Seattle-born, third generation Japanese-American, bright as a "button," looking like any college student in jeans. All the helplessness of not being able to communicate slips away!

Dr. Miyauchi came and we left for Senju by subway, stopped at his office on the way to the Chiyoda station to pick up some books which turned out to be gifts to us! Subway station noisy with a troop of young boys in baseball uniforms escorted by a young woman who seemed to be their coach. Bad News Bears?

The Nippon Television Network (NTV) film crew was setting up when we arrived at Kiyota's sushi restaurant. The streets in Senju were gay with pink plastic cherry blossoms hung on the young trees for **Sakura,** *the cherry blossom festival. Streets crowded—it is also a Buddhist holiday celebrating the spring equinox—shops displaying interesting fruits, garments and gadgets at extremely high prices.*

Masuaki began trying to bend spoons and the filming began. It is to be part of a "World Wonders" series, Elaine said, and the crew were already displaying what became a day-long, cooperative, low-key patience. About 3 p.m. the Kiyotas served a meal in the downstairs restaurant for all—raw fish with rice, soy sauce and condiments, mischo soup and tea—quite delicious! Mr. Kiyota told me the names of the fish; but I only remember tuna and squid. Thank heaven, no octopus! I did not feel up to that—not right away.

Eight-year-old Yukizi and 20-year-old Kazuko were not in sight, but we met grandfather who makes peasant sandals of cloth strips and straw. He gave us a pair and said he would make some to fit our feet—to be ready next Friday.

Masuaki, dictionary in hand, was eager to talk with us and showed us his stereo, records, books and souvenirs. He had us stand by as he bent several spoons (try as I might, I could not actually see the bending—it was that fast) and then presented them to us. Two were airline spoons which we had sought to buy on the plane but were told it was simpler to just take them.

Masuaki said he was hungry and could do better after he had eaten. After lunch he started thoughtography (nengraphy) with Mr. Fukuda, a professional photographer supervising. The lens-less polaroid camera was attached to sensors which were so displayed that the TV cameras could also photograph them. Two packs of Polaroid produced different images of the same object which could not be identified at this time. This seemed to be a new development which was quite exciting. Also some of the equipment began picking up what sounded to us like "psychic raps." Elaine was on hand the entire day to explain and interpret for us. About 10 p.m. it was decided to call it a day. The TV crew took Masuaki, Kazuko, Masuaki's friends, Elaine and us to a warm little coffee place down the street where the young people played TV games (a kind of electronic pinball) at the tables. Then Masuaki and his friends escorted Elaine and us all the way to our hotel. . .

March 22
Breakfast at a pleasant little cafe across the street from the Tokyo-Green Hotel where we are staying and to a nearby bank to change dollars for yen. People seeing us look at our little street map would stop to ask if they could help. In the imposing bank, a man motioned us up the stairs to the "Foreign Exchange." Apparently one glance told him we were American "tourists"—we didn't have to say a word!

. . .Masuaki, Hiroto and Toru—his friends who were at his home yesterday—and another young friend came for us at 1:30 and we went to Dr. Motoyama's Institute of Parapsychology and Religion by train. It is a lovely day—we walked to the Institute through a big park with a

bridge, lagoon complete with ducks, and crowds of people. Walter had been at the Institute in '76 so we had no trouble finding it. . .Dr. Motoyama was busy with patients, so after greeting us, we were shown around the institute by Dr. Harada, his assistant. Masuaki and Hiroto had fun working with an "ESP testing machine" with blinking red lights which I did not understand except that Masuaki appeared to be doing very well on it.

March 23

This forenoon we took a train to the Keio Plaza center where Walter wanted to take some pictures of the Keio Plaza hotel, one of Masuaki's best "targets." Then we went into the hotel (what affluence—these monster international hotels!) where we checked flight connections. Next we went to the Keio department store—the ultimate in department stores—buying gifts for the children at home and a supply of tablespoons for bending.

Dr. Miyauchi was at our hotel at one. Waited for a time for Elaine and then he left word where she could meet us. He led us up a street where within a block we encountered Elaine headed for our hotel. At a dark-shuttered little place, the Dr. stopped and led us in. He had been asking us if we liked what sounded like "eagle"—it turned out to be "eel"! We were ushered into a little private room with mats, low table and cushions. We are becoming accustomed to slipping off our shoes now and trying to keep those bright-colored, what our granddaughter calls "flip flops", on our feet.

We were brought beer, glasses and platters with scallions and a mound of pearl barley in a red fish sauce. Then came the broiled eels in sauce with rice, all in red lacquered "boxes". . .Suddenly Masuaki, Hiroto and Toru appeared and I wondered how they knew where to find us. They were persuaded to eat the extra eel the Doctor had ordered. . .

Lunch over, we went to Senju by subway, walking to the Kiyota home by different streets after leaving the station this time, past wares displayed outside the stores; throngs of women, children; bicycles, cars and trucks making their way through the masses of shoppers. Suddenly Masuaki darted into the doorway of a coffee house and we followed upstairs, Elaine explaining that he wanted to "warm up" for experiments by playing the TV (electronic) games for a while. These games are presently a "craze" among Japanese youth and must make a mint for the proprietors. The games are set into the booth tables and are coin-operated. Knobs are turned to send lights blasting targets with strange pings and squeaks. Masuaki's favorite game is one which shoots down "UFOs."

After an hour of sipping very strong coffee and watching the players, then buying film, we arrived at the Kiyota home. Mr. Fukuda was already there. The upstairs rooms which were filled with the TV crew's paraphanalia the previous day are now clear except for two low tables and the floor cushions. We distributed ourselves around the tables and out came the spoons and cameras. After toying with the cutlery a bit, Masuaki picked up the camera containing a pack of Polaroid color film we had brought and went into his small study with Walter who came out shortly with a paranormal showing a large spot of light, TV antennae, roofs—very impressive. Masauki then asked me to come in and hold the camera to "make a picture." He instructed me to relax and think of something and he would "help" me. All I could visualize was light. My left thumb began to tingle noticably. Masuaki thought we had something and pulled out the film. We did indeed have "light"—the whole photo was white, with a small green brush across the lower left hand corner. (There was no tripping of the shutter so the film should have been black.) Masuaki seemed quite pleased.

After a few more attempts at thoughtography, one of which resembled the Statue of Liberty, he turned to a telepathy experiment, first with me and then with Mr. Fukada, but nothing significant came of that. Next the spoons. Hiroto meanwhile, who can also bend spoons and metal, kept working on a spoon which sometime later was handed to me nicely bent. Mrs. Kiyota interrupted this with bowls of noodle soup for all nine of us, apparently at Masuaki's request, although earlier he had had a dish of meat and rice because he felt hungry and thought he could work better if he had something to eat. We all had tea earlier and had been nibbling on potato chips, crackers and tangerines since we arrived. The noodles, served with pork slices and strips of kelp in broth were a rather large meal after the rice and eel; and we had lunched on a slice of Oscar Mayer ham before we left the hotel, not anticipating the excellent meals that were to follow!

Mr. Fukuda and I tried to see if we could 'send' Masuaki a design of wire with two closed doors between, but this was a "wipe out."

More photo work. Masuaki ran a few feet of the film in the movie camera and then we tried another experiment. Synchronized our watches and Mr. Fukuda, Toru Ozaki and I took Fukuda's camera loaded with film and walked out into the street instructed to go a hundred meters in any direction we pleased, then without snapping the shutter, to pull the film. Meanwhile Masuaki, Walter, Elaine and the others who were there, held hands in a circle while Masuaki concentrated on producing an image on the film in "our" camera. Fukuda carefully checked his watch. We were standing at an intersection with traffic going by. We were very anxious to see if there would be a picture. Standing there in the street lights (it was already dark) Fukuda pulled off the covering of the polaroid film and exclaimed in astonishment. There was a double inverted image recognizable as the Statue of Liberty.

A trial with Walter and me produced a color which might be our house at Oregon which we were trying to visualize. Masuaki had never seen our home or a picture of it. I thought the house with the adjoining garage with its white doors a would be easiest to visualize, while Walter said his mind kept going to the nearby granary. There is something like a tower at one side of the reddish and green Polaroid print and two areas of blurred white which correspond to the garage doors and the light yellow driveway leading up to them.

People were fatigued by 11:30 p.m. and we headed "home" with Elaine *and Dr. Miyauchi and Toru. Interspersed with all the afternoon's activities were several conversations with Yoshinori Kiyota, Masuaki's father, translated by Elaine, with Masuki and Mr. Fukuda joining in. . .*

The first piece of cutlery infuenced by Masuaki Kiyota during our visit to Tokyo, March 1979. A Northwest-Orient Airlines cabin attendant had said it would be simpler just to take a few pieces of cutlery for PK experiments rather than to complete purchase forms for them. This fork was given to Masuaki shortly after our arrival and within one minute the handle fell to the floor, the tines remaining in his hand. In this case there was no stroking or rubbing—a very impressive demonstration of PK. Where the break occurred, the metal appeared to have been momentarily softened or plasticized. There was no sign of a sharp break.

March 24

. . . . Walter went with Masuaki, Hiroto and Toru to Nippon Television Network studios for dinner with Mr. Jun-Ichi Yaoi. . . He found the TV studios one of the most impressive things he had seen as to production, technology, etc.

March 25

. . . Our friends from Okayama arrived yesterday. It was a gray rainy day and the best thing we could decide to do which would also be interesting for our friends' 14-year-old son was to visit the National Museum. What was a drizzle when we arrived at this great gray stone survivor of imperial splendor had become a downpour when we were to leave later in the afternoon. Not even the pink plastic cherry blossoms could do much to brighten the day. Inside the museum we walked through the great unadorned halls admiring the marvellous tapestries and hangings, the ancient bronzes and porcelains and the scale models of national shrines and famous buildings.

Today the sun is shining. . . Furusawa and his family would like to see something of Tokyo since it is his son's first visit, so I will go with them on a city tour which leaves from the central bus terminal. . . Walter will meet the boys again this morning. They want to show him the old Akasaka part of Tokyo and are disppointed that I am not going along.

Hiroto wrote a touching note to us which he gave to Elaine to give to us for he is shy and thinks his English inadequate. . .

There was a note from Walter in our room when I returned. He and Masuaki waited for me until 1:35 and had to leave to meet Prof. Sasaki out in Senju, and would I phone? Finally reached him at Kiyotas about 4. Toru was coming out later and would stop by for me. About 5:30 Toru appeared and we went together. Toru will begin medical school in May

although he has completed his schooling in fisheries management. He is a quiet, thoughtful young man. It is his interest in the phenomena around Masuaki that made him decide to go into medicine and psychiatry.

At Kiyota's, snacks are on the low table upstairs and an array of instruments is on the other, tended by Prof. Sasaki's assistant. Masuaki has just bent a fork for Elaine and is "working" on another. We go over to the instruments from time to time to watch the pen-recorder which gets "agitated" when Masuaki begins to "rev" up. Prof. Sasaki has been showing Walter some of his reports and we go through photo albums full of Masuaki's nengraphy photos and photos of Masuaki and Hiroto bending metal when they were much younger.

Another and last sushi meal; talked with Prof. Sasaki about Findhorn; his limited English and my total lack of Japanese—it is a wonder that I understood he wanted us to send him information about Findhorn.

Packed up a box to mail home, including the two pairs of cloth sandals which Grandfather Kiyota made for us. He came dashing up on his heavy bicycle as we walked to the station in Senju Friday night to give us "the big pair" he hoped would fit Walter. The weaving of these sandals from cloth and straw is becoming a lost art and Grandfather is proud of his skill. We feel we have experienced a few insights into life in Japan which not many are privileged to have.

March 26
Masuaki came to the hotel to bring the movie camera this morning. It grew near to the time we had to leave for the air terminal for check-in but no sign of Masuaki. At three minutes to 10, Walter had the desk clerk at the hotel call the Kiyotas and learned that Masuaki was just leaving. At 10:15 he walked into the door of the hotel, camera in hand. We have not figured out how he made that trip by subway and on foot in about 18 minutes! We cannot imagine doing it in half an hour. He went with us to the Tokyo Central Air Terminal where we said our good-byes and Masuaki was almost tearful. Walter gave him the handful of coins from his pockets and he smiled when he told him to use it for playing TV games.

On the hour-long drive to Narita airport, we looked at the construction, housing and clumps of forsythia in bloom on the medians. The entrances to Narita International Airport were heavily guarded by police in riot gear who checked carefully all incoming cars and persons. We had been thoroughly checked out at TCAT—an immense place—by polite, white-gloved guards who ask if they may do so! Narita is relatively empty and very quiet. The architecture, though modern and unusual, seems gloomy and sterile. After the pass control, our hand luggage is inspected and Walter's Swiss army knife taken into "custody" to be returned to him when we get to Manila.

Masuaki Influences Both Color and Black-and White Film

Photos lose some sharpness when reproduced, especially when they are half-toned for printing. These two pictures (Nos. 5 and 6) are not sharp but the forms are recognizable. Instead of reproduction in color—

an expensive process—a more detailed description is given to convey what we experienced.

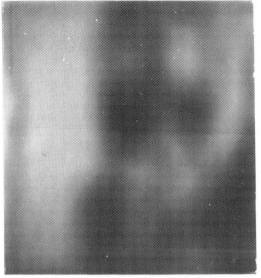

No. 5 paranormal photo—Big Ben

Photo No. 5 (Polacolor 083561-2) was produced by Masuaki about 7:30 p.m., March 23, 1979 at his home in Tokyo. Both of us watched while he concentrated on the camera loaded with film we had supplied. After about a minute, he pulled out the film without tripping the shutter; the photo showed what looked like two faces of the Big Ben clock tower in London's Parliament building. On the original picture, the vertical structure appears to be black and grey-ish, the left side of the picture is a blue shade like the sky.

At no time during the entire set of experiments with polaroid film did Masuaki trip the shutter. He explains that when he tries to project a picture onto film by PK, it is often as if he is leafing through a book of pictures. Usually the picture in his conscious mind at the moment he gets the urge to project a picture is the image that actually appears on film. However, there are times when the picture he visualized just before or after the one he has tried to project, gets onto the film. Things do not always turn out that way, though, so no one explanation is adequate to cover the range of phenomena we observed. It seems as if some images are so well imprinted in his "mind" that objects like Big Ben, the Statue of Liberty, the Tokyo Tower, the Keio-Plaza Hotel in Tokyo, etc. recur from time to time. If the phenomenon were limited to such pictures, and if they were always produced from a perspective where one could determine how the picture was taken, there might be some basis for suspecting that

Masuaki resorts to a gimmick. Considering all the pictures he has produced and the circumstances involved, "gimmickry" is totally inadequate as an explanation. Too often images have been obtained when others had control of the camera, in some cases, hundreds of feet away.

Here is what appeared on the other prints of the Polacolor pack on March 23rd:

No. 1—At about 5:30 p.m., Masuaki's first attempt produced a picture which shows the lower half of a large ball of light at the top which somewhat resembles a light fixture on the ceiling. The rest of the picture, which is in fairly sharp focus, shows the corner of the roof of nearby buildings and some TV antennae that can be seen out of the small window of his study. I took a photograph of that scene with my own camera that evening and again the next morning and got recognizable similarities *but not the same image.* Even though I am sure that no trickery was involved, I can appreciate that anyone not there to observe might conclude that we were not observing enough to see him influence the film by some "normal" means. We know that Masuaki did not point the camera at the ceiling nor through the window.

No 2.—Masuaki gave the camera to Mary Jo and asked her to visualize something for a picture and he would "help." All she was able to think of was white "light." She experienced a tingling in her left thumb and then handed the camera back to Masuaki who said he thought there was something on it. He pulled out the film and when the negative was separated from the positive, the photo was all a creamy white except for a small blue-green area along the lower left side of the picture. (5:54 p.m.)

No. 3—At 6 p.m. Masuaki, with no visible concentration, pulled another film which turned out to be a "blackie" as should be expected, since he did not trip the shutter.

No. 4—At 6:30 p.m. he pulled out another "blackie."

No. 5—with the image of Big Ben was described earlier.

No. 6—The biggest surprise came when Masuaki asked us to concentrate on our house in Wisconsin—a place he had never seen, personally, or in pictures, at that time. At about 8 p.m., Mr. Yutaka Fukuda, a professional photographer who had conducted many experiments with Masuaki, and myself were asked to take the camera out on the street, while Masuaki stayed inside the house and concentrated. After about four minutes passed, Mr. Fukuda said he was experiencing a headache and we went back in the house with the camera. When No. 6 was pulled from the camera, it showed structures which both Mary Jo and myself recognized as part of our house in Wisconsin. Even the colors matched. Our split-level house is painted red with white trim. The two-car garage is attached on the north side. The garage doors are white and can be seen as such when closed. Fifty feet north of the garage stands an old granary which has been rebuilt, parts added on,

NO. 6 A very unusual photo produced by thoughtgraphy on Polaroid film without tripping the camera shutter. Masuaki had asked the Uphoffs to think about their home in Wisconsin which he had never seen, nor had he seen a photo of it. This photo shows recognizable shapes and colors consistent with the two-car garage attached to the house and a view of the remodelled granary nearby, super-imposed on the main part of the house.

Photos of relevant parts of Uphoff's house, garage and granary referred to above. Picture at right shows a south view of the granary with its two roof sections. An east view of the granary with its two roof sections. An east view of the granary, showing the square window (also visible in the paranormal photo) is superimposed on part of the house, as described in text.

and also painted red with a white trim. When viewed from the south side, the roof of that building's addition starts about three feet below the edge of the original roof, thus showing two separate areas of the roof.

The picture Masuaki produced showed most of the two-car garage on the right side. The granary, as seen from the East, with its big square window and two roof areas, is superimposed on the main part of the house, except that the granary roofs had a perspective as if photographed from about a hundred feet above and East of the building. The roof on the addition, which has only a slight pitch which is barely visible from the ground, appears at least as wide as the roof on the old part of the building.

Something extra appeared above the granary which we cannot identify. The background is sky-blue.

We do not presume to know how Masuaki was able to cut through time and space to get that picture in Tokyo. When asked to think about our house, I wondered if I should visualize a close-up or a panoramic view of the house and yard, including the granary. Mary Jo had concentrated on the garage with its two white doors and the driveway which has been filled with crushed lime. Had Masuaki picked up some of our thoughts and combined them in a composite picture, or had he made a quick "trip" through space to get the image?

Nos. 7 and **8** were then pulled in a succession as controls, with no concentration, and both were black as was to be expected.

A Double Statue of Liberty

After using the 8-pack Polacolor film, I loaded the camera with black and white Polaroid film I had brought. Again the shutter was not tripped for any of the pictures made during the next hour. No 1, pulled out without concentration, was a "blackie." Nos. 2 and 3 turned out to be "whities" similar to those Ted Serios often got in experiments with Dr. Jule Eisenbud before Ted projected images. At 8:45 p.m. Masuaki concentrated on the camera only for about ten seconds, shook his head and pulled out No. 4. It quite clearly showed the base and most of the Statue of Liberty as can be seen in the picture.

Then about 9:20 p.m. Mr. Fukuda, Masuaki's friend who is a medical student, and Mary Jo were asked to take the camera with them and walk a distance down the street and pull the next film after five minutes had elapsed. Mr. Fukuda kept track of the time and also kept the camera, swinging it on the wrist strap as they walked. Meanwhile, upstairs in the Kiyota house, Dr. Miyauchi, Elaine Morikawa, Hiroto Yamashita and I held hands in a circle with Masuaki for about three minutes while he concentrated on a picture. He predicted that this would be an unusual picture and it certainly was.

Out on the street corner, Mr. Fukuda pulled No. 5 out of the camera and peeled off the negative after allowing for development time. On the picture was a double-inverted image of the Statue of Liberty; in one image, the outstretched arm of the figure was only partially visible.

Naturally this created some excitement when Mr. Fukuda brought the picture into the house. After the excitement died down, Mr. Fukuda suggested pulling two more films from the pack on which Masuaki had not concentrated (as controls) and these were both "blackies."

The series of Polaroid pictures, numbers 2 through 7, which Masuaki Kiyota produced without tripping the camera shutter. (See text for details.) NO. 5, which shows a double, inverted Statue of Liberty, was produced when the camera had been carried out into the street while Masuaki remained in the house and concentrated on projecting the image.

Paranormals on Movie Film

A Canon-514 Super-8 movie camera was loaned to us for the trip by Ken Coffman of Oregon, Wisconsin. After the successes with Polaroid, we thought it would be interesting to see if Masuaki could also influence movie film, since we had already seen other movie film he had affected by PK. We loaded the camera with color film and gave it to him in the afternoon of March 24th. He worked with it for at least five minutes, running about ten feet of the film. He then decided that he was "not in the mood" and had not been able to "get anything." Mr. Fukuda then suggested that we tape the lens cap and the film cassette opening with heavy plastic tape and mark with a felt-tip pen across each layer of the tape so that any tampering could be detected. We left the camera with Masuaki with the suggestion that he try to produce something on that film if he felt in the mood later on.

The next day was Sunday. Masuaki and his friends wanted to show us a part of Tokyo before we left for the Philippines so he forgot to do anything with the camera. He promised he would try that evening and would bring the camera to the Tokyo Green Hotel where we were staying before we were to leave for the air terminal on Monday forenoon.

Since the camera was not mine and I needed it in the Philippines, I spent some anxious moments Monday morning as 10 a.m. approached and Masuaki had not yet appeared with the camera. Our baggage was in the hotel lobby, ready for the taxi to the terminal. At 9:57 a.m. I wrote the desk clerk a note asking him to phone Masuaki's home to ask that if Masuaki had not yet left with the camera, he should meet us at the air terminal instead, as we had to be there by 10:30. The clerk reported that Masuaki told him he was just ready to leave for the hotel and that we should not worry. Having travelled the distance between the hotel and the Kiyota home in Senju a number of times, I figured it would take at least half an hour. But at 10:15 Masuaki walked into the lobby with a big smile on his face, saying, "I think I got some picture for you!"

Uphoff marks the tape wound over the film cassette opening of the movie camera before giving it to Masuaki to try his powers of "thoughtography".
(Photo by Y. Fukuda)

I remembered what Toru Ozaki had told me and what his father had written about Masuaki teleporting himself to school occasionally when he did not leave home on time, and I wondered if he had accomplished this distance by the same means. He would have had to walk or run well over half a mile, go down into the subway station, buy his ticket, wait for the next train, ride five station stops, get off at the sixth, walk or run up another long flight of stairs, and then cover three more blocks on foot—all in 18 minutes. In any case, Masuaki said he felt that the first image on the film would be the Statue of Liberty and there would be others of the Tokyo Tower and some scenes of London. The footage counter was at 50, indicating that the remaining 40 feet of film had been run through the camera. I took photos of the movie camera, with taping and counter, to show that the lens and film cassette opening had not been tampered with.

The super-8 movie camera used by Masuaki when he projected images on color film. The lens cap and film cassette opening were securely taped as described in the text. Photo *(above)* shows the footage counter at 10 when the camera was taped; the photo *(below)* shows the counter at 50 when the camera was returned with the taping intact.

The movie film was processed by Kodak after our return via Europe and run through our projector before any of the other films taken on the trip. The first ten feet of film were black and I wondered if the entire film might be blank. Then came about 7 seconds of the Statue of Liberty;

53

another blank section; then the middle section of the Tokyo Tower; more blank film; then what looked like a section of a large office building with tiers of windows as if "photographed" from an aerial perspective with the windows slanted at a 30-degree angle; more blank film; an unclear image of some structures with what appeared to be bright red roofs; and finally a close-up of a face with great dark eyes, something like a Goya painting—about 27 seconds of images on 3 minutes of film. All the images appeared bathed in a soft golden light.

In order to keep the original film in as good condition as possible, extra prints were made. Glenn Austin, a professional photographer, worked with the original film to make enlargements of sections where the images appeared. He used 35 mm. color film which shows the sprocket holes of the original film as part of the reproduction. At one point Glenn asked for some pieces of film which had been cut from other rolls taken on the trip. Only later did he tell us that he had wanted to examine that film under a magnifying glass to see if the paranormal film had been run through the same movie camera. He said that a bit of detective work will reveal whether the same camera was used—that each camera leaves its tell-tale "finger prints" on the edge of the film in the form of some slight irregularity on the margin or edge of the photograph and that this varies from camera to camera. He concluded that, in fact, the same camera had been used for producing the paranormal pictures—something we were sure of all the time.

How does Masuaki do this? We do not know but we are certain that no trickery was involved. Several sections of the film Glenn Austin enlarged are reproduced to show how the image shifts gradually from frame to frame.

 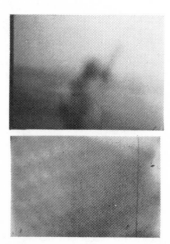

Enlargements of four frames from the Super-8 paranormal film.

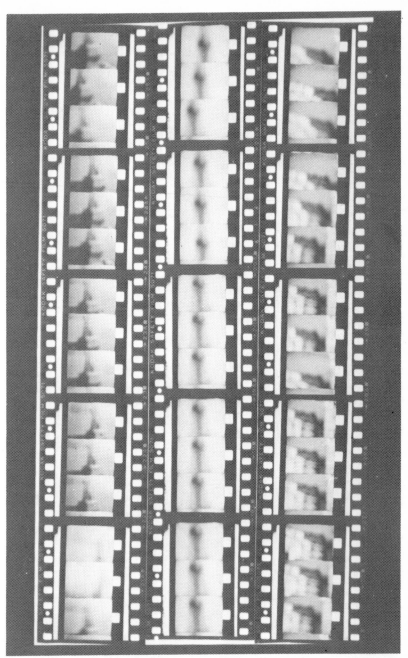

Section of super-8 Kodak color film, showing frames with the Statue of Liberty, the Tokyo Tower, and a building which Masuaki said he saw when he was in London. The enlargement to 35 mm. with the sprocket holes of the original film shown, was done by Glenn Austin.

The Uphoffs, with the assistance of Elaine Morikawa, discuss the paranormal photos Masuaki has produced with his father, Yoshinori Kiyota, while Masuaki relaxes by blowing bubblegum. (Photo by Y. Fukuda)

Mary Jo and Walter Uphoff, with Masuaki and Elaine Morikawa at the Kiyota home in Tokyo. The "thumbs up" gesture is a favorite pose of Masuaki's.

VI.   The Nippon TV Documentary

The first filming of experiments with Masuaki Kiyota for this program were scheduled for March 1979. Knowing that we were coming to Tokyo that month, the Kiyota family had suggested that this start when we could be present as observers. Our arrival had been scheduled to coincide with school vacation when Masuaki and his friend and "fellow-psychic" Hiroto Yamashita, who is nearly two years younger, would be free to give more time to the project.

During the time we were guests at the Kiyota home, we had the good fortune to have with us most of the time, a young American, Elaine Morikawa, who for the past three years had been teaching English in Tokyo and who was willing to serve as interpreter. She had already become acquainted with the Kiyota family and was a friend of Masuaki.

The film crew was setting up equipment on the second floor of Kiyota's *sushi* restaurant when we arrived there about noon the day after we had arrived in Tokyo. Japanese household furnishings, as the reader may know, are traditionally simple, consisting of low tables and mats, or cushions for seating. Shoes were left at the door and we were supplied with red plastic sandals to wear which did not fit our over-sized American feet very well. Masuaki immediately took us to his "study"— a very small room filled with his books, desk, a stereo, souvenirs, posters, records, camera, gym shoes—except for the Japanese characters, it could have been any American teenager's favorite nook.

While the film crew set up, Masuaki showed us his Japanese-English dictionary, his school texts for his English class, his school annuals and his favorite rock records. We were soon to discover that rock music, played good and loud, was an indispensable part of the experimental activities because it "put him in the mood" for revving up his psychic state of mind. Dr. Miyauchi, a physicist interested in "thoughtography" and managing director of the Japan Nengraphy Association, was on hand, as was a professional photographer, Mr. Yutaka Fukuda—both of whom had also been present when Alan Neuman filmed Masuaki in 1976. Both of them knew Walter. Mr. Fukuda was actively involved as a professional, in helping set up and monitor the experiments in which Masuaki was to try to influence the film.

The spoon bending, as we were to discover, was a kind of peripheral activity. Masuaki and 15-year-old Hiroto, who had also come for the filming session, both kept toying with spoons while awaiting the experimental filming to take place. They fondled, rubbed and juggled the pieces of tableware, while they roamed around in various parts of the room or talked with the people who were there. Yoshinori Kiyota, Masuaki's father, a handsome, pleasant-faced man, clad in his restauranteur's white coat, looked in occasionally to see how things were coming along. Masuaki's sisters shyly observed the activities from a doorway from time to time and then unobtrusively disappeared.

The film crew, particularly the cameraman, was an extraordinary model of patience. Sitting cross-legged on the cushions, chain-smoking cigarettes, they conversed in soft voices and provided us a contrast with the conditions imposed on Geller, for instance, when he appeared on TV programs in the U.S. and was prodded continuously to perform. These men knew one waited and imposed no constraints of time. Both days that we witnessed filming, the crew demonstrated this attitude of endless patience throughout the day, waiting prepared for the right moment. The documentary produced shows that their patience and understanding were rewarded.

When Masuaki came to the U.S. on July 26th, he brought with him a copy of the videotape of the NTV documentary programs, most of which were filmed after we left Tokyo. Jamie Hubbard, a graduate student in Oriental languages at the University of Wisconsin, was engaged to translate the Japanese sound track and dub in an English commentary for showing this videotape at the workshops in Madison.

Edited version of Jamie's commentary

Those phenomena which occur in our world and cannot be understood by science are termed supernatural or paranormal. One such phenomenon which several years ago enjoyed great popularity in Japan was that of bending or twisting spoons by psychic power—psychokinesis or PK. This phenomenon, however, left many doubts and unanswered questions which the producers of this show proposed to investigate in a scientific manner.

[The videotape shows a spoon bent by PK and then the force required to produce a tight twist in a spoon in the same way by normal force. It required so much force that the feat was impossible to replicate with bare hands. Even then the twist produced by the machine was much gentler than the abrupt twist seen in the spoon bent by psychokinetic power.]

About 1100 kilograms (2420 pounds) of pressure was required to break the spoon which was broken through the power of PK. There is no discernible difference between the two spoons to the naked eye. But when examined with an electron microscope, some interesting differences appear. The surface of the spoon broken by PK exhibits great stress and structural confusion—a phenomenon even more apparent when the

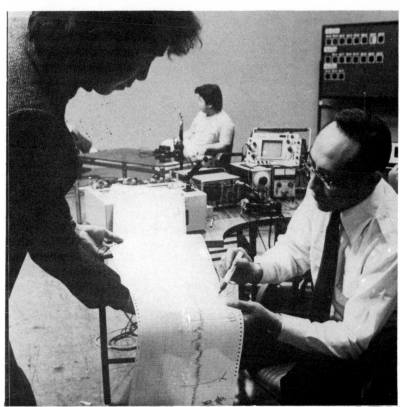

(Above) Masuaki in the background, surrounded by elaborate monitoring equipment, with Mr. Hideya Yamaguchi, director of Nippon TV Network, and Dr. Suzuki, at right, studying the unusual tracings produced. *(Below)* a closeup of the tracing.

magnification is increased 300 times. There is evidence of great weakness induced in the metal; obviously the spoon's structure is weakened to a great extent. The spoon broken by the machine, however, exhibits only the usual wave patterns associated with metal fatigue. Seen in comparison, the differences are readily apparent. The research team was now ready to admit the existence of paranormal phenomena. . .

The "Source" of Psychic Phenomena

[NTV then proceeded to investigate Masuaki Kiyota to determine the "source" of this psychic or paranormal phenomenon.] *Masuaki first noted his psychic abilities in 1973 and though he has supernormal abilities, his school and home life are no different than that of a normal 16-year-old boy. In addition to being able to bend spoons, he is also capable of thoughtography, or mentally projecting images onto unexposed film. . .*

The film and camera used in this experiment were prepared by the research crew. The camera is an ordinary Polaroid camera with the lens and shutter locked so it cannot be released. When asked how he felt while trying to project an image psychically, Masuaki replied that he felt a slight tingling in his thumb and a warm feeling in his body. . .Masuaki went on to say that the energy he transmitted was not so much within him as it was an energy around him that he was able to channel and direct. He added that it was precisely because he was not using up his own energy that he does not become extremely tired or fatigued while performing such feats.

Although he said he had been concentrating on the Keio-Plaza hotel, one of the largest buildings in downtown Tokyo, the image produced in this experiment is the Statue of Liberty, a view which he often produces. Masuaki explained this by saying that although he was trying to concentrate on the Keio-Plaza, nonetheless many other images and thoughts pass through this mind and at the moment he transmits his psychic energy, that image which is foremost in his mind is the one which will be transmitted to the unexposed film.

He added that he has never actually seen the Statue of Liberty. Both of these photos of the Keio-Plaza in Tokyo were produced paranormally by Masuaki, the one on the right by automatic polaroid and the one on the left by manual polaroid. Both of these photos appear to have been taken from a high vantage point such as a nearby building. [or from a helicopter.Ed.]

Helicopter Establishes Paranormality

The research team then set out in a helicopter to see if they could find such a vantage point. The photo which Masuaki produced psychically is exactly as one which would have been taken from an altitude of 200 meters, or just about 600 feet. At first glance the photo produced paranormally and the actual photo appear to be very similar, but on closer inspection one notices that the building in Masuaki's photo is slightly tilted to the left and the bottom of the building is wider than the

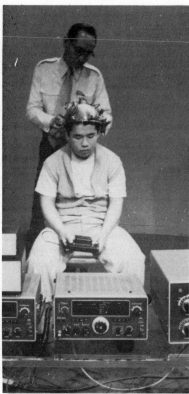

Hiroto and Masuaki wearing helmets wired to measure brain waves from different parts of their heads. At left Hiroto concentrates on bending a spoon. At right Masuaki seeks to influence Polaroid film in a box which has no shutter or lens. (See Chapter XI for details on megaherz emissions.)

top—a perspective which is opposite from what one would get if the photo were taken from above the subject*. . .Then photos were psychically produced in rapid succession by Masuaki and the unusual designs and pictures were the results of his not having concentrated on any particular image when he transmitted his psychic energy.

The research team and staff at NTV then decided to take psychically-produced photographs as one main topic in the study of paranormal activity. In addition to light, heat and pressure are known to also be factors influencing photographic film. Thus, for the purposes of these experiments, the staff constructed a special camera and attached a three mm. thick aluminum covering to the front of the camera, making it impossible for light, heat or pressure to influence the film in any way. The camera was then submitted to tests, using infrared light to determine whether any heat or light would be able to penetrate this cover. After temperatures up to 85° C. [185° F.] the film is absolutely black, showing no signs of exposure and thus showing that neither light nor heat is

---

*Nippon TV actually engaged a helicopter to get aerial views.

capable of entering the camera and influencing the film.

Using this specially constructed camera, the experiment was then begun in one of Nippon TV's sound studios. Of course, unopened film was always used for these experiments. Although it is not widely known, psychic photography or thoughtography was first discovered in 1910 by a Japanese psychologist, Dr. T. Fukurai, a teacher at Tokyo University. Prof. Fukurai subsequently announced his findings at an international conference in London in 1911. Unfortunately Dr. Fukurai lost his job as a result of the controvery over his book about his findings.

Masuaki Influences Unexposed Film

Although Masuaki normally has about an 80% success ratio in psychically transmitting images on film, during the filming of this documentary, his success rate fell to approximately 10%. Masuaki attributed this low rate to distractions caused by his nervousness in the presence of the film crew, as well as the psychological handicap of having to work with a specially-constructed camera box which was not really a camera. It took approximately 50 attempts before he was able to produce the first image during these experiments. After he produced the first image, he felt more relaxed and as a result he was then able to produce images in about 50% of the remaining attempts, inspite of the 3 mm. aluminum cover on the camera.

Although neither heat nor light is able to penetrate such an aluminum covering, radiation of a higher frequency than light, such as x-rays or gamma rays would be able to penetrate it. The camera was then exposed to x-rays in order to determine whether or not this would expose film in the same way as young Masuaki and thus raise the possibility that there was some form of x-ray radiation involved in Masuaki's psychic abilities. The film was 100% exposed with results similar to those often obtained by Masuaki. Next the camera was exposed to gamma rays with the same result as obtained from the previous experiment.

Masuaki was then checked with Geiger counters and other instruments to see if there were any form of radiation present when he concentrated on transmitting psychic energy. However, no matter how many times they repeated the test, there was never any evidence of the presence of radioactivity. If radiation were not the cause of Masuaki's abilities, where then was one to search for the source of the psychic energies he was capable of transmitting? Again, if this source of energy was such that it could not be measured by any scientific instruments, would we then have to posit that it found its source in a different dimension?

The research team had exhausted all of their ideas when suddenly during a viewing of the tapes of the experiments they had made, they discovered an unexplained noise which had been picked up by the wireless mike when Masuaki was concentrating on producing an image on the film. Using sophisticated sound monitors, all the films they had made during the experiments were then carefully checked. It was found that a white line on the left side of the screen represented a recording of that sound.

(Left) Dr. T. Miyauchi *(standing, left)* looking on as the Nippon TV crew focus on Masuaki *(right)* who has successfully influenced the Polaroid film which Mr. Y. Fukuda is shown peeling off the negative. Elaine Morikawa is seated at the table on the left.

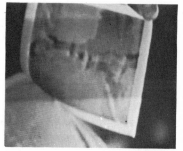

NO. 1 Polaroid camera with lens and shutter removed, sealed with an aluminum plate. Exposure to intense light shows box to be lightproof.

NO. 2 An image of the Statue of Liberty produced by "thoughtography" during a session of continuous filming.

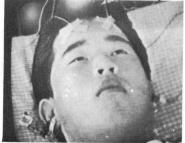

NO. 3 Photo taken from a helicopter over Tokyo to determine the perspective from which Masuaki's image of the Keio Plaza Hotel might have been obtained.

NO. 4 Masuaki being tested at Dr. H. Motoyama's laboratory for physical responses occurring during PK activity.

Such a noise should have been impossible in the closed sound stage where they were working. They decided to follow this lead. They asked Dr. Matsumi Suzuki, the discoverer of voice prints, to investigate this phenomenon. When measured on the spectograph, this sound proved to be an electrical wave with a frequency of approximately 30 megaherz—a little used frequency between the short waves used in wireless radios and the VHF frequency used for television broadcasting.

Electrical Waves From Left Frontal Lobe

Masuaki was then checked to see if he could be the source of these electrical waves. . .When Masuaki began to concentrate, the needles on the pen-recorder used to measure the strength of the electrical waves began to move, indicating the increased presence of these electrical waves and it was thus determined that the electrical waves produced by Masuaki were the source of the noise recorded earlier.

What was the meaning? What significance did these electrical waves have? What part of the body did they come from? Could they be the cause of Masuaki's psychic ability? The research team decided to pursue these questions to investigate the phenomenon. Further investigation showed that there was a clear relationship between the strength or weakness of the electrical waves and Masuaki's concentration and whether or not Masuaki was concentrating. When the experiment was repeated with Mr. Hideya Yamaguchi, the director of the program as the subject, there was no evidence whatsoever of the emission of electrical waves. Masuaki is able to produce at will. . .electrical waves which others are not capable of producing. The electrical energy which he produces is not generated immediately when he begins to concentrate. It requires a slight warming up period. Also it does not stop abruptly when he stops concentrating—rather it tapers off.

Next they attempted to determine which part of Masuaki's body emitted these electrical waves and it was found that they came from the upper part of his head. Next they repeated this experiment on someone from the crew with no results whatsoever.

In order to determine from which part of his head these electrical waves were emitted, Prof. Suzuki designed a special helmet with 13 separate poles from which to record the electrical waves. In this way they were able to determine that the electrical energy was strongest from Nos. 7, 8 and 10. The data was analyzed by computer and it was determined that an electrical wave of 34.5 megaherz was emitted from the left frontal lobe of the brain. [See Chapter VIII concerning an incident of a garage door opening at a home where M.K. and H.Y. were guests.]

The left frontal lobe is that part of the brain which controls our motor nervous system and of course it is not part of the normal function of this part of the brain to produce electrical waves. To determine whether this phenomenon—transmitting electrical waves—is common to all psychics, the research team then repeated the experiments with Hiroto Yamashita, a 15-year-old boy who also has the ability to bend spoons. Hiroto is also capable of producing electrical waves. Again, like Masuaki, depending on his level of concentration, Hiroto is able to control the strength and weakness of the electrical waves. Prof. Suzuki explains that the wave length produced by the two boys is of such nature that it could not be produced artificially. Although the electrical waves emitted by both

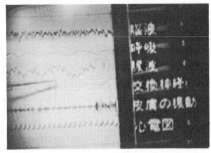

NO. 5 Tracings recorded by Nippon TV showing the brain wave activity when Masuaki was producing PK energy.

NO. 6 Testing equipment used to determine force required to break a spoon with the same visible effect as a paranormal break.

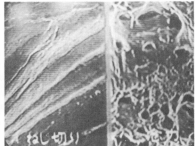

NO. 7 Tablespoon which broke at the point that the instrument recorded approximately 1100 kilograms applied force.

NO. 8 At 300X magnification, the spoon broken by mechanical force *(left)* is distinctly different from the spoon broken by PK *(right)* showing what is termed by Dr. Suzuki as structural confusion.

Masuaki and Hiroto share many similar characteristics, Masuaki's are more difficult to record because of the greater variance in the frequency of the wave length. Although ten times greater in strength than the electrical waves emitted by Masuaki, the frequency of those produced by Hiroto (26.5 megaherz) are 8 megaherz lower than Masuaki's

In order to determine what physiological changes occur while emitting such electrical waves, Masuaki was examined at Prof. Hiroshi Motoyama's Institute for the Study of Religion and Parapsychology. There he was given many tests, among them an electroencephlagram, electrocardiogram and tests designed to measure responses of his motor and sympathetic nervous systems. While he was relaxing, the fourth needle, measuring brain waves, showed no movement changes. However, when he is in total concentration, both the fourth needle measuring the brain waves and the seventh needle measuring the responses of the sympathetic nervous system show great movement—a physical response similar to that exhibited in a state of excitement.

Faraday Cage Used

Next, while measuring physiological changes in Masuaki, they also checked changes which occurred in the magnetic and electrical fields which surrounded him. In order to prevent any outside electrical influence, these tests were conducted in a Faraday cage, shielded by copper and lead. The first needle measured any changes in the magnetic field,and the third needle in the electrical field. While he is relaxed there is no significant movement in either needle. However, when Masuaki began to concentrate, the instruments recorded significant changes in both the magnetic and the electrical fields within the cage. The magnetic field which surrounds the Earth is produced within the planet in the same way as an electrical generator produces electricity. Although this magnetic field cannot be seen or felt, it covers the entire earth. This magnetic field is also present inside the Faraday cage as well.

Next the research team tried to answer the question of just how the supernatural and paranormal events could occur. There are many and various types of energy in this world of ours. There are, in addition, vast amounts of energy continuously being produced in the far reaches of our universe. In 1931 Prof. Karl Jansky discovered electrical waves which originated outside our earth. In our galaxy alone there are many thousands of so-called "radio stars" which continuously emit electrical waves. In 1942, Prof. George Southworth* discovered that the sun gives off electrical waves. Although electrical waves produced by those who have psychic powers is not a very significant form of energy, could it be possible that the paranormal phenomena that they are capable of producing occur when their waves come into contact with another, different form of energy? The staff set up an experiment in order to test this hypothesis. For example, it is known that when electrical waves come into contact with electrical current, a fluorescent light can be lit without a cord. This occurs because when electrical waves come into contact with another form of energy, they are greatly amplified. In the case of light, when the mercury vapor inside the tube is set in motion by the electrical waves, it collides with the fluorescent material thus causing the illuminescence.

Hiroto's Electric Waves Light Fluorescent Tube

For this experiment the transmitter used to produce the electrical waves was replaced by Hiroto and again the fluorescent tube is lit. In the same way that the fluorescent tube is lit when electrical waves,produced by Hiroto, come into contact with the electrical current, could it be possible that paranormal or psychic phenomena occur when these electrical waves come into contact with a different, as yet undiscovered form of energy?

Through these experiments, the research team came to feel that if one could find the answer to this question, phenomena which have been dismissed as magic or incomprehensible would come to have a more rational explanation.

---

*According to Prof. Ed. Churchill at the University of Wisconsin, J. S. Hey of Bell Telephone discovered the waves in February 1942, several months earlier.

VII.   Conversations with Professor Hasted in London

By Mary Jo Uphoff

On two European visits we have had the pleasure and the opportunity for conversations with Prof. John B. Hasted, of the Department of Physics at Birkbeck College of the University of London.

The first visit in 1977 was something of an unknown quantity for all three of us. Academicians are not necessarily stuffy individuals, but we were quite unprepared for this warm, informal man with the lively brown eyes and shock of gray hair who came to the entrance of the college building to meet us, attired in shirt sleeves, and greeted us enthusiastically. When we visited him again in 1979, he wore a red vest, reminescent of our Wisconsin governor who campaigned in a red vest which he had adopted as a mode of "communication" with students while at Stevens Point branch of the University.

A conversation with John Hasted is an intellectual smorgasbord of philosophy, information and ideas. He has fun with them and exudes a freshness and enthusiasm which is contagious. This is quite in keeping with a small wire artifact from experiments with young English metal-benders—a wire bent by one lad into "This is fun" which lay on his desk.

It was his studies with these young "mini-Gellers" which led us to arrange these visits. Prof. John Taylor at King's College had written a book, *Super Minds,* about his studies of some of these young psychics and he had contributed articles about them to several publications which had come to our attention. But he reversed his early position and had backed off from further investigation after his work had been attacked by some academic colleagues and in the media. It required courage then and even in these later years to admit to interest in phenomena of this kind and we wondered how John Hasted was bearing up under the prevailing scientific climate.

Prof. Hasted bears up very well, thank you, as a man with peace within himself does. Something unusual is going on and he wants to learn more about it. The experiments he has done with a number of children whose ages range from six years to late teens have convinced him that it is no longer a question of whether PK abilities are genuine or

that they exist at all. His quest now is to discover how, what and why—
or in better order, what, how and why.

The characteristics of the kind of energy termed *psychokinesis* are
emerging little by little in the studies with these children in Japan by
Miyauchi, Sasaki, Suzuki and others; in the studies by Braud, Shafer,
Tiller, Stanford Research Institute and others in the U.S. and Hasted
in England. The Japanese have found evidence for a "wave" emitted
from the left frontal lobe of the brain; scientists who studied Matthew
Manning, the young British psychic at Toronto in 1974, reported
finding a brain wave pattern which they called the "ramp function"
which occurred when the subject was generating PK.

The questions arise: Does this brain pattern exist in all psychics?
What is the role of thought and concentration in activating these brain
waves? Is it inherited or acquired? How is this "energy" able to overcome
time and distance (space)? Does "belief" have a role, and if so, what is it?
What are the implications of the alteration of structure of matter and
the de- and re-materialization of matter which seems to occur? If energy
cannot be destroyed, does it imply that this energy exists independent of
the physical body, i.e. in so-called mind travel, out-of-body experiences,
astral travel—which seem to be involved or implied? New concepts of
reality seem to be called for, challenging what we think we already
know. So where are most of the physicists? the biologists? the
psychologists and psychiatrists? John Hasted, so far, is in a rather lonely
place, and when one speaks about his research, one also thinks of
courage.

John Hasted does not appear scared, however; he is having fun and
he is absolutely not bored. Time was too short for all the interesting
thoughts and experiences to be adequately talked through; we hope
Prof. Hasted will not mind if we share some of the recollections we have
of the discussions about the diverse phenomena we had encountered in
Europe, the Philippines and Japan. His perspectives are measured
against the experimental data of the laboratory even while he
communicates with laymen. But keep in mind, too, that it is becoming
somewhat more difficult these days to separate the philosphers from the
physicists from the physicians from the psychics. Look at the
acceptance of psychosomatic origins of illness. The other side of the coin
is psychosomatic health. Except for mechanics and technology, have
things changed all that much? As the ancient wisdom goes, "As a man
thinks, so he is."

Hasted told us about some of his observations of his young subjects
which are of great interest to us [See Appendix for Hasted's paper on
some of his research.] Some of these children seem to have other
unusual abilities. Some of them see color (auras) around the object they
are inducing to bend; some *know* or have a knowledge of, when the

Above: **Glass spheres containing paper clips twisted by children studied by Hasted.**

Right: **Prof. John B. Hasted, Birkbeck College, University of London, holding a sphere containing the 'scrunch' of paper clips. A closeup of one of the spheres is shown above.**

event is about to take place. Hasted and others are intrigued by the apparent connection between PK phenomena and healing ability. Matthew Manning no longer does metal-bending; he is following his bent toward psychic diagnosis and laying-on-of-hands healing. Masuaki also has discovered this ability in himself; for example, one evening he sensed that tension was causing pains in my back and that he could help by holding his hands over the area and directing "energy" to it, which afforded immediate relief. One little girl Hasted has worked with was moved to attempt contact healing at which she has turned out to be quite successful. One child has shown in drawings that he senses vortices or centers which correspond to the head, throat and spleen chakras. The child insists that they are there because of observations of himself in front of a mirror. He sees them sometimes in other people.

Heredity, Hasted thinks, has something to do with psychic ability.

One finds that relatives in these children's families have some psychic ability. (In Masuaki's case there are sensitives in both maternal and paternal families.) One speculates about the extent to which genetics may have something to do with these abilities. Hasted mused, "I generally don't like match-making, but. . . ."

Some ingenious experiments have been devised by Prof. Hasted to test the young "mini-Gellers." One he has come up with utilizes a glass sphere with a small opening into which straightened paper clips can be inserted. Different colored clips are used in order that the movement and contortions can be observed as they are bent. The young metal-benders were given the task of mentally twisting the paper clips into a mass. One eleven-year-old was so successful at this that the "scrunch," as Prof. Hasted calls it, inside the sphere does not even rattle. A row of these "scrunch"-filled glass spheres lines the top of a case in his office. He also has one sphere with which a laboratory assistant tried to replicate the feats of the children manually. It contains many less clips, the sphere is cracked, the clips still rattle, and it required hours to do it.

What is exasperating is that it is tricky business getting these things to take place exactly as desired in a laboratory setting. Scientists are often rigid about this despite the fact that psychic events often occur when there is a change in the psychological state of the subject—when tension is either relaxed or built up.

Although some of the children tire or become hungry or thirsty when working with objects, others do not. Some believe, as Masuaki does, that they can "collect" energy from around them. Dr. Barbara Ivanova, a Russian parapsychologist who is also a healer, states that a talented healer is able to utilize energies of others and transmit them to heal the "patient"—the Pranha concept of Eastern religions.

We were talking about the paranormal voices on tapes. Hasted remarked, "There are a lot of stray radio signals knocking around. . .where you don't have to depend on an antenna" which prompted one of us to comment that sometimes you apparently do not have to have a microphone either. There have been words found on tapes which have not gone through the recording head. "But it's always nice to have a microphone," Hasted countered, amused. "I'd be a bit shy of messing around without a microphone."

This led to a discussion of the significance of symbols—something which seems to trigger the process of building the psychic event or phenomenon in the way of simulation or a resemblance—as if a kind of make-believe or imaginative play shaped a reality. The cancer healing program devised by the Simontons* relies heavily on visualization, an aspect of imagination. This is a modification of what is called the

---

*Simonton, O. Carl, M.D. and Stephanie Matthews-Simonton, with James Creighton, **Getting Well Again.** Tarcher-St. Martin's, Los Angeles (1978).

70

Prof. John B. Hasted - London U

Cutlery twisted by PK by one of the children participating in Hasted's experiments.

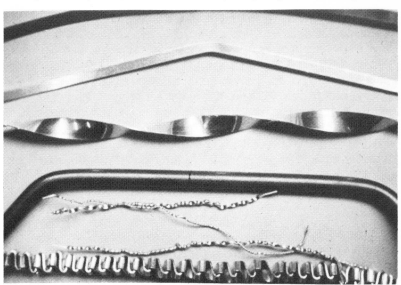

Metal strips in varying sizes and materials which were twisted by children in Hasted's PK experiments.

placebo effect—a "stand-in" doing the work of what is generally accepted as the REAL thing.

This, of course, tends to do violence to that which we call *reality*, but raises again the basic question that centers on PK phenomena—mind over matter—apparently affecting the shape of solidly-structured things like metal and affecting things formless and invisible such as healing, sound, etc. Some experimenters who record the paranormal voices on tape now think that white noise and other background sounds are modulated (bent?) to shape words perceived by ear.

Hasted reminded us that many studies and experiments that have been done in Europe show that all kinds of radio components: resistors, **diodes, magnetic tapes, capacitors, bits of wire, etc. can be effected by** strong psychics. We mentioned that we had a new tape recorder which produced a garbled tape and ceased to function during an interview **with Masuaki and his father the evening before we left Tokyo.*** Masuaki was obviously "up tight" at the time and the atmosphere fairly prickled. The tape recorder was a new instrument, purchased on March 3rd, just before we left on our trip to Japan and the Philippines, returning by way of Europe. In order to have a recorder for the remainder of our travel interviews, a new machine was purchased in Manila. For whatever reason, the first recorder would not function during the entire trip. To our astonishment when we took it back to Radio Shack in Madison where it was bought (it was guaranteed for 3 months) after our return, it began working again.

With little formal training in physics (and that some years ago) much of what is talked about in physics today is not completely comprehensible to us. We can appreciate how challenging the paranormal experiences must be for the world of science—feats performed by human beings in which matter is affected or altered by what appears to be the power of thought. Obviously these events can be upsetting and disturbing too, but if they exist, nothing is gained by ignoring them.

We heard the last part of Prof. Hasted's lecture at a Mind/Body/Spirit Festival in London last spring. With informality and good humor, he presented his lecture, illustrated with charts and sketches—a rare demonstration of a scientist communicating with a lay audience. Near the end he postulated that perhaps we now have to think of other dimensions of existence—a fourth, or perhaps more—to fit what we are learning about ourselves and the universe. The audience applauded his forthright views and gave him a standing ovation.

When he came to Wisconsin for the PK workshops last August, we discovered other "dimensions" about Prof. Hasted too: his delight in natural surroundings and such simples pleasures as a raspberry patch, his harmony with time and place; and when the pressures on the culinary department had grown somewhat frenetic, he fixed eggs foo yung for supper for the boys from Japan and himself.

We had a similar experience five years before when we met Matthew Manning at Gerrards Cross, England. After the first few minutes of conversation, the tape recording became unintelligible. Matthew was matter-of-fact about it, explaining that this happened to instruments around him on other occasions. The recorder functioned properly for the rest of the trip.

VIII. Masuaki and Hiroto Invited to the U.S.

The psychic abilities of the two young Japanese psychics so impressed us that after we completed our extended trip in May 1979, we invited them to spend part of their summer vacation with us. This would give them the opportunity to see parts of our country and make it possible for others to meet them and learn what these young fellows had already done, and also permit others to observe or participate in some paranormal experiments with them.

We hoped that most of the direct expenses would be covered by registration fees for a two-day private workshop at the New Frontiers Center, ticket sales for Prof. John Hasted's lecture and a public workshop in Madison, plus contributions from some individuals and from organizations in California where further experiments were planned. Even though the time for planning and adequately publicizing such an ambitious program was short, the response was excellent and the income did cover about 80% of the direct expenses.

Our Japanese "Grandsons"
Mary Jo Uphoff

Have you ever wondered what it would be like to have a psychic youngster in your family? We have not had that experience for long periods of time but we have had Matthew Manning with us for weeks on two occasions and in 1979 Masuaki and Hiroto were our guests for almost four weeks. Having two psychic teenagers in one's household can be an enlightening and somewhat baffling experience. Please do not get the wrong impression. Not too much of our own cutlery was bent into unuseable contorted shapes, although there were times when I had to snatch a fork or spoon from some enthusiastic visitor who wanted one for an "experiment"—it never seems to be enough to read about, see, or have someone else's spoon bent—it has to be one of your own and be in your possession. However, there were times when I fervently wished I could get my hands on a helpful book, entitled probably, "The Care and Feeding of Psychics."

Cokes and Hamburgers

Since World War II, Coca-cola and McDonald's hamburgers have succeeded in addicting many inhabitants of the Western world and made deep inroads into the Eastern hemisphere as well. We, accustomed to what we think is a "healthful" diet, were somewhat perturbed to find that all our young guests really relished were 16-ounce bottles of cokes, morning, noon and night, along with a steady intake of McDonald's hamburgers, alternating with Kentucky fried chicken. We expected at any time to see an outbreak of trembling hands and jumpy nerves, which never happened.

Our garden produce was unfamiliar to our young guests and they were not particularly fond of vegetables anyway, with the exception of sweet corn, so our garden bounty which we greatly enjoyed was little help in menu planning. Masuaki did not touch any milk products—so much for our famed Wisconsin cheese. On several occasions Walter brought in a supply of the Colonel's finger-lickin' chicken and I prayerfully hoped that the excess of batter and oil would not bring on attacks of indigestion. The lack of a good fresh fish supply presented no problem. Masuaki, growing up in a home connected to his parents' *sushi* restaurant, didn't care for fish anyway.

I was really concerned about keeping them well. Heat, change of diet, Hiroto's sensitivity to our environment which brought on a severe attack of hay fever, all had to be reckoned with. The experiments tired them, even if they did not "drain" their energy; between experiments the boys adopted an easygoing, somewhat indifferent "life style"—their only exercise was playing at times with bats and balls. Their reluctance to go exploring around the farm was understandable. The August heat was tiring, the mosquitos vicious at times, and they had not had much chance to recover from jet-lag.

To ensure that he had a relaxing atmosphere, Masuaki brought with him a supply of tapes. He had a passion for rock music—good, loud rock music—most of the lyrics in English. Although one might conclude that Masuaki was the extrovert and Hiroto somewhat more introvert in personality, both had a tremendous amount of nervous energy which was worked off in drumming fingers and swinging, tapping foot movements. Only toward the end of their Wisconsin stay did they really "sack out" and sleep over-time as we had expected them to do sooner or later.

Communicating Without an Interpreter

Communication, until Elaine Morikawa, our interpreter, arrived, was a laborious business of consulting Masuaki's Japanese-English and English-Japanese dictionaries. The frustrations of language for the two boys must have been enormous. Particularly was it difficult to be sure that plans and schedules were understood. I am certain that they used their telepathic abilties to some extent and my own were enlisted as well. With Hiroto, whose English was more limited than Masuaki's, it seemed we rather quickly developed a kind of telepathic communication. He knew what I was saying and I often knew what he wished to say. Both had their "antennae" out most of the time. One day I thought I had my frustrations under control—with the schedules, the interruptions (particularly the phone calls)—the constant "gear shifting" that was necessary throughout the time. Masuaki picked up my desperation and asked Walter why I was angry with him. The truth was that I was irritated by everyone: my husband, the phone, the hamburgers-and-cokes, and the general confusion in our lives that was taking place.

Although the Tokyo climate compares with ours, the boys were bothered by the steamy heat, particularly in August when the workshops were in session at the farm and we were serving meals to about 40 people that weekend. We had able and willing helpers, but it was still a "pressure-cooker" situation. The boys transported an electric fan wherever they went and clothes were changed three and four times a day which meant doing laundry practically on a daily basis.

They enjoyed our small grandchildren who live next door. Sarah, five, and Jim, three, found them fascinating company and were bug-eyed when the boys bent spoons. One afternoon I suggested to Sarah, "Go ask Hiroto to show you how to bend a spoon." Taking the stainless spoon I handed her she gave it to Hiroto who got it started bending a little. She brought it to me in an adjoining room a little later and Masuaki who had been talking with us, came over and held his fist, clenching and unclenching it, over the spoon while I held it by the end of the handle. Before our eyes the bowl of the spoon began to droop until eventually it made a gentle U. This was not the way this usually occurred. When a spoon began to bend, Masuaki would usually toss it in the air and when it landed it would show a tight twist of about 180°. I was curious to see if the children would respond as other children did on seeing Geller and Manning on TV and try to do it themselves, but so far they have made no serious effort to do so.

Was it Coincidence?

Several events occurred which may or may not have been connected with our psychic guests. When we got into the car at the Chicago airport where we met them, Masuaki started to roll down the left rear window and the glass simply dropped so that we had difficulty pulling it back up. Walter took the car to the shop where the mechanism was put back in order. He was not permitted in the repair area, so he does not know the nature of the problem. But in any case, there has been no problem with the window since. The day the boys were to appear with Walter and Jamie Hubbard on Channel 3 WISC-TV, I dropped them off at the station on Hammersley Road, and started driving out of the parking lot when the car's power-steering failed. I nearly panicked; fortunately the car was barely moving, so I quickly turned off the ignition and tried to figure out what to do next. I had some shopping to do a few blocks away and had visions of being stalled with precious time ticking away. But before going for help I decided to start the car cautiously and see what would happen. "Nothing." I steered the car very slowly and apprehensively out of the lot and into the street toward the nearby shopping center; it has functioned properly ever since.

The Girls

The big event, for the boys, was their meeting "the girls." J. Cary Caraway, who lives near Spring Green, had seen the story about the boys in the local paper and phoned us, offering to take them to visit the House on the Rock and to meet his teenage grandchildren who were visiting him. Language proved no barrier whatsoever to their enthusiasm for the girls' company and from all appearances it was mutual. After that there were telephone calls, another day spent at the Caraways and several times the Caraways brought the girls to our home and stayed for part of the workshops. Masuaki had a good sales talk— the girls, he assured us, got them "in the mood" for successful experiments and it probably helped. What better inspiration for demonstrating masculine prowess than a couple pretty spectators at hand? One of the visits to see "the girls" provided Masuaki and Hiroto with some unexpected excitement. A summer storm, accompanied by strong, tornado-like winds and sheets of rain, passed over the Spring Green area. It was so violent that they could not start their return to our home until it had blown over. Some minor damage was done to the Caraway house, but the boys did manage to be on time for an appointment in Milwaukee, thanks to friends of the Caraways who took them to Milwaukee on their way to Chicago.

Masuaki and Hiroto had only a casual interest in natural surroundings and seeing the country. The outdoors tempted them not at all. Jamie Hubbard who was the interpreter for some of the media interviews, invited them to his home in Milwaukee and took them to see a Brewers' game there. The baseball game—baseball being a reigning passion in Japan—was a highlight in their visit. One afternoon our son Charles took them to see a local rodeo, which was exciting for our grandchildren, but less so for our visitors. It probably seemed quite pointless a sport to them.

We can understand, since we spent some days in Tokyo, some of their disinterest in our surroundings which we find restful, refreshing and interesting. Great cities surround such children with a completely man-made environment. In Senju when we were there for Sakura, the Cherry Blossom festival, even the cherry blossoms on the small trees on the street were pink plastic. The miracles of life and growth are not a familiar, integral part of their experience. Flora and fauna are reserved for parks maintained for viewing, like television, rather than experiencing, and achieving rapport with living, breathing things which have a life of their own.

The Boys' Families

We had met Masuaki's family in Toyko in the spring, but had no occasion to get acquainted with Hiroto's. I often thought it must have been a difficult decision for his parents to send him to the care of an "unknown quantity." With the assistance of a friend his father had phoned us before the boys came, inquiring about what his son's needs for his trip might be. We wrote to the parents several times before the boys were to leave Japan, trying to anticipate their concerns and questions.

Masuaki has an older sister, Kazuko who is 20 and a college student, and an eight-year-old little sister, Yukizi. Both his parents and his grandfather work in the *sushi* restaurant in Senju which adjoins their home. Originally the family were farmers and fishermen, but they have been in Tokyo for some time; Masuaki's childhood photos which we saw show him in this place. Hiroto's mother is a hypnotherapist who works with doctors in Tokyo; his father is in investment banking—a kind of savings and loan institution, as we understand it. He has a younger sister whom he regards in much the same way as Masuaki does Yukizi—a tolerable nuisance.

It was only on the last afternoon we were with the boys in San Francisco and were about to leave that we learned about Hiroto's no small talent as a pianist. Henry Dakin had invited us for a late lunch at his home and while we were there Hiroto discovered their grand piano. He played as if he had come upon a long lost friend. Surely we had missed something very special by discovering this too late.

Hard to Say "Goodbye"

Most of the boys' visit was filled with so much activity that it was only the last day or so when we were with them in San Francisco that we learned how much they had become attached to us as surrogate parents. Trying to decide whether to stay in San Francisco for a day before flying to Los Angeles, or to go with us to San Jose where we were to speak (a dull way to spend a day from a teens' point of view, we thought), they vacillated between going with us and staying, almost to the point of tears. They did not know then that one of the most fun-filled weeks of their trip lay ahead of them in Los Angeles where they were guests of relatives of friends in Japan, and were to spend some time with Alan Neuman, the Hollywood film producer who had included a segment about Masuaki in the NBC-TV program, "Exploring the Unknown."

Now when they write to us in English, which improves with each passing month, they send greetings to Sarah and Jim; and Sarah and Jim from time to time want to know if and when Hiroto and Masuaki are coming back again. All the research and investigations aside, it seems that we have acquired two more "sons" in addition to the ones from India, Germany, Mexico and Japan, who over the years came to consider themselves a part of our extended family.

Schedule of Activities — W. H. U.

Although we never run out of interesting things to do, the period of July 26-August 19 kept us even busier than usual. There were radio and TV programs to prepare for, newspaper interviews, phone calls from those wanting to attend one or more of the activities planned, and arrangements for translation of the commentary from the Nippon TV documentary into English so that viewers could follow what they were seeing on the screen. There were trips to be made to Madison, Milwaukee and Rochester, Minnesota; cutlery and film to be provided for experiments, etc. for we were not prepared to offer our own silver-ware for the cause of investigating PK. (We still have the souvenirs of Matthew Manning's first visit in 1977, when one of our Rogers 1847 spoons was twisted in a drawer about eight feet away from where Matthew sat.)

Here are some of the things in which Masuaki and Hiroto got involved: Visits from reporters and photographers from both Madison, Wisconsin newspapers; (These are discussed in Chapter IX) interviews on radio stations WIBA and WORT and TV channels 3 and 15, as well as Cable 4 in Madison, and WTMJ in Milwaukee. We wondered how much value these programs had, since many viewers are unfamiliar with the PK phenomenon and would therefore be more impressed by actually seeing spoons bend than merely talking about it. The brief time available and the problem of language did not contribute to an atmosphere where Masuaki and Hiroto would be likely to bend spoons on command. At Cable 4, where more time was available and the relaxed nature of the program had brought Masuaki nearly to the point where he could have bent a spoon "on the air," he handed Selena Fox, co-host of the program a twisted spoon within two minutes after the program was over.

Prof. Roger Severson had met Matthew Manning when Matthew visited Madison in 1977 and was interested in having something that had been influenced by PK. Masuaki obligingly bent one of his keys for him shortly after the boys arrived.

Did "Mind Waves" Open a Garage Door?

Our interpreter and translator during the first two weeks Masuaki and Hiroto were with us was Jamie Hubbard, a graduate student at the University in Madison. His mother's home is in Milwaukee and when we drove to Milwaukee to discuss arrangements for the boys' appearance on WTMJ-TV's talk show on August 6th, the boys decided to stay overnight at Jamie's mother's home in north Milwaukee and return to Madison next day by bus.

Jamie had to go to the airport early in the morning to meet his fiancee who was flying in from Japan. When he got downstairs to the garage, he discovered to his amazement, that the electronically-controlled door was open. This had never happened before and has not happened since. We had been working on an English commentary for the Nippon TV documentary (see Chapter VI) and began to wonder if there were a connection with the door opening and Dr. Suzuki's discovery of the electrical waves emitted from Masuaki's left frontal part of his head. Could there have been the possibility that the frequencies emitted by one of the boys caused the electronic equipment to open the garage door? How many explanations occur to the readers? How should they be ranked?

From Mrs. Hubbard we learned that the door unit was a Vemco Door Opener which had been installed by Geis Overhead Door Company. We called on Jim Melotte, an electronics technician for the company, who told us that their units function within a range of 265 to 400 megaherz. He said that their equipment will respond to what is known as the "harmonics effect"—that is, multiples of the frequency in question. When we told him about the door opening incident, he quickly multiplied the frequencies reportedly emitted by Masuaki and Hiroto (Chapter XI-progress report by Dr. Suzuki and Mr. Y. Fukuda) and found that both fell within the range of their door openers.

He had never heard of such a thing before but granted that the effect on the unit was a possibility. He looked up the frequency of the unit in the Hubbard house and found that it was in the range of ten times the frequencies reported for the boys. That the door opened only at the time the boys were in the house raises the question whether coincidence is the most likely explanation.

Experiments at the Mayo Clinic

Berthold E. Schwarz, M.D., a psychiatrist in Montclair, New Jersey, who has extensively investigated psychic phenomena and published widely, wrote Dr. Earl Wood at the Mayo Center, suggesting that if someone at that institution were interested in conducting some experiments with Masuaki and Hiroto while they were in the U.S., it might contribute to a better understanding of PK. "Naturally a psychiatrist would be helpful" he wrote, "but for the short period of time available and because of language barriers, etc. it might be most practical to concentrate all the efforts on the possible physical-chemical-mechanical effects: and their documentation. . .I think it would be a fundamental step forward in this most necessary area of investigation..."

Dr. Wood turned Dr. Schwarz' letter over to Dr. Maurice J. Martin, chairman of the Department of Psychiatry and Psychology at Mayo and through him plans were completed for an all-day visit to the laboratory at Mayo on August 7th. Toshihiko Maruta, M.D. had come from Japan eight years earlier to work in the Psychiatry department at Mayo and his presence and participation was invaluable in carrying out the scheduled experiments. Prof. Severson and I had driven to Milwaukee early on August 6th to be at the State Fair grounds where WTMJ had scheduled Masuaki, Hiroto, Jamie Hubbard, our interpreter, Prof. Severson and myself to participate in a live telecast. Amid the noise from the crowd at the State Fair, and the interruptions of spot commercials, the boys were unable to get "into the mood" to bend anything. Prof. Hasted's plane was delayed from London so he missed being on that program. That afternoon he joined us for the drive to Rochester, Minnesota, where early the next morning, after "breakfast at McDonald's," we all went to the Mayo Clinic.

After preliminary introductions and a tour of part of the facilities, the boys were taken to a laboratory equipped with electroencephlographic equipment and videotape cameras. Staff members from psychiatry, the EEG department, physics, etc. spent hours watching and waiting while the boys tried to bend Kahler Hotel spoons while they were wired to the EEG equipment. The long wires which were attached to their scalps with collodion were disconnected from the machines for lunch, but not from the boys' heads. They looked the stereotype of Chinamen as we went down to the cafeteria with the long strands of wires hanging down their backs. Videotape cameras were kept running and the EEG equipment used reams of paper during the forenoon and the early afternoon. About mid-afternoon it was decided to end the formal experiment. The collodion was dissolved so that the wires could be removed from the boys' heads, but some of it remained and had to be removed by cutting off some of their hair when they returned home that night. Hiroto was particularly bothered by this part of the experiment because of his sensitivity.

After the EEG wires were removed, Masuaki was successful during the next hour in putting tight twists in the handles of five cafeteria spoons, but by the time this happened, most of the staff who were involved in the experiments had returned to their work—not expecting anything to happen. Dr. Maruta and some of the laboratory staff were still in the area where the spoon-bending occurred, but the results could not be termed "conclusive" because they had taken place after the boys were disconnected from the testing equipment.

As the saying goes, "hindsight is better than foresight." Since we were guests of the Clinic and appreciated their efforts to measure any unusual physiological functions which might manifest while the boys were

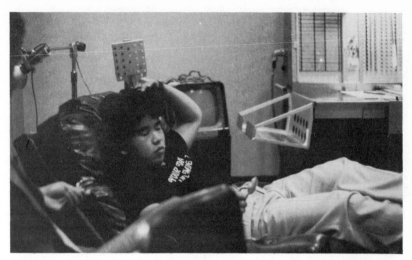

Masuaki reclining at the Clinic with spoon in hand and Dr. Maruta nearby.

Dr. Toshihiko Maruta keeping an eye on Masuaki's behavior.

attempting to influence spoons by PK, I did not make any suggestions about alternative methods under which experiments might be conducted. In working with subjects with PK abilities (demonstrated or claimed) there are several ways of carrying out tests. One is to establish so many controls at the beginning that if something unusual or paranormal happens, even skeptics will have difficulty dismissing it. The other is to start with a minimum of controls and then see what happens; then to tighten the controls, step by step, to see if the phenomenon persists. If the phenomenon does indeed persist, even after rigid controls are in effect, the chances of the event being paranormal are just as great as if tight controls were used at the beginning of the

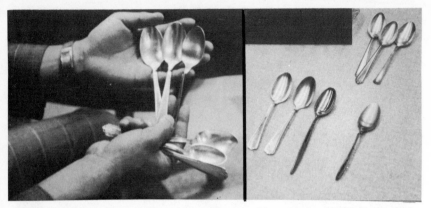

Dr. Maruta holding three of the spoons twisted by Masuaki after the EEG wires had been removed from his scalp. On the right, the spoons are laid out on a table nearby.

experiment. I personally favor the latter approach but realize that there are occasions when there is not sufficient time to start with a relaxed atmosphere and gradually "tighten" the conditions for the experiment.

It was interesting to observe that some staff members had less difficulty than others in imagining the possibility of such a thing as a psychokinetic effect, even though Masuaki was successful in twisting spoons only after he was released from the EEG equipment and the videotape cameras were turned off. A report we got from Dr. Martin later stated that no abnormalities were found in the EEG tracings but he has one of the spoons Masuaki bent and is still intrigued by the event. [When Matthew Manning was tested in Toronto during metal-bending experiments in 1974, a very unusual brain wave pattern, which was called "the ramp function," appeared on the tracings when Manning was concentrating on bending metal.]

The Private Workshop

When the word came that Masuaki and Hiroto were to visit us, I phoned Prof. John Hasted in London and he immediately agreed to come to Wisconsin to spend six days with the boys. Although the time was short, a two-day private workshop was scheduled to which investigators and experts from various disciplines, who had an interest in psychic phenomena, were invited. The gathering was to be private to permit discussion free from the inhibitions imposed when reporters, who may not be familiar with the subject misquote or quote out of context, are present. Several who came said their jobs could be jeopardized if word got out that they were attending the workshop, even on their own time. It is an unfortunate situation that some of the groups who vow allegiance to the scientific approach are intolerant toward subjects which do not fit into their belief system. Several must have felt

Prof. Hasted (standing) leading discussion on metal benders. Those closest to the speaker *(left to right)* Marjorie Sibley, Walter H. Uphoff, Prof. Peter Phillips, Sit Bar Khalsa, Prof. Otto Schmitt, Ruth Harvey, and Pamela de Maigret.

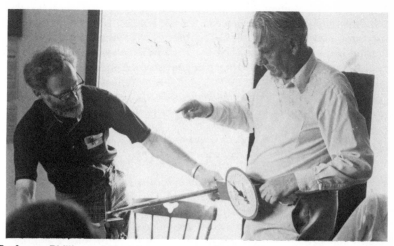

Professors Phillips and Hasted carry out a crude experiment with a heavy spoon in a vise to which is attached a vise grip tool with an elongated handle and a scale to measure the pounds of force required to produce a twist. It was agreed that such twisting could not be done manually.

some of the apprehension which we presume accompanies a visit to "a house of ill-fame," but once the group assembled we had two lively and productive days together.

Attenders came from Arizona, Arkansas, California, Colorado, Delaware, Michigan, Minnesota, Missouri, New York, Ohio, Oregon, Pennsylvania, South Carolina, Utah, Wisconsin and Toronto, Canada. The thirty-plus participants were all that could be accommodated in our home; they had a variety of backgrounds: biology, bio-psychics and bio-engineering, electronics, genetics, photography, neuro-physiology, parapsychology, physics, psychiatry and psychology. The subject matter discussed is dealt with in papers and in the *Appendix,* and in some of the quotations from other publications throughout the text.

Presented here are some excerpts from the sessions to indicate the free-ranging philosophical and theoretical scope of the discussions:

I am interested in becoming what I am potentially. . . .

There is just as much objective evidence of nonphysical causation as there is for physical causation. . .It might very well do to become aware that the only sources of knowledge are not in the natural sciences: physics, chemistry, biology. I have become interested in telepathy and clairvoyance and psychokinesis, not so much from the study of contemporary physics or even of contemporary chemistry and biology, but rather of world literature. For instance, how many of you have ever considered Shakespeare's 94th sonnet?. . .Shakespeare has one of his characters say what this sonnet is about in Measure for Measure: "Oh, it is excellent to have the strength of a giant, but it is tyrannous to use that strength like a giant." I have learned more about evidence for the existence of extrasensory perception from books. . .than I have from all the arguments that go on among the scientists as to whether or not telepathy, clairvoyance and these other psychic phenomena exist.

We are a part of a world that is not physical, it is not a part of the world of motion. Not all of us are a part of that—our bodies are physical—but that does not mean the human being is merely a physical being. We are also controlled by agencies that are beyond the universe of motion, which is what the physical universe is all about, and are beyond space and time. . . .I have no diffculty being convinced without all these strain gauges that a physical effect has occurred when metal is bent. . .I can see with my own eyes that the metal has been bent. . .

I vigorously denounce this notion that there is a physical system that obeys rules and another sytem that is nebulous, and disorderly. . .What I was seeking is simply next steps that have helped, historically, each of the things that have become sciences. They started as folklore, witchcraft, art—and became natural philosophy, then hardened into chemistry, physics, and astronomy that we feel we know a little about. I am trying to build a ground to incorporate these phenomena you are talking about as more of a science. . .

(response) You have not given up the sound principle of science that so many scientists have; namely, that the physical universe, and in fact the universe as a whole, is a rational universe. It is not a big blooming confusion that has no laws, no order, and anything goes!

A psychiatrist, acquainted with psychic phenomena, described some experiences of a person well known to him, who has frequent "out-of-body" experiences. On one occasion she found herself, in a "dream," visiting an Indian chief in a cliff dwelling and being given an old bone cone that belonged to a princess of the tribe. When she awoke, the bone cone was in bed with her, and they plan to have it radiocarbon-dated. This person has also experienced passing through locked doors and finding herself locked on the other side. She also gets paranormal images on film and can write in many languages she has never studied. He would call psychic photography "quasi-photoparakinesis."

There was much interest in the Owens' report on the "imaginary" Philip created by an experimental group in Toronto, who conversed with "his" creators with raps and on one occasion got meaningful responses onto a tape recorder while the experimenters were inside a sound proof room in a hospital. This led to a discussion of multiple or interpenetrating universes, "side by side," identical in nature in every respect except that of momentum—"it could be angular momentum as well as linear momentum, slightly different from the last one. Then if you are able to travel between these universes—1, 2, 3, 4, 5, 6, 7,. . .fast enough, you wouldn't notice the jerks, in fact it may even be a continuum." Prof. Hasted observed that PK effects usually occur when there is a change in mental state: anger, concentration, anxiety, fright, relaxation, laughter or euphoria. The phenomena was inhibited, Iris Owen, Toronto, observed, when one or more participants in the experiment were in a state of sadness or depression.

In between the informal sessions, Prof. Hasted used a strain gauge and chart recorder in some experiments designed to test the boys' abilities. He returned to England convinced that there should be further study of them. He made plans to visit them in Tokyo where he was attending a conference next month.

Pieces of assorted cutlery bought at a Goodwill store in Madison were bent and twisted by two boys during the private, as well as the public workshop on August 11th, and later on August 14th and 15th before going to San Francisco—about 40 pieces in all. (See photos of cutlery on page 98.)

Influencing Film—An Entire Pack at a Time

Masuaki had brought with him, the Polaroid camera box which was used during the filming of the Nippon TV documentary. The lens and shutter had been removed and a light-tight aluminum cover put over the film compartment. On Friday forenoon, he suggested that he would try to influence an entire pack of Polaroid film at a time. Most of the workshop attenders watched as he concentrated intensely for at least ten minutes, holding the "lens-less" camera in both hands.

Elaine Morikawa was at hand as interpreter while Prof. Hasted and Pamela de Maigret kept track of the film which was pulled out of the box after Masuaki turned the "camera" over to them. All the positives should have been black, but they were not. Numbers 2, 3, 4 and 5 were "whities"; No. 6 was much darker and showed a "texture" which resembled a woven fabric under a microscope (see illustrations). I was within five feet of Masuaki and watched both his concentration efforts and witnessed the film being pulled from the box and numbered. Prof. Hasted later took the entire series and pasted them in a notebook from which the illustrations here were reproduced.

In true scientific tradition, someone raised a question about what had happened to No. 1, since only Nos. 2 through 8 had been influenced by Masuaki in the presence of the group. The explanation that No. 1 had been pulled from the "camera" as a control and was a "blackie" did not satisfy everyone, so they asked, "Could Masuaki try to influence another, unopened pack of film?" Even though the first attempt had been quite an effort, he agreed to try.

Prof. Roger Severson had brought some extra Polaroid film that morning and it had been kept by Pamela de Maigret until it was loaded into the "camera." I distinctly recall tearing the seal on the film pack before it was put into the box. Masuaki concentrated on the "camera" again until he was visibly exhausted. All eight pieces of the film pack were pulled out, one after the other, and when the negatives were separated, the positives all turned out to be "whities" except that No. 3 showed considerable fuzziness and hair-like quality, somewhat similar to No. 8 in the previous pack, and No. 7, showed a light gray spot near the top which did not reproduce when half-tones were made for this book.

Some readers may wonder why so much space is devoted to this one experiment. The answer is that we consider it an important event that occurred in the presence of about 30 witnesses and that it raises interesting questions about mind over matter as it relates to film. We hope that other psychics, as well as skeptics, will try to replicate these results under the same conditions, using a light-tight Polaroid camera box without lens or shutter and fresh film supplied by outsiders and inserted in the presence of a number of witnesses. We would be greatly interested in hearing about such experiences as, I am sure, would Prof. Hasted and Prof. Peter Phillips, Director of the McDonnell Laboratory for Psychic Research, Washington University, St. Louis, MO 63130.

About 30 observers were present at the workshop on PK at the Uphoff home, August 10, 1979, when this experiment was carried out. Since No. 1 of the film had been pulled (a "blackie") before formal observation started, some participants asked if Masuaki would be willing to try once more to influence an entire pack of film. He agreed even though it was quite exhausting for him. Pamela de Maigret had the unopened film pack in her possession all forenoon until it was needed for the experiment and Walter Uphoff tore the seal on the pack before it was inserted in Polaroid film cassette opening of the box. Since there was no exposure to light, all the photos should have been black, but as the illustration shows, six of the eight were "whities."

The black lines were drawn to indicate the edge of the Polaroid films since "whities" would otherwise not be easily recognizable.

8/10/79 at Uphoff home.

#2

first series — This is Prof. Hasted's hand writing

#3

Original Polaroid Pictures peeled off and numbered by Prof. John B. Hasted.
#1 had been pulled out before experiment and was reported as being a "blackie."

#1 was bled — Black

#4

#5

Masuaki Kiyota concentrated on Light-proof Polaroid Box with film in it
where lens & shutter had been removed for Japan NTV Experiment. He attempted
to influence (By PK) First Series all 7 pictures in pack at one sitting

87

Prof. Hasted and Pamela de Maigret examined the pictures as the negatives were peeled off the Polaroid film. The pictures were then numbered and Hasted mounted them in a loose-leaf notebook for a permanent record. On the first page he wrote "#1 was trial—black." The half-tones reproduce much of the detail on the originals but are natually not as sharp. Photocopies are reproduced on following pages.

#6   first series   #7

#8   first series

1 was black.
#2, 3 + 4 turned out to be "whities"

#5 has a bit of grey on right side
#6 shows more grey on right side especially lower right corner

#7 has still more grey, covering most of picture
#8 is mostly grey and black under magnifying glass upper part resembles a wool weaving pattern

When Masuaki tries to project an image onto film, he usually gets either a recognizable image or "whities." This was his first attempt to influence an entire pack of film at one time.

8/10/79

This is Prof Hasted's handwriting → **Second Series**

Masuaki Kiyota concentrated on entire Polaroid Film pack. Pack was

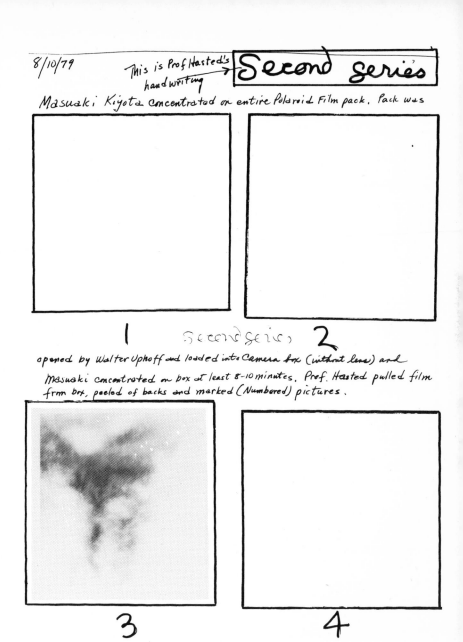

1   Second Series   2

opened by Walter Uphoff and loaded into Camera box (without lens) and Masuaki concentrated on box at least 8-10 minutes. Prof. Hasted pulled film from box, peeled of backs and marked (Numbered) pictures.

3   4

No 3 showed substantial gray areas which looked like animal hair and No. 7 had a light gray spot at top center, not pronounced enough to reproduce here.

Second series

1, 2, 4, 5, 6 + 8 turned out to be "whities." #3 shows considerable fuzziness and hair-like quality when magnified. #7 shows slight grey spot at top center.

5

6

Second series

7

8

*(Left)*Harold Sherman and Ruth Harvey talking with Gordon and Margaret Clarke during a break in the workshop sessions. (*(Right)* Prof. Peter Phillips poses with Iris and A.R.G. Owen who came from Toronto, Canada, for the workshop.

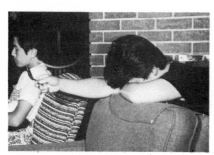

(Left) Hiroto and Masuaki in a meditative mood, concentrating on spoons during a refreshment break at the PK workshop. *(Right)* Prof. Roger Severson, of the department of Educational Psychology at the University of Wisconsin and director of an Institute of Clinical Hypnosis, was very helpful in planning and implementing both the private and public workshops on PK and in arrangements for Prof. Hasted's lecture.

Prof. Hasted's Lecture at the University of Wisconsin

Since Prof. John Hasted, one of the best informed physicists on PK was coming all the way from London, we thought the community should have an opportunity to hear him tell about his research in PK. A lecture was scheduled at the University of Wisconsin Humanities building in Madison for the evening of August 10th, jointly sponsored by the Wisconsin Student Association and the New Frontiers Center.

The lecture was attended by about 175 persons. Early in the evening, someone stood in the audience and wanted to know why the Amazing Randi's offer of $5,000 had not been accepted, in which case, if the demonstration of PK were successful, there would be no need to charge admission to defray expenses. (Curtis Fuller, who follows Randi's activities more closely than we do, points out that it is easy to establish terms which make it virtually impossible for anyone ever to "win" the award.) We were interested in hearing Prof. Hasted in an atmosphere free of suspicion and charges of trickery.

Jacquelyn Mitchard, who had written sympathetic articles about the boys in the *Capital Times* (May 12th and August 9th) brought with her to the lecture, Prof. Waclaw Szybalski from the University's medical school, as a "technical consultant" and asked that he be admitted without charge. Later we learned that Mitchard's "consultant" was one of 32 scientific consultants for the Committee for the Scientific Investigation of Claims of the Paranormal (see Chapter X). During the lecture he left with Mitchard but later returned to the auditorium.

The "Statistically" Impossible Happens

We realized that the audience that evening would naturally be interested to see what the boys could do. I had given each of the boys, who were seated in the audience, some unbent spoons which I had brought along. These were Northwest Orient Airlines spoons which I had thought would not be like any in the possession of anyone else who was there that night. Masuaki and Hiroto had had two busy days at our home and Masuaki had greatly exerted himself to produce those 15 paranormal "pictures." They could not do anything with the spoons that evening, which caused Prof. Szybalski to conclude that the whole affair was fakery and he had caught the boys "red-handed." He had come up to the stage when the lecture ended and I was curious about the the consultant Miss Mitchard had found to bring along. I engaged him in conversation and he seemed very upset and angry and had very harsh words to say about Prof. Hasted. When the anger was out of his system, I learned what had produced his emotional state. He had brought along a Northwest Orient spoon and had given it to the boys! When the meeting ended he had gone to where the boys were sitting about 25 feet from the stage, to reclaim his spoon, only to discover later that he had been inadvertently given a different one—the Northwest Orient spoon I had brought.

Szybalski had marked his own spoon and when he got in return an unmarked spoon, he was certain that trickery—in this case, substitution—was what the boys engaged in. The *Capital Times* article which appeared after the Hasted lecture quoted Szybalski as saying (Chapter IX) that "he saw a briefcase full of hundreds of spoons, among which his was finally located."

Here are the facts:

I had brought along a small case containing my collection of about forty twisted forks, spoons and metal strips produced by Masuaki and Hiroto, as well as Matthew Manning, to show to interested persons after the lecture. My case was on the stage throughout the entire evening while the boys were seated in the left section of the audience about 25-30 feet from the stage. I had walked down to where they sat before the program began and given them the Northwest Orient spoons. The boys were never near the twisted cutlery I had brought along to show members of the audience.

This was a most unusual "coincidence"—whatever that is, but it helped explain Prof. Szybalski's reaction. Masuaki, Hiroto, Elaine Morikawa and I went to talk with Prof. Szybalski at his home early in the following week. He was calm and civil after our first encounter the previous week. I inquired as to how long he had been working with the CSICOP and he gave me the impression that he had little to do with them, only having been consulted on some legislative matter about two years earlier.

I had taken my collection of paranormally twisted items with me to show to him, and we left with the feeling that he was much more objective than he appeared at the lecture. Should he have occasion some day to observe PK abilities at first hand, he might well come to modify his position.

Hasted's Statement

Experiments with Masuaki Kiyota and Hiroto Yamashita at Oregon, Wisconsin

During the summer of 1979, I had the opportunity to meet with Masuaki Kiyota and Hiroto Yamashita and conduct experiments with them, particularly on the paranormal bending of metal.

Both of the boys are able to produce twists of approximately 180° in the handles of stainless steel teaspoons and dessert spoons, without the apparent use of force. The necessary normal torque for such an operation can readily be shown to be of the order of 6-7 Nm. However, I have observed the production of these twists and am of the opinion that normal manual forces of this magnitude were not used by either of the boys. It seems that a local sudden temporary paranormal softening of the metal occurs in the presence of the boy; it is associated with his handling of the spoon.

*I had the opportunity to test the boys with my no-touch strain gauge technique (described in **Journal of the Society for Psychical Research**, 45, 1976). In this experiment a small strip of metal is fitted with a miniature strain gauge, which is connected to a bridge and amplifier circuit with output taken to a chart recorder. The metal is suspended from its electrical connections, and the subject is seated in front of it, but is carefully observed and is not permitted to touch the metal. Normally some auxiliary precautions are taken, but these were not possible with the apparatus available. Nevertheless, my observation that neither boy touched the metal or the apparatus before or during the experiment was quite definite. Indeed when parapsychologist Iris Owen deliberately tested my observation by surreptitiously touching the metal during a test of her metal-bending ability, I was able to report the touch.*

The exposure of the metal to the boys afforded positive evidence of their

93

metal bending powers. Although no permanent deformation was obtained, bursts of dynamic strain were recorded; in our experience these are to be interpreted as being of paranormal origin.

Signed,
John Hasted

NOTE: Readers interested in Prof. Hasted's experiments will find his paper summarizing some of his research in the *Appendix* of this book.

(Left) C. Caraway, Theresa Wolfson, Prof. Frank Meyer and Wm. Wolfson, M.D. chatting with Prof. Hasted *(center)* at private workshop.
(Right) Michaeleen Maher, City College, N.Y., and J. Packard Laird, New Castle, Delaware, examining twisted spoon Masuaki had just tossed in the air toward them.

The Workshop Session in Madison

The workshop at the Howard Johnson Motor Lodge in Madison on August 11th was attended by about 80 persons who came to hear Prof. Hasted elaborate on his experiments with young British metal-benders, to see the videotape of the documentary about the boys which was made in Japan, and to discuss the phenomenon with those who had been at the private workshop the preceding two days.

Masuaki and Hiroto felt some pressure to demonstrate their PK abilities and probably would have preferred to spend their time with the girls from Spring Green. Someone asked if the boys could demonstrate before the entire group but after explanation that it was very difficult to concentrate and get into the mental state required for doing this in the presence of a large group of curious and often skeptical people, it was agreed to chose five persons to be observers, who would report back to the workshop.

Those who would like to observe were asked to put their name tags into a "hat" for a drawing; most of the participants, as would be expected, wanted to observe. Jacquelyn Mitchard, the *Capital Times* reporter, spoke up, arguing that since her newspaper reached 30,000 readers, she would like to be one of the five. There seemed to be general agreement with her request so I agreed and that left four names to be drawn by lot. Gordon Clarke, who had been helping with registration, was given charge of the drawing and Masuaki was asked to take four name cards. The first was Richard Leshuk's; he had come all the way from Manassas, Virginia and was the person who had asked on the evening of the Hasted lecture, why Randi's offer (which, of course, had never been made to us) had not been accepted. The others drawn were Jim Davis, Milwaukee; Elaine Erickson, New Berlin, Wisconsin; and J. Packard Laird, New Castle, Delaware.

Masuaki and Hiroto, with Elaine Morikawa, Gordon Clarke and the five workshop participants went into a large room adjoining the conference room where the workshop was held and were joined by Larc L., Masuaki's young friend. A sketch which Elaine made shows where each person sat during the experiment and where the spoons were etc.

Based on discussions and taped interviews with participants, here is

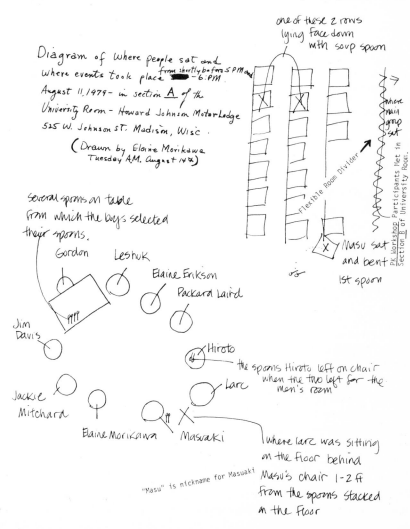

one of these 2 rows lying face down with soup spoon

Diagram of where people sat and where events took place from shortly before 5 PM and —6:PM. August 11, 1979— in section __A__ of the University Room - Howard Johnson Motor Lodge 525 W. Johnson ST. Madison, Wisc.
(Drawn by Elaine Morikawa Tuesday A.M. August 14th)

where main group sat

Flexible Room Divider

PK Workshop Participants Met in Section B of University Room.

several spoons on table from which the boys selected their spoons.

Gordon   Leshuk
                    Elaine Erikson
                         Packard Laird

Jim
Davis

Masu sat and bent 1st spoon

Hiroto
the spoons Hiroto left on chair when the two left for the men's room

Larc

Jackie
Mitchard

Elaine Morikawa   Masuaki

where larc was sitting on the floor behind Masu's chair 1-2 ft from the spoons stacked on the floor

"Masu" is nickname for Masuaki

95

the consensus of what occurred:

The group assembled as shown in the sketch. A collection of spoons was laid on a table nearby. Masuaki took three spoons and Hiroto took two and they began to rub and stroke them and twirl them, but had no success in bending them. After almost half an hour passed, the boys excused themselves to go to the lavoratory. Hiroto laid the two spoons he had been holding on the floor. Masuaki laid two on the floor but kept one in his hand. They returned after about five minutes, restless and frustrated because they had not been successful so far in bending any of the spoons. He stretched out across several chairs while he continued to play with the spoon he was holding. At a moment when no one was watching closely, he put a double twist in the handle of the spoon.

Elaine Erickson and J. Packard Laird told me that before the spoon bent, Richard Leshuk had been eager to go back to report to the workshop that nothing paranormal had happened. After the spoon bent, Leshuk volunteered to report to the workshop on the group's behalf and, spoon in hand, came into the conference room to make the report, the others remaining behind. He told about the boys going to the lavoratory and said that Masuaki had taken one of the spoons with him, implying that he might have twisted the spoon while there. (He did not elaborate what would have been required to put such a double twist into the handle by normal forces and the others on the observers' committee were sure that the spoon he had with him was not twisted when

No. 1 First spoon twisted by M. Masuaki at 5:25 p.m.

No. 2 The spoon Masuaki had taken to the lavoratory. Masuaki became irritated when he learned about Leshuk's report and twisted this one in a matter of seconds.

No. 3 Spoon Leshuk gave Prof. Severson as an example of what he could do manually. Note very gentle twist in handle.

Masuaki returned from the lavoratory.)

Leshuk's report was heard over the public address system by the other observers, the boys and the interpreter. At first they thought his report was amusing, but as he continued, they began to question his motives and why he had been so eager to make the report before any spoons had been bent. Elaine Morikawa translated Leshuk's comments for the boys and this irritated Masuaki enough so that in about 30 seconds he twisted another spoon. Morikawa distinctly recalls that Masuaki had taken three spoons—two teaspoons and one soup spoon, and that it was the soup spoon he had taken to the lavoratory while the two teaspoons were nested, one in the other, something which cannot be done with spoons of different sizes and shape.

As soon as Masuaki had twisted the soup spoon, he and Elaine walked into the workshop room to tell the audience that *this* was the spoon which Masuaki had with him in the lavoratory. This completely changed the atmosphere of suspicion that had begun to develop as a result of Leshuk's report. After this he had no further comment.

When the session was over, Leshuk handed Prof. Roger Severson a spoon which he had bent by physical force. That spoon had a long and very gradual rather than a tight twist in the handle as can be seen in the accompanying photograph.

More Twists in Forks and Spoons

Sunday, August 12th, was a day of sightseeing and relaxation for the two boys while two healers from England, Rose and Peter Gladden, discussed their work with about 70 people at our home.

A number of workshop participants wanted to have an example of PK bent forks or spoons as a souvenir but I hesitated to part with the collection I had accumulated because I needed it for evidence. Masuaki and Hiroto, aware of the eagerness of particiants to have souvenirs, went on a "flurry" of metal-bending. Hiroto produced six twisted spoons and two forks on Tuesday forenoon, and shortly afterward, Masuaki came with four spoons and two forks, one of which had the tine separated from the rest of the fork. The door of their room next to our living quarters was open all that morning and we are sure they had no tools to use for twisting.

Why are all these details given if we are convinced the boys' PK abilities are genuine? The answer is simply that others who have not witnessed such phenomena may wonder if we are certain that the metal bending had not been done by physical force. Anyone who has taken the trouble to run tests on the foot-pounds of force required to twist cutlery by physical force and knows the precautions which must be taken to protect cutlery so that scratches from the pliers or vise will not show, can recognize the differences in paranormally bent metal and metals twisted by mechanical force.

Photo of some of the cutlery bent by Masuaki and Hiroto at various times. The grouping at lower right shows six spoons and two forks influenced by PK by Hiroto on August 14, 1979. Lower middle grouping of four spoons and two forks which were twisted by Masuaki on the same day. Both youths felt "in the mood" and wanted to show their appreciation for being invited to the U.S. Note the tine of the fork in the middle group which fell off during the experiment.

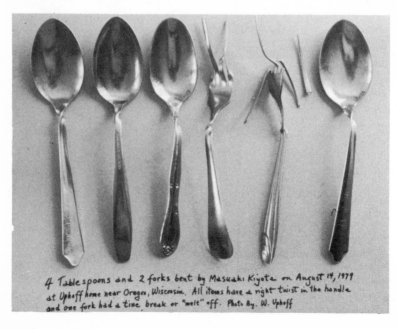

4 Tablespoons and 2 forks bent by Masuaki Kiyota on August 14, 1979 at Uphoff home near Oregon, Wisconsin. All items have a right twist in the handle and one fork had a tine break or "melt" off. Photo By. W. Uphoff

On August 15, 1979, after a late breakfast, Masuaki went to his room adjoining the living room at the Uphoff home. Mrs. Uphoff had straightened up this room every day and there were no signs of tools or equipment around which could be used to produce the contorted forks Masuaki excitedly brought to us. He explained that he had held one fork in each hand and that they had twisted simultaneously while a third one twisted on the small table near his bed without it being touched. He said he had never gotten such an unusual shape before and asked if he could take one back to Japan to show to his father.

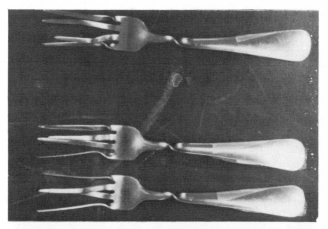
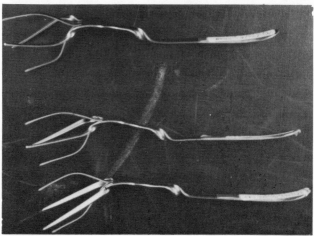

Close examination revealed no marks which would indicate physical force had been applied. We have witnessed him produce enough twisted cutlery to be confident that these were also done by PK. Top and side views of the forks are shown here. Note the tight twist in the handles and in the outside tines of all three forks. According to Masuaki, the fork on the left twisted while lying on the table near him.

A close examination of the six pieces he twisted the day before shows that one of the forks, shown in the previous picture, also had very similar twists but apparently he had not noticed this.

In California

We—Masuaki, Hiroto, Elaine, Mary Jo and I—took a flight to San Francisco on August 16th, rented a car at the airport and drove to the Washington Research Center (WRC) where Henry Dakin, the director, showed us the facilities and the lab and settled us for the night.

On the 17th, Jeffrey Mishlove and I went to the 22nd annual convention of the Parapsychological Association hosted by John F. Kennedy University, about an hour's drive east of the city. Mary Jo stayed in San Francisco to observe the experiments planned at WRC. Mr. Yutaka Fukuda, the professional photographer we had met at the Kiyota home in the spring had flown to San Francisco to take part in whatever experiments might be scheduled. He had brought along a pen-recorder to use if the opportunity presented itself and naturally the boys were happy to have someone from home come to join them.

The three busy weeks in Wisconsin and having to say the inevitable farewells to the two girls whose company they had greatly enjoyed had not put Masuaki and Hiroto in an enthusiastic state of mind for experiments.

Notes made by Mary Jo state:

> The boys don't want to do anything—they "want to go out and play." Elaine told me. She's getting irked with their attitude. Both Masuaki and Hiroto were intrigued with the computerized typewriter, but eventually Hiroto worked again with the camera in an effort to produce some paranormals under Mr. Fukuda's direction. Masuaki had a fork which Jean Millay had given him and carried it around with him, upstairs and down. At 3:45 p.m. he pulled the fork, which was somewhat bent out of his pocket. He had been playing with it, scratching his back with it and talking animately to Fukuda and Elaine. He showed the fork to us, explaining that he "stopped" the twist and thought it would continue bending. It did, humping a little while it lay on the table.

> Masuaki had been in a good mood since lunch. He seemed restless, walking around, showing what seemed to be a short attention span in whatever was going on. He told us that he wanted to "save" his energy for the experiments and the evening program planned for the next day.

> Jean Millay drew outlines around the fork and made a number of photocopies of it. The machine intrigued the boys who tried to influence it, without success. Before the afternoon ended, Hiroto tried another photography experiment which resulted in another "blackie." In retrospect, Friday's occurrences were not nearly as impressive as the events on Saturday.

> Masuaki, Hiroto and Elaine had been Jean Millay's guests at her apartment across the street from the Washington Research Center, with which Jean was associated. She opened her home for experiments and buffet meals on Saturday, August 18th. There was more space for observers at her apartment than in the area at WRC where the monitoring equipment is located. Included among those who came to

meet the boys and to observe whatever paranormal activities might occur, were Frederic Blau, a researcher; William E. Cox, parapsychologist and magician, Rolla, MO; Henry Dakin, director of WRC; Dr. Jule Eisenbud, psychiatrist from Denver who has had extensive experience with paranormal photography, and his wife Mollie; Yutaka Fukuda, the professional photographer from Japan; James Hickman from WRC; Barbara Honegger, parapsychologist; Jean Millay, Ph.D.; Peter Phillips, physicist from Washington University, St. Louis, MO; Harold Puthoff, Stanford Research Institute; Saul Paul Sirag; Sola Smith; Russell Targ, Stanford Research Institute; in addition to Masuaki, Hiroto, Elaine Morikawa and ourselves. Dakin and the Eisenbuds came after activities were underway.

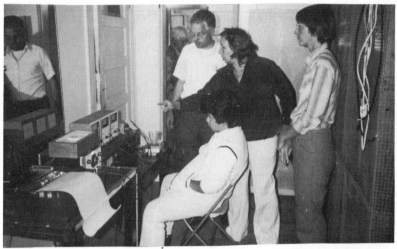

Masuaki *(seated)* **in the laboratory at the Washington Research Center, San Francisco, along with Henry Dakin, the director of the Center, Jean Millay and Adrienne H.**

The Experiments at 3118 Washington Street, August 18, 1979

On Saturday, August 18th, it had been agreed to shift the experiments from the formal setting at the Washington Research Center, 3101 Washington Street, San Francisco, to Jean Millay's apartment just across the street. Elaine and the two boys had been staying there (we were house guests of Jeff and Janelle Mishlove some distance away) and part of the morning was spent in packing and gathering their belongings. Jean and Henry Dakin had provided lunch for the crowd and the buffet table was a popular gathering place for those who drifted in. Jean and Fred Blau discussed the "protocol" to be followed for some PK experiments with spoons if Masuaki and Hiroto felt "up to it" after the activities of the day before. Jean and Fred, we agreed, would supervise the experiments.

Fred and Jean had taken an assortment of spoons which I had bought at a small variety store the day before and marked them with a metal-engraving tool, numbers one through eight. Masuaki and Hiroto each chose one and started playing with them. Hiroto returned his spoon to Jean after a short time because he felt he was not "in the mood" to do anything with it. Fred Blau, as custodian of the spoons, put Hiroto's unbent spoon in with the other six in the manila envelope. Masuaki and Hiroto wandered through the apartment and through the room where Elaine was packing.

One enters Jean's second story apartment up a long flight of stairs. Then one can turn right and go down the short hall to the large living room which fronts on the street, or go into the area which leads to the kitchen, bedrooms and bath. After a time, some of those present, moved from the living room into the kitchen to drink coffee and to talk. Targ, Puthoff and Hickman went into the kitchen first, later to be joined by Barbara Honegger and Fred Blau. They stood around or leaned on the kitchen-counters at the far end of the kitchen. I took a chair at the small table where I could look out into the hall and stairway as well as observe what was going on in the kitchen. I sensed some disappointment in some of the observers that no metal-bending had yet ocurred in their presence, but the conversation was mostly 'shop talk' about the inadequacy of funds for research in parapsychology, the papers given at the Parapsychological Association convention, etc.

While the conversation was taking place in the kitchen, Masuaki came into the doorway across from me, and after looking over the group, sat down on the floor near the door with his back against the wall. He gazed around, scratched his shoulders, and tossed and played with the spoon he had in his hand. I recognized this "antsy" behavior which I had observed before when he was in a spoon-bending state, and decided to keep my eyes on him. He conveyed an air of indifference or boredom—I don't know which—and did considerable fidgeting. After some minutes he rapped the spoon several times sharply on the floor, gave me a quick knowing glance and slid the spoon across the floor toward the people gathered there. As he sent the spoon across the floor, I called out to them, "Here's your spoon!" Someone scooped up he spoon and they all clustered around to examine it. Masuaki got up from the floor and walked over to them. Although I did not hear what was said in the excitement, he must have told them in his limited English that he thought they would find another spoon twisted in the envelope in the other room, whereupon everyone moved quickly into the front room. I overheard "Let's check the envelope" and "Where's the envelope?" I witnessed Masuaki tap the spoon on the floor and then slide it across the floor, but I cannot say that I saw the spoon bend and twist because it went so fast. I do know that it was not bent when he was playing with it and there was no pliers or vise-grip tool around which could have been used to bend it physically.

To everyone's amazement, a twisted spoon *was found inside* the envelope. Although these are the events as I observed them, explaining them is not easy. How and why did the second spoon bend at a distance? It was assumed that Masuaki was the active agent because he had suggested that the envelope would contain another twisted spoon. But could it have been a delayed PK effect on the spoon Hiroto had worked with? And, in any event, how did Masuaki know about the bent spoon in the envelope? and what might this experience give us about the powers of the mind and the possibility of assistance from other intelligences or other dimensions?

Front and side views of the spoons mentioned in the text. No. 2 was found twisted in the manila envelope after Masuaki had twisted No. 3 in the kitchen of the Millay apartment.

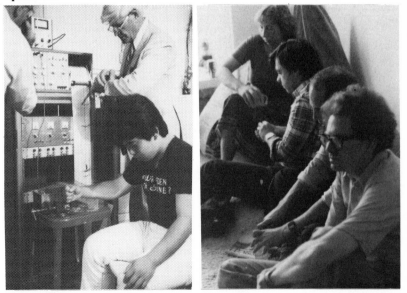

(Left) Closeup of Masuaki at the Washington Research Center with Henry Dakin and William E. Cox monitoring and timing an experiment.

(Right) Jean Millay, Harold Puthoff, Jeffrey Mishlove, and Russell Targ at Jean Millay's apartment, August 18, shortly before the spoon twisting occurred.

Peter Phillips and Yutaka Fukuda *(left)* looking at the twisted spoons Jean Millay holds. Surrounding her are photocopies of the spoons made from different angles.

Masuaki, W. E. Cox, Stanley Krippner and Henry Dakin at the San Francisco airport. Krippner had deliberately created an opportunity in which Masuaki could presumably have "cheated" in bending a key, had he wanted to, but Krippner found no evidence for this.

Enough observers were present so that it was very difficult for deception to occur. All those there were interested in meeting the young Japanese psychics and seeing if anything would happen which could be attributed to PK.

Jean Millay's paper, from which portions follow, reported her observations and those of several others. To avoid repetition, some of the most pertinent comments will be given here.   —*M.J.U.*

Phenomenology and Psychokinesis
by Jean Millay, Ph.D.

Nothing happened that could be scientifically validated in the strict sense of a controlled experiment. However, the many different experiential reports, written or taped immediately after the events, tell a story which raise a number of phenomenological questions.

A physicist looks for what can be measured. Not finding measurements which are concise both before and after an event, s/ he must conclude that nothing happened, no matter how many bent spoons or keys are produced as evidence during the event. A dedicated believer in the power of mind over matter might look at the evidence with wonderment and reverence at the scope of human potential abilities, but without the necessary critical judgement to assess the methodology accurately. A magician looks for deception, and explains how "tricks" are done, assuming that all PK attempts are some form of deception. None of these disciplines are, in themselves, sufficient to reveal the multiple dimensions involved in many types of PSI activity, although all have their place in the analysis of events.

My field is humanistic science. My research involves exploring the belief systems of people with extraordinary abilities, in order to discover how these abilities might be trained in myself and in others. I have taught parapsychology and biofeedback since 1972, and in that time, I have received many reports from students who did indeed learn to improve their telepathic ability. In the summer and fall of 1979, Sola Smith and I conducted a regular weekly meditation healing circle at the same apartment where some of the PK experiments would be attempted. We also taught group and personal classes in deep relaxation, stress management, and focusing techniques for enhancing mental development and psychic sensitivity. We had not, however, learned to do or to teach PK. We were both interested in meeting the young visitors in order to explore informally what they believed about their own activity and about their definitions of normal and paranormal.

The first thing I noticed about M.K. and H.Y. was that they were very active. Like many teenagers, they preferred loud, fast, disco and rock music, large quantities of sugared cola drinks, and wanted to be "on the go" all the time. (I have observed that some people who claim to be adept at PK exhibit sometimes agitated, even hyperactive type behavior. This is in contrast to the relaxed calm, focused behavior often exhibited by others who are practicing telepathy. Though we usually play meditation music in the apartment, I was prepared to observe these very different vibrations because of my intense interest in the chance to observe PK. Perhaps the fast pace may be an essential part of the PK occurrence.)

Both young men believed in their own ability to do PK. They spoke of the need for conditions to be "right" for the best results. They could not describe just what these "right" conditions or feelings were, but they knew what might cause an experiment to go wrong. If people around them were very skeptical, insulting, or unfriendly, then the phenomena was more difficult to produce or else it didn't happen at all, no matter how much effort they put into trying to force an effect. If the feeling was right, very little effort produced better results.

On the first day, several WRC associates, and Yutaka Fukuda (Y.F.), had arranged to do a series of informal measurements and observations of physical effects frequently associated with psychokinetic abilities. Equipment was improvised on short notice to measure electric fields and temperature changes inside a shielded aluminum enclosure. I was there to take notes and to observe. M.K. and H.Y. took turns concentrating on the high impedance volt meter, the double probed thermister, and the voltage controlled oscillator. Because of the difficulty of translating technical information, they both thought that the slight movement of the dial meant that they were actually registering a psychic event on the meter. As soon as H.D. realized that such an assumption was being made, he asked E.M. to explain to the young men that the slight movement of the dial was normal to the action of the meter. Both M.K. and H.Y. became very angry and told E. M. that they did not want to do any more experiments. Rather than being involved in the spirit of exploration, since none of us know what measurements will produce meaningful results, they chose to feel insulted. They felt they had exerted a lot of focused energy uselessly without proper explanations. E.M. spoke to them at length, and finally M.K. asked, "What is the effect that would convince you that my mind is doing something to this box?" (This is a very important question to be negotiated in advance. A skeptical person could find a way to confound almost any result. In this situation, however, the language problem had confused the issue.) H.D. very gently explained again the action of the various devices, and as this was translated, the young men agreed to try once more. However, the mood was changed and there were still no results, so they decided to go sight seeing instead.

Prior to sending her report, Jean had written:

All of the reports that I gathered from the people who were here in attendance are, of course, very different. We have more a study in phenomenology than about PK. . .

She added that she was now working at the University of California Medical Center's Langley-Porter Institute on brain wave research and from what she was learning about the problems of brain wave measurement, she was inclined to think that the radio frequencies reported to come from the left hemispheres of the two boys' heads (discovered when making the Nippon TV documentary) were simply the result of a loose electrode in an environment of radio frequencies. She went on to say:

Yet the headache that was experienced (by Hiroto after he started a watch Saturday evening) in the left hemisphere and the exorcism that was required to remove it, suggested some possible disturbance in the left hemisphere that might be detected in brainwave analysis had we measured it then. However, brainwaves could be measured that would be as fast as radio frequencies, compared to normal brain rhythms. So if we can strike a balance between physics and meta-physics, we will not scare away the skeptics, nor the true believers.

It will be interesting to see what response or explanation is gotten from those in Japan who were involved in recording the results reported in Chapter XI.

The final event planned for San Francisco was an evening meeting at Cogswell College to which those attending the Parapsychological Association convention and the community were invited to attend. The Nippon TV videotape was shown, the two boys introduced to the audience, and reports given on experiments with the two young psychics. The meeting was sponsored by the WRC and the Institute for Noetic Sciences.

Events of August 18-19, 1979 Which Involved the PK Factor:

* A spoon twisted by Masuaki in the kitchen of Jean Millay's apartment. Of those present, Jim Hickman and Mary Jo had been observing him most closely.

* A second twisted spoon was found in the manila envelope into which Blau had put the unused, marked spoons, after Masuaki said he thought they would find one.

* Six attempts at producing paranormal effects on polaroid film resulted in "blackies" or failures. Recorded by Fred Blau.

* Masuaki twisted a silver heirloom fork for Adrienne H. before the program began at Cogswell College, the evening of August 19th.

* Hiroto started, by mental concentration and effort, an old gold watch given him by one of the people in the audience. The watch had not run for about 25 years.

* A spoon which Frank Tribbe brought to the Saturday evening program, was wrapped in plastic and secured with a rubber band and given to Masuaki who twisted it without signs of damage to the plastic film. The wrapped spoon was carefully examined by William E. Cox, parapsychologist and professional magician.

* William E. Cox gave Masuaki a watch which had been stopped with metal foil. Masuaki was successful in starting it. See Cox's paper in the *Appendix* for his account of this and other phenomena he recorded.

* Masuaki who sensed that Mary Jo had tension pains across her shoulders during the time she was attending the Saturday night meeting, held his hands above the shoulders, instantly relieving the pain.

It becomes obvious, as one investigates PK events, that the extent to which they are considered paranormal or "impossible" has a bearing on how they are interpreted. Often little if any thought is given to alternative explanations. For example: When Masuaki remarked that he thought they might find another twisted spoon in the envelope in Millay's living room—after he had twisted the spoon in the kitchen, and they did find the second spoon—why had activity not been stopped in order to discuss all the possible explanations for it? After all, it was a very significant event, or some very clever sleight-of-hand.

How many spoons were in the envelope? Were all of them marked? Exactly where had the envelope been placed, by whom and when? Was it found in the same place? Had the clip on the envelope been closed? How continuously had the envelope been guarded after all except spoon No. 3 which Masuaki had taken with him, had been placed back inside it?

Such questions should always be considered both by those who accept and by those who deny the possiblity of PK phenomena, if we are to move toward understanding and consensus as to what it is all about.

On July 10 Masuaki's father had written us as follows.

> In my last letter, I told you about the incidental discovery -----they are emitting electric waves from the left sides of their frontal heads as long as they concentrate themselves. Masuaki emits electric waves of 30 ~ 40 megaherzs; Hiroto 21 ~ 28 megaherzs. Examined by the received mechanism of a wireless apparatus, these waves could reach the distance of about 50 meters. The existence of telepathy, I am sure, has been substantiated by this discovery, but the science at present can't afford to give us a satisfactory answer to it.
>
> If you could make preparations for an electric-wave-receiver beforehand, you will be able to have the opportunity to make certain that they can emit electric waves. They can also put on a fluorescent lamp. If a computer and a radio-receiving-set were used together, I suppose it would be no longer an impossible matter to put their hertzian waves into such words as "bend!" or "come out!".
>
> When they produce PK by their concentration, they can emit electric waves from the left sides of their frontal heads towards the backward direction.

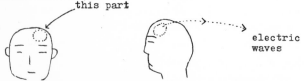

this part

electric waves

Please send our very best wishes to Mrs. Uphoff.

Sincerely yours,

Yoshinori Kiyota

Yoshinori Kiyota

Unfortunately that letter was not found until after the workshop so we did not even discuss Mr. Kiyota's speculation about using a computer and radio to "bend."

IX The Media and Psychic Phenomena

By Walter H. Uphoff

In Japan

Since Uri Geller and Matthew Manning visited Japan in the early and middle 1970's the media generally has given considerable coverage to psychics who have been investigated, and has reported the phenomena fairly. The interest generated among the populace when Geller and Manning appeared on television there resulted in hundreds of reports of metal-bending and other psychic happenings which occurred in the homes of viewers. The number of these latent psychics appearing on the scene created a sensation that was given extensive coverage. Similar reports have also come from England, Denmark and other countries where Geller's appearances on television stimulated interest among parapsychological investigators and it has understandably polarized those who believe his PK abilities are genuine and those who view such abilities as impossible or unlikely and who could not give credence to such reports. It was reported from Copenhagen that an interview with Geller had been videotaped and broadcast after he had left the country; yet when the program was aired, hundreds of viewers reported that their cutlery bent and watches began running again. Should this all be dismissed as fabrication by mischievous viewers?

Japanese media—radio, television and newspapers—give good coverage to psychic events, judging by the number of articles which appeared in the press about the Nippon Television Network documentary featuring Masuaki Kiyota and Hiroto Yamashita. When I was in Tokyo with Alan Neuman in October 1976, I learned that Gerard Croiset, Sr., the internationally-known healer and clairvoyant from Utrecht, Holland, had been brought to Japan by one of the TV stations to see if he might be able to locate a seven-year-old girl for whom 750 police had been searching for four days. (See Chapter II for article from the *Japan Times,* May 7, 1976)

While we were at the Kiyota home in Tokyo, the film crew from NTV (Chapter VI) came to photograph metal bending and thoughtography for what was to become an hour-long documentary. The advance coverage given this program which was shown on July 5th and 12th was impressive. Here in the United States, brief announcements of important radio and TV programs appear shortly before they are to be aired, but rarely is the content of the program given regular news coverage as was given the Nippon TV program. One of the many articles (with pictures) about Masuaki Kiyota to illustrate the press coverage is reproduced below:

昭和 **54**年（1979年）**6**月**8**日（金曜日）　　　　　（第3種郵便物認可）

超能力騒動

今度は 念力電波 発す少年!?

"スプーン曲げの日本テレビ"がまたまた超常現象に挑戦。今度は超能力少年の頭から、念力電波?! が発せられていることを科学的につきとめたとして、七日午後、記者発表と番組の試写会を開いた。十六歳の少年に密封し

追跡

たポラロイドカメラを持たせて「念写」の実験をしたところ、不思議な電波を探知したというもの。「世界的にも初めて」というこの発見?! 七月五日に放送されるが、これを機に再び超能力論争が巻き起こるか?!

VTR試写中、正体不明のノイズ

数年前ユリ・ゲラー青年のスプーン曲げを始め、超能力少年二人を呼んで実験を続けていたものので、この三月から、超能写の年、二人を呼んで実験を続けているもので、この三月から、超能写の先があらわれた日本テレビが、今度は放映が、実験というわゆる〝念力〟で、実験というゆる〝念力〟で、映像を感じさせるという実験。同局のドキュメンタリー番組「驚異の世界」（木曜後7・00）が、この三月から、超能写真の実験。同局のドキュメンタリー番組「驚異の世界」（木曜後7・00）が、この三月から、超能写真の

実験中の清田益章君と桜ろは鈴木教授

放送電波以外の、普通人には、きわめて起こりにくい能力を持っているが、実験機器に感じかめて。
実際、電波だけの能力に対しても実を始めたが、日本テレビでは、この電波が、頭から発射、コードなしで蛍光灯輝くあらゆる電離者や数者が、〝避雷針の〟

30メガヘルツ帯の電波

電波そのものは念力で、念を起こすだけの能力に対しても実を始めたが、日本テレビでは、この電波が、頭から発射、コードなしで蛍光灯輝くあらゆる電離者や数者が、〝避雷針の〟〝後も〟、いわゆる電離者や数者が、〝避雷針の〟〝後も〟、いわ
〇─の実験の波を感じたり、選ばれたのは立
清田益章君、小学生時代に、テレビにも登場するが、念写のほか、スプーン曲げの少年〝として

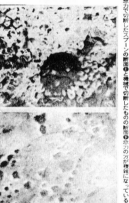
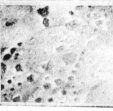
念力で切断したスプーンの断面❶と機械で切断したものの断面❷念力のスプーンが複雑になっている

──16歳・清田益章君──
ポラロイドカメラで「自由の女神」を念写

取材は、まず清田益章君発案を、VTRに収めるところから始まった。実験に当たっては、スタッフが準備したカメラ、フィルムを装てんしジャッターはロックし、スタッフ六人が監視。五枚程失敗したあと、四時間後〝写れ〟

が始まった。"実験用カメラ"を使って、清田君の〝念力〟により放射線機器で測定してみると、これは、放射線のようなエネルギーが出てくるのではないか? という推測から失敗したあと、分析の手がかりを失う

ロイド写真を撮ったところ、でちゃんとロイド写真を撮ったところ、でちゃんと写っている。ただ、実際の念写の写真はビルの階数も同じように、空から写ったような映像をように、これは同局と別に測定したところ、かなり精確に、新宿・京王帝都のビルが写っており、この室を確かめるのである。動〝音響〟模様のものだ。

来月5日、NTV「驚異の世界」で正体を確かめるのである。動〝音響〟模様のものだ。

〇─清田君の〝念力〟の念で実験以外で念写したピントの正確、〝念〟を入れた簡単の遠の状況さえも見えた実際の念写の写真はブレ実際の念写の写真はブレが、実際〝念写〟の写真はだれもが〝違う部分が小さくなって写る〟ことに欠けており、〝「一方、鈴木教授は

がでちゃんと写るのではないか? という、これは、放射線のようなエネルギーが出てくるのではないか? という推測から失敗したあと、分析の手がかりを失う

放射線機器で測定してみると、かなり精確に、新宿・京王帝都のビルが写っており、これは同局と別に測定したところ、なお、この断面電波が放射されるがつくという。また、電波が放射されるがつくという。さらに、変化が起こるという。
に、変化が起こるという。念力のスプーンの左図断面が34・5の断面倍に撮ったところ、山〝曲げ〟中で、山村ルツ帯の電波模様をキャッチした。

自宅で念写した〝自由の女神〟

（解説）研究の第一人者、（筑波大学）氏が、この断面電波が放射されるがつくという。ガルツ帯の電波模様が、念力の〝曲げ〟中で、山村ルツ帯の電波模様をキャッチした。

As a rule, newspapers and other media pay more attention to personalities from within their own country and feature events which are considered of general interest. Thus it is to be expected that Kiyota and Yamashita would get more press coverage in Japan and that Matthew Manning should get more space in the British press. Major political events, natural catastrophes, etc. generally get world-wide coverage, but psychic phenomena, until recently, have gotten very little serious attention. There was very little publicity given to the content of the film, "Exploring the Unknown" produced by Alan Neuman and shown on NBC, either before or after the event.

As an example of the treatment Alan Neuman's film, "Exploring the Unknown," received in the American press, we quote parts of an article which appeared in *The Nevadan,* October 30, 1977, by Paul Henninger of *The Los Angeles Times:*

> *Hollywood—In keeping with the Halloween spirit of the night of October 30, NBC is presenting some spooky happenings that far transcend anything that little trick-or-treaters could dream up to scare adults. "Psychic Phenomena: Exploring the Unknown," is more than a Big Event, as the network likes to label special shows, it's a series of mind-boggling big events; psychic healing, parapsychology, metal-bending, psychic photography, past life regression, communication with the spirit world and psychic surgery.*

> *Over the years since he first produced NBC's pioneering* **Wide, Wide World** *series, through which he became aware of unusual phenomena, Alan Neuman has become personally interested in the subject. Burt Lancaster shares that same interest. . .He went on location with Neuman and the camera crew to become an eye witness to some of the phenomena performances.*

> **Reached in London by phone, where he was putting the final touches on his show, Neuman was quoted as saying:**

> *"Only in recent years of this Space Age have scientists devised the hardware to record the truth that is truly stranger than any fictional 'Star Wars' plot. . ."*

> *In each instance Neuman had an authority in front of the camera as each psychic occurrence took place. . .To further authenticate what is shown, NBC sent Dr. Glenn Olds, currently president of Alaska Methodist* **University and a former ambassador to the Economic and Social Council of the United Nations, to London to observe and consult Neuman and reassure the network of the basic ethicality of the show. He found the show was 'handled with great care and objectivity' and was 'scientifically valid.'**

Much more space could be given this subject than is available here. We have reproduced a number of news items as they appeared in the press and have added our commentary and observations. The treatment accorded psychic phenomena varies greatly from publication to publication, and provides the basis for an interesting socio-psychological study of how belief and disbelief, as well as pressure from interest groups and opinion-molders, plays a role in what is printed and how the subject is presented. Some of the relevant facts about our experiences with Masuaki Kiyota and Hiroto Yamashita are contained in articles reproduced in this chapter and are therefore not repeated in Chapters V and VIII.

Anyone who has followed the phenomenal circulation growth of *The National Enquirer* (and other tabloids to a lesser extent) in recent years, must be aware of the space given to psychic phenomena and other subjects seldom covered in the daily press. One can assume that the tabloids are interested in selling papers, just as other newspapers and magazines are. The fact that so much space is given to psychic phenomena can be interpreted as reflecting a growing interest in this subject. Many of the articles are based on personal experiences and are considered anecdotal in nature by those who seek laboratory or scientific verification before breaking into print.

We are certainly not in a position to pass judgement on the degree of accuracy of items printed, either in the tabloids or in the daily press, but we do know that within the past four years, fourteen reporters and members of the editorial staff of *The National Enquirer* have phoned me regarding stories they were investigating, often asking for names, addresses and phone numbers both in the U.S. and abroad for further verification before making the decision whether to print a story. As mentioned in Chapter III, John Cooke of *The Enquirer* phoned about Masuaki Kiyota after seeing our report on Masuaki in our book, *New Psychic Frontiers;* then a reporter and a photographer for *The Enquirer* spent three days at the Kiyota home before a decision was reached to publish the article which appears later in this chapter. As reported in Chapter VIII, it had been decided to conduct a private workshop on PK for scientists and investigators at our home, August 9-10, 1979, prior to a public lecture and workshop in Madison. Somehow, some staff members from *The Enquirer,* learned that the two young Japanese psychics were guests in our home. After some discussion, we agreed that a reporter and a photographer could meet with Kiyota and Yamashita *after* the private workshop was over. The boys had produced a number of twisted forks, spoons, etc. and Polaroid pictures between July 26th and August 10th, but did not produce anything worth writing about during the time Lee Harrison from *The Enquirer* spent with them and "second-hand" evidence was not enough for a follow-up story on the article which had appeared in the March 14, 1978 *Enquirer.* Although it is to their credit that they did not write a feature article based on second-hand evidence, a brief news item mentioning Prof. Hasted's coming all the way from London to investigate, the Nippon TV documentary, etc. for which there *was* first-hand evidence, would have been in order. The feature story about Masuaki which appeared in the March 14, 1978 *Enquirer* is reproduced here in full.

15-Year-Old Psychic Puts Pictures on Film —With His Mind

A 15-year-old psychic wonder has transmitted mental images of incredible detail onto unexposed film under rigid scientific conditions — and stunned eyewitnesses say he has astonishing paranormal powers.

"He's an amazing boy — there's no question that he's genuine," declared noted psychic researcher Prof. Walter Uphoff, who conducted experiments with the boy in Tokyo.

And leading Japanese psychic investigator Tsutomu Miyauchi — who has conducted more than 300 separate experiments with the boy over the last two years — told The ENQUIRER:

"I am convinced that the boy has a genuine paranormal power."

The Japanese boy wonder, Masuaki Kiyota, was tested by Uphoff as part of an NBC-TV "Big Event" special on the paranormal.

A loaded Polaroid camera the boy had never seen before was put on a table in front of him.

The youngster concentrated on the camera — and amazingly produced on the film an aerial view of a nearby hotel. On other film frames, he produced pictures of the Tokyo Tower. Incredibly, the lens cap was in place and the shutter never pressed.

"This is one of the most astonishing cases of the paranormal I've ever investigated," said Uphoff, coauthor of "New Psychic Frontiers" and former lecturer in parapsychology at the University of Colorado.

Prof. Shigemi Sasaki headed a team at the prestigious University of Electro-Communications at Chofu, near Tokyo, that published a scientific paper on the boy's psychic abilities.

In one experiment, Prof. Sasaki's team inserted light-sensitive diodes in a sealed lightproof steel box. The 15-year-old focused his powers on the container — and the diodes recorded mysterious electronic disturbances on a sensitive graph recorder.

"Masuaki's power cannot be fully explained by normal laws of science," said Prof. Sasaki.

"His power was something extraordinary. The experiment was carried out under strict scientific controls."

So impressive were the results of various experiments on the boy that The ENQUIRER decided to run its own test on Masuaki.

Two ENQUIRER reporters supplied a brand new Polaroid camera and black and white film, and chose an almost bare room in Tokyo — containing just a table — to conduct the experiment.

The boy was asked to produce a picture of the Statue of Liberty. With the camera pressed against his forehead, Masuaki's first attempts failed. But several of the prints snowed inexplicable exposure to light.

As the youngster's confidence grew, he asked one of the reporters to stand 15 feet away on the other side of the room. The lens was covered with a lightproof black card and pointed to the ceiling by the reporter. Masuaki summoned all of his powers, then declared, "O.K. . . . check the next picture."

One of the reporters excitedly pulled the film from the camera, and there was a blurred but clearly recognizable image of the Statue of Liberty.

Masuaki was then able to produce pictures of the reflecting pool in front of the Washington Monument, and of Britain's Houses of Parliament and of Big Ben when asked for a British scene.

He climaxed the staggering display by staring at the camera and producing two pictures at once. Two frames were pulled from the camera, one after another. They showed a wider view of the Statue of Liberty and one of the Manhattan skyline.

— *JOHN COOKE*

'NO QUESTION HE'S GENUINE,' says expert of teenage psychic Masuaki Kiyota, shown during ENQUIRER test.

ASTOUNDING PHOTOGRAPHS of the Statue of Liberty and of Big Ben were transmitted onto film by Masuaki during experiment conducted by The ENQUIRER in a room in Tokyo. **March 14-1978**

PK Effects on Movie Film

When we returned from Japan and had the super-8 movie film, which Masuaki attempted to influence by PK, developed, what we saw convinced us that the very unusual abilities of Masuaki Kiyota deserved wider attention. We scheduled a press conference for the local area newspapers which at times get their story on the national wire services. Prof. Roger Severson made arrangements for the press conference held on May 11, 1979. Knowing the level of knowledge about psychic phenomena on the part of most reporters and editors, we would have been pleasantly surprised if the full significance of what we had to report had been comprehended by the media generally. A *Capital Times*, photographer and a reporter who had written other articles about the paranormal, and a reporter from the University of Wisconsin student publication, *The Daily Cardinal*, were the only media representatives present for a showing of the super 8-movie film which young Kiyota had influenced psychokinetically while the lens cap and film cassette of the camera had been securely taped. Mr. Yutaka Fukuda, a professional photographer, and I had done the taping and had photographed the sealed camera for the record. We had prepared basic background information for a press release and were prepared to answer questions after showing the movie film, the images produced on Polaroid film by Masuaki Kiyota, and twisted forks and spoons produced by both Masuaki and Hiroto.

The main parts of the press release follow:

Local Couple Participate in Experiments With 17-Year-Old Japanese Psychic Who Produces Images in Color on 8 MM Movie Film With Camera Lens Capped

Walter H. Uphoff, Professor Emeritus, University of Colorado, and Mary Jo Uphoff returned last week to their home near Oregon, Wisconsin, after an 8-week trip around the world during which they investigated paranormal phenomena. Their trip was sponsored in part by the ESP Research Associates Foundation of Little Rock, Arkansas.

The Uphoff's recent trip took them via Japan, the Philippines, Sri Lanka and four European countries where they visited and conferred with researchers and psychics, accumulating first-hand evidence related to psychic phenomena. The most important implications for science may be the amazing feats of a 17-year-old Tokyo youth, Masuaki Kiyota who for a number of years has bent and twisted cutlery and metal similar to the phenomena identified with Uri Geller and Matthew Manning, but is also able to project images on film at will by mental concentration.

Prof. Uphoff first met young Kiyota in October 1976 while he was consultant to the Alan Neuman Productions, Hollywood, in filming for a 90-minute special program shown on NBC-TV, October 30, 1977. Masuaki Kiyota, then 14½ years of age, was able to project images on polaroid film—among them an aerial view of the Keio Plaza Hotel, Tokyo, where the film crew was staying (about 10 miles away from the Kiyota home in Senju) and of the Tokyo Tower shown on the NBC program.

The Uphoffs spent six days, March 21-26, experimenting with young Kiyota

114

and another gifted young psychic, Hiroto Yamashita, observing the filming of Masuaki for a Japanese TV program and conferring with several scientists who have worked with both youths for a number of years.

Although they witnessed metal bending and spectacular photos produced on Polaroid film, the most phenomenal of the experiments has just been verified when an 8 mm movie film processed by Kodak was picked up at Regent Photographic in Madison on the Uphoffs' return.

Yutaka Fukuda, a professional photographer; Toru Ozaki, a medical student; and Mrs. Uphoff took Fukuda's polaroid camera (containing a film pack purchased by Uphoff) and after synchronizing watches with Uphoff and Masuaki, walked about a hundred meters down the street while Uphoff and Masuaki remained in the **residence with Yamashita, Elaine Morikawa, the interpreter, and Dr. Tsutomu Miyauchi, who held hands while Kiyota** concentrated. After the agreed-upon five-minute interval, Fukuda without tripping the shutter of the camera which had the lens capped, pulled out the film. On the black and white Polaroid film was a most unusual picture—a *reversed* mirror image of the statue of Liberty which Kiyota has never seen except in pictures.

Masuaki was then asked to try to produce images on movie film. He held the Canon 514 XL movie camera, which Uphoff had brought, but after less than a minute's effort felt that he was not able to produce anything. Fukuda, the photographer, then suggested that Masuaki keep the camera and try to get pictures when he was in the mood to do so. Fukuda and Uphoff taped the lens cap and the film cartridge firmly in place with plastic tape and marked and initialled it with a felt-tipped pen so that any disturbance could easily be detected. This procedure was witnessed and photographed. The footage indicator stood at 10.

When the camera was returned it was again photographed. The tape was intact; the footage counter showed "50," indicating that the film had been run through the camera "blind."

Masuaki told the Uphoffs that he was quite certain there would be an image of the Tokyo Tower and several London scenes on the film. When the developed film was viewed, the Uphoffs were surprised and pleased to find paranormal effects on the film. In between blank sections, they found not only the Tokyo Tower but a number of buildings, the Statue of Liberty and a glimpse of a handsome face, all bathed in golden light. Under normal circumstances nothing whatsoever should have appeared on the film.

In the course of the experiments with polaroid film, young Kiyota produced images on black and white and color film, among these were the clock tower of Big Ben, London, several of the Statue of Liberty and a composite of the Uphoff's two-car garage at Oregon Road and the nearby remodelled granary with its two-tiered roof and picture window, all produced by mental concentration.

Miss Mitchard had arranged for David Sandell, a *Capital Times* photographer to attend the press conference. Her article, on the next two pages, was a serious effort to report objectively what she considers significant. To call attention to the misconceptions and some of the wording in the Mitchard article, I prepared the following:

Comments and corrections on *The Capital Times* article of May 12, 1979, entitled "Blurred 'Psychic' Film Could Open Door to Research," prepared by Walter H. Uphoff.

Paragraph 4 Our dictionary defines *reportedly* as "according to report

Blurred 'psychic' film could

By JACQUELYN MITCHARD
Capital Times Staff Writer

A blurred, five-second film of the Statue of Liberty may be the key to major advances in the study of psychic phenomenon.

Former college professor and psychic researcher Walter Uphoff of Oregon, Wis., Friday showed film with images of the statue, a face, and a tower, all blurred and wavering, which he says were placed on the film by the paranormal mental powers of a young Japanese student.

Uphoff and his wife Mary Jo spent six days in March experimenting with Masuaki Kiyota, a 17-year-old Toyko youth, who first became noted for placing images on film as part of a 1977 documentary for NBC-TV.

During the visit, Kiyota reportedly produced the indistinct images of buildings and streets on Polaroid and home movie film without ever touching the shutter or opening the lens.

Uphoff showed photos, film and affidavits from witnesses to students and reporters Friday at a press conference in Madison.

In the presence of several Japanese professors and students as well as the Uphoffs, Kiyota said he used "mental concentration" to place images of the Statue of Liberty (which he has seen only in photographs) on film purchased by the Uphoffs and placed in a camera owned by professional photographer Yutaka Fukada.

After an agreed-upon five-minute interval, film pulled from the camera showed a reversed image of the statue.

Uphoff used slides to show how he prepared his Canon movie camera for the film experiment. He used plastic tape to seal the lens cap and film cartridge firmly in place, then wrote his

These images allegedly were placed on Polaroid film by the "mind power" of 17-year-old Masuaki Kiyota, 17, who appears in two of the photos.

name several times on each seal with a felt-tipped pen so "any disturbance could be easily detected."

He took the precautions because the young Kiyota requested that he be left alone in a room with the camera. When the boy later returned the camera, the footage counter showed "50," indicating that he had run several minutes of the film through the camera blind.

The four-minute film, which Uphoff showed today, was processed at Regent Photographic Studios in Madison

on the Uphoffs' return to the United States.

Most of it is blank, but there are several seconds of recognizable, though wavering, images of the Statue of Liberty, an image of the gold-painted Tokyo tower and a clear, brief image of a young woman's face, which looked as though it came from a painting.

With the exception of the face, these had been the images Kiyota told Uphoff he had placed on the film when he gave the camera back to the

or rumor." What we observed and the evidence we brought back from Japan is not a matter of rumor. It would have been accurate to say that "Uphoff *reported* that. . ." It should be added that one does not *touch* the shutter of a camera, but one does or does not *trip* the shutter. When the Polaroid camera was used, the shutter was not tripped and in the case of the movie camera, the lens cap was securely taped on and had not been tampered with.

Paragraph 5 The Uphoffs showed photos and films. The color slides taken of the sealed camera with the footage counter at 10 (when it was first sealed) and at 50 (when returned without the tape having been tampered with) were the evidence we presented. There was no occasion for any affidavits, since the film was run through the camera in Japan but processed by Kodak (via the Regent Photographic Studio) in the U.S.

Paragraphs 6 & 7 What was significant here is that three persons were

116

open door in research

researcher.

Uphoff said Kiyota (who first showed paranormal behavior by "metal-bending," a phenomenon commonly associated with Israeli psychic Uri Geller) placed the images on the film by fixing a picture in his mind and willing it to appear on the film.

The Uphoffs first recorded this ability in their textbook on parapsychology, "New Psychic Frontiers" published in 1977. However, these experiments were the most extensive they had conducted with Kiyota.

A professional photographer who viewed the film and examined the Polaroid pictures said they could have been faked, but he could not figure out how — if the experiments had been conducted and witnessed as Uphoff attested.

Uphoff said he is making an effort to bring Kiyota, a high-school student studying fish farming, to Madison during the boy's summer vacation so that further experiments can be conducted under laboratory conditions.

Uphoff also showed pieces of Continental Airlines cutlery he had given the boy to bend. Spoons and forks had tight double and triple twists in the handles, and knives were bent at right angles.

Uphoff said Kiyota stroked and tossed the spoons between his hands but never used any force in bending them, and that he bent the metal in the presence of at least six witnesses.

Uphoff admitted spoons could have been bent by force, but said the minute twists could not have been made by hand without the use of a machine. Without first heating metal, observers said, it would be impossible to bend it so tightly without breaking it off.

Uphoff, a former professor at the

DAVID SANDELL/The Capital Times

Psychic researcher Walter Uphoff, right, and his wife Mary Jo explain some of the experiments they conducted in Japan to UW psychologist Roger Severson, left. On the table are some of the cutlery Masuaki Kiyoto caused to bend paranormally and the movie camera he held in his hands while reportedly causing images to appear on several seconds of the film.

University of Colorado and longtime political figure in Wisconsin, and who once ran for governor, began his study of psychic phenomenon several years ago. He is director of the ESP Research Associates Foundation, a non-profit group headquartered in Mountain View, Ark.

---

given the polaroid camera and told to walk about 100 meters into the street and after 5 minutes to pull a film out of the camera without tripping the shutter. Masuaki, during this time was upstairs in his home concentrating on producing a picture. The photographer's name is Fukuda not Fukada.

Paragraph 8 Uphoff and Fukuda worked together in taping the lens cap and the film cartridge compartment.

Paragraph 9 It is not accurate to say that "young Kiyota requested that he be left alone in a room with the camera." *We* asked *him* if he would try to project some images onto movie film after he had been successful in getting some on polaroid film. After letting the camera film run about 10 feet (less than a minute) he said he did not think he was getting anything. Mr. Fukuda, the photographer, then suggested we might tape the cap on the camera lens, as described in the article, and let him try to project some images if he felt in the mood to do so. This is quite different from

117

"requesting to be left alone." When Masuaki returned the camera to us, the footage indicator stood at 50, showing that the film had been run through the camera with the lens capped.

Paragraph 10 We had Regent Photographic Studio, Madison, send the film to Kodak for processing. They did not process it themselves.

Paragraph 11 We specifically viewed the film again after reading that the images amount to "several seconds." Our count shows the first sequence running about 7 seconds, the second about 4, the third about 13, and the fourth about 3, or a total of 27 seconds. After the last image there also appears a less bright image of a face with moving lips.

Paragraph 15 What does it mean to say ". . .they could have been faked but he could not figure out how—if the experiments had been conducted and witnessed as Uphoff attested"? In all fairness, the sentence should have read "if the experiments *were* [not 'had been'] conducted. . ."

Paragraph 16 A friend of Masuaki who was present during the experiments is the person who studied fisheries management. This friend, Toru Ozaki, is now a medical student. Masuaki, who turned 17 on April 30th, is still in high school and plans to study psychology after graduation.

Paragraph 17 The cutlery which Masuaki twisted or broke came partly from Continental and Northwest airlines and the Keio Plaza department store in Tokyo. The fork and spoons were severely twisted, but the knife was only partly bent—and not at right angles. I do not want the "Amazing Randi" to ask me to see the knife bent at right angle when it was only slightly bent. I am always prepared to document what I write.

Paragraph 19 "Uphoff *admitted*. . ." implies that I was questioned. I *explained* that the spoons could be bent normally, but not the way that Masuaki does it, and then only if a strong mechanical force or intense heat were used.

Paragraph 20 I do not understand what relevance "longtime political figure in Wisconsin" added to the story, but since it was used, the facts ought to be stated at least. I have been away from Wisconsin most of the time since 1951. I was on the faculty of the University of Minnesota from 1951-63 and the University of Colorado from 1963 to 1976. In the 1940's I was candidate on the Socialist ticket for U. S. Senator when Norman **Thomas was candidate for President in 1944, and for governor of** Wisconsin in 1946 and 1948. I viewed that as an educational effort and not as a "political" activity in the usual sense. I also served on the national executive committee of the Socialist Party from 1942-50 and was active in the state organization.

I have been less active in the 29 years which followed only because the two major parties—which agree on much more than they disagree—have seen to it that in many states it is very difficult to get on the ballot and to **receive fair treatment by the media. The world would be a better and** more peaceful place to live if the ideals of Norman Thomas and the Socialist Party had been applied in a larger measure.

It was about 45 years ago that I started to study psychic phenomena—very skeptically for more than 30 years—not "several years ago" as stated in the article. I came to the conclusion that the evidence was worthy of investigation and too extensive to ignore. I taught classes in parapsychology at the University of Colorado as long as ten years ago. Harold Sherman is the founder and board chairman of the ESP Research Associates Foundation, with headquarters in Little Rock, Arkansas. I am only one of 11 directors. I can understand how that error was made, since the cards printed for us by the Foundation merely identify me as "director."

The caption under the first pictures used the word *allegedly* which according to our dictionary means: 1. to declare with positiveness; assert. 2. to declare before a court or elsewhere as if under oath. 3. to assert without proof. 4. to plead in support of; urge as reason or excuse. . .This was an unfortunate choice of word. It would have been accurate to say "it was *reported* that these images were placed on film. . ." The word "allege" has a negative connotation for many people.

Under the second picture the word *reportedly* is again used when it would have been accurate to say, "it was reported that. . ."

I realize that these comments and corrections may be more extensive than your paper is prepared to print but for the sake of accuracy and for the record—especially in a field where so many sweeping charges are made by skeptics and debunkers who seldom take the trouble to investigate—I believe it is important to reply to this article, not so much for ourselves, as for the reputation of young Masuaki Kiyota who is a truly gifted person. We had prepared a two-page information statement for the press conference in the hope that inaccuracies would be kept at a minimum.

We have seen enough reporting of events in the last half century to realize that most mistakes are not deliberate. Certainly Miss Mitchard is open-minded and fair in her reporting and does a good job within the severe contraints of time and space which prevail in the daily newspaper business. It may be that we are too closely involved in this investigation to see the phenomena from the same perspective as reporters, but it does seem that the significant thing about the Kiyota experiments was that he was able to get *anything* on film with the lens capped—not that the image was "blurred." We hope that the article will stimulate others to at least look at the evidence with an open mind. We do hope that Masuaki Kiyota and his friend Hiroto Yamashita may be able to come for a visit during their vacation this summer—not to be treated as "laboratory subjects" but as human beings from whom we might be able to gain some insights about the nature of life and of the mind.

We realized that this statement, commenting on 13 of the 20 paragraphs in the article, was too long to have much chance of being printed in full but it was written to keep the record straight. A 3-page letter from Jacquelyn Mitchard, the first page of which is reproduced below, will indicate to the reader something about the problems facing a newspaper reporter, especially when writing about a subject surrounded by more prejudice and emotion than knowledge. She added that she hoped I would understand that none of the mistakes were deliberate; that she had endeavoured to avoid giving critics and debunkers "grist for their mill."

THE CAPITAL TIMES

1901 Fish Hatchery Road
PO Box 8060
Zip Code: 53708

ELLIOTT MARANISS
Editor
ROBERT MELOON
Executive Editor
DAVE ZWEIFEL
Managing Editor
JOHN PATRICK HUNTER
Associate Editor
MARIE PULVERMACHER
Associate Editor

Madison, Wisconsin

Phone: 608-252-6400

May 15, 1979

Walter Uphoff
Route 1
Oregon, WI 53575

Dear Walter,

The Capital Times will be more than happy to print a letter containing the corrections made regarding the Kiyota experiments, but I first want to take the opportunity to respond to some of them - for the reason that I think we are "on the same side of the fence, and I believe that an explanation from me will help clarify some of the reasoning behind several of the things you found objectionable.

When approaching a subject of this nature, reporter and subject are, of course, setting themselves up for charges from "skeptics and debunkers" so the utmost care and RESTRAINT are advisable in the writing.

I could have written the story in such a fashion as to indicate that I believed every word you said about Kiyota (which I did, personally) but then it would not have gone into the newspaper. I had to fight two editors to get it in as it was. And though it grieves me, you realize that the wire services did not bother with it, nor did any of the other newspapers, though I did send a copy right off to Sheyboygan. This indicates what I believe is an important factor in reporting on material of this nature - too many times newspapers consider it "silly," far-fetched or "Enquirer stuff." I don't believe that, nor does our city editor David Zweifel, who went to bat for the story as legitimate news. But what I ask you and MaryJo to realize is that I, as a reporter, have to function as the voice of all those skeptics and debunkers, and the tone of the article reflects that. I believe that tone is to your credit, and the credit of the story. It says, in effect, "we tried to debunk it, and we couldn't and here it is."

Let me respond to some of the points you made. As you said, perhaps it is difficult for you, being so eagerly involved with the subject, to see it as a reporter does, and must. The

We were told that we could submit a shorter letter, which she hoped would be published in the readers' column. We did prepare a short letter which was printed but the paragraph we considered most important was left out, namely that interested readers could contact us for more details.

Uphoff disputes psychic article

OREGON — On May 12 The Capital Times ran an article about the psychic abilities of young Masuaki Kiyota of Tokyo whom we visited in March. Jacki Mitchard wrote an interesting report of the phenomena we described. Being intimately involved in all details of the experiments we conducted, naturally we recognized errors which inadvertently crept into the article.

We hope the following points can be printed:

(1) At least 27 seconds of images — not several or five — were produced on the super-8 movie film with the lens cap securely taped on and the film cassette also securely taped in place. This was witnessed and photographed before and after.

(2) Masuaki did not ask to have the camera. Mr. Yutaka Fukuda (not Fukada), a professional photographer who took part in the experiments and taping the camera, suggested it be given Masuaki so he could try to project images when in the "psychic mood" to do so. The results were phenomenal and we have just learned that NTV, one of the major Japanese networks, will show a documentary on young Kiyota in June, based on films they made while we were there and one successive weekend.

(3) I did not appreciate the word "allegedly" used in the caption with the picture of images of the Tokyo Tower produced paranormally by young Kiyota. I am certain the phenomenon is genuine and that there was no chance of fraud. Under those circumstances I would have had no objection to the article stating that "Uphoff reported that . . ." Had there been the slightest doubt about my integrity, your paper should not have used an inch of type to report the experiment.

We are inviting two young psychics from Japan to visit us this summer and there will be an opportunity for those interested to meet them. — **Walter H. Uphoff**

After we had been assured by Masuaki and Hiroto that they could spend their vacation with us, arriving July 26th, we made arrangements for a two-day private workshop at our home, a public lecture for Professor Hasted at the University of Wisconsin, and an all-day public workshop at Howard Johnson's Motor Lodge in Madison. A University news service sent out a release to the in-state media announcing the Hasted lecture.

Because the *Wisconsin State Journal* is the morning paper, it "scooped" the *Capital Times* when the two young psychics arrived. Reporter Chuck Martin and photographer Carolyn Pflasterer came out to our home to meet Masuaki and Hiroto. Jamie Hubbard, a graduate student in the University's Asian Studies Department, served as interpreter. They stayed well over an hour and we have a tape recording of the interview. Many pertinent questions were asked and Jamie did an excellent job of two-way translation, essential for the interview.

The two feature stories, written by Chuck Martin, are reproduced on the following pages. The first article, with pictures, started on the front page of the *Journal* and continued on the second page, followed by a story about the Uphoffs and their experiments with Masuaki and Hiroto in Japan.

Both Masuaki and Hiroto were given heavy stainless steel tablespoons on which to try their "PK." Most of the interview took place in the relaxed environment of a small guest house next to our house. Most of the attention during the interview was centered on Masuaki and it was he who produced the twisted spoon that was shown on the front page. The articles stimulated considerable interest and apparently some controversy in the community. More about that later.

Spoon-bender's a mind-bender and came from Japan to prove it

By Chuck Martin
Of The State Journal

A spoon Kiyota said he bent by thought power.

When Masuaki Kiyota, 17, arrived in the United States last Thursday from his native Tokyo, he knew he would be an object of curiosity.

As he stood in a sunlit room at the New Frontiers Center on Highway MM about 5 miles south of Madison, he smiled at the first newspaper reporter he met in America.

"You want me to bend a spoon for you?" he asked.

About 90 minutes later, after being interviewed and photographed, he returned to the same room carrying an ordinary spoon he had been holding for about 30 minutes. As five other persons talked about his apparent ability to bend and twist tableware without applying physical force, he tapped a table with the spoon and held it up, the handle twisted and bent just above the bowl.

The others stopped talking and reached for the spoon. He shrugged his shoulders and grinned.

Kiyota is one of several hundred persons throughout the world who have been observed to perform such acts as contorting or breaking metal objects or repairing broken watches apparently by using a mental force.

In 1977 he appeared on the television program "Exploring the Unknown" broadcast on the NBC network. In front of television cameras and photographic experts he projected an image of the Tokyo Tower, an Eiffel Tower-like landmark, on film in a sealed Polaroid camera, apparently by concentration.

In the last three years he has been examined on several occasions by physicists, psychiatrists and parapsychology researchers, demonstrating his ability with varying degrees of success and failure.

He and another Japanese boy who has performed similar acts, Hiroto Yamashita, 15, were brought to Wisconsin by Walter and Mary Jo Uphoff, Oregon.

The Uphoffs have written a book, "New Psychic Frontiers," on phenomona of the mind from the perception of things beyond the normal senses (extra-sensory perception) to the use of the mind to alter matter (psychokinesis). They established the New

Turn to Page 2, Col. 1

Continued from Page 1

Frontiers Center at their Oregon farmstead to provide a place for interested persons to discuss and study psychic phenomona.

The boys will appear at a two-day public workshop on the alteration of motion or objects by influence of the mind to be held Aug. 10 and 11 in Madison.

Speaking through an interpreter, Kiyota, the son of a restaurant operator, said last week he has had the ability to contort small metal objects by thought for as long as he can remember.

Until he was about 10 years old, he assumed everyone possessed the same ability, he said. But when a visit to Japan by the Israeli psychic Uri Geller attracted much news media attention, he realized his ability was unusual, he said.

He said after seeing Geller bend spoons on television, he told his parents he could perform the same acts. They believed him, he said, when he bent a spoon without touching it.

He said bending spoons and transferring images to film is to him a natural process. He said usually when he begins a session of spoon-bending, he must concentrate on contorting the metal. But after he has performed the act once or twice, he sometimes is able to continue without concentrating, he said.

"It's like an engine," he said. "You have to crank it to get it started. But then it goes by itself."

Spoon-bending and image transfers are his "specialties," he said. He said he often wishes he could perform more practical acts than bending spoons.

He said he once placed a container of water near a container of instant noodles. By concentrating he made the water to boil, he said. He then transferred the boiling water to the noodle container by thought power, he said.

He also has unlocked doors and windows by concentration, he said.

One of the most unusual acts he has performed, he said, was to cause a coin to enter a tangerine without marring the skin of the fruit.

He cannot perform on demand, however, he said. During an interview he attempted to project an image on film in a State Journal photographer's camera.

After about three minutes of silent concentration on the camera, with lens removed and body cap fitted, he pulled back from the table at which he was seated. He said he was not confident that he had caused an image to appear on the film.

When developed the film was black.

He said he does not believe he uses his own energy to contort metal objects or create images on film. Rather, he said, he believes he is a conduit for an outside force.

The workshop at which Kiyota will attempt to demonstrate his ability will begin at 7:30 p.m. Aug. 10 in room 3650 of the Humanities Building at the University of Wisconsin-Madison. On Aug. 11 the workshop will begin at 9 a.m. in the University Room of the Howard Johnson Motor Lodge, 525 W. Johnson St.

Uphoff said about 50 physicists, biologists, psychiatrists, metallurgists and photographic experts will attend. Registration costs $6 for the Aug. 10 session and $30 for the Aug. 11 session. Further information can be obtained from the New Frontiers Center at 835-3795.

Masukai Kiyota, 17, attempts to create an image on film.
— State Journal photos by Carolyn Pflasterer.

122

Many experiments offered and teen is up to them

OREGON — Walter Uphoff, 66, author and former professor at the universities of Wisconsin, Minnesota and Colorado, met Masuaki Kiyota, then 15, in Tokyo in October 1976.

Uphoff had been asked by a television producer to assist in the production of "Exploring the Unknown," a program on psychic phenomena including psychokinesis, the alteration of matter by mind power.

Knowing Kiyota had said he could bend spoons without physical force, he took a spoon to the boy's home to investigate his ability. The boy stroked the neck of the spoon, shook it quickly and held it out, twisted just above the bowl.

Uphoff and his wife, Mary Jo, 67, returned to Tokyo last March to meet and conduct experiments on Kiyota again. In one experiment, Uphoff said, he and a Japanese photographer gave Kiyota a Canon Super-8 movie camera to determine if he could create images by thought on movie film as he apparently had done previously with Polaroid film.

"After about 10 feet of film had been run, he said he wasn't getting anything," Uphoff said. "So we gave him the camera to work on alone when he got in the mood."

Uphoff said he and the photographer taped the lens cap on the camera and taped the cassette compartment to insure the film could not be tampered with. Later Kiyota returned the camera and said he believed he had created images on the film. He told Uphoff the first image on the film would be the Tokyo Tower, Uphoff said.

When the Uphoffs returned to Madison, they had the film processed by Kodak. When they ran the film through a projector, the first 12 feet were blank, Uphoff said. Then, for about seven seconds, the Tokyo Tower appeared.

Another blank section followed. Then, more images appeared, including about 13 seconds of the Statue of Liberty, separated by blank sections.

"This was all on about three minutes of film run through the camera with the lens securely taped," Uphoff said.

From March through June a series of experiments was conducted on Kiyota for two half-hour documentaries shown on a Japanese television network earlier this month.

In one experiment, conducted by physicists, Kiyota was found to emit electric waves of a frequency between 30 and 40 megahertz from the left side of the frontal lobe of his brain. Other persons were found to emit no electric waves that registered on the measurement instruments.

The electric current in most American homes has a frequency of 60 hertz. A megahertz is 1 million hertz.

In another experiment magnified photographs of a spoon broken by machine and a spoon broken by Kiyota were compared.

The photographs revealed the molecular structure of the two breaks to be significantly different, according to the physicists.

Uphoff said he was a skeptic when he began studying psychic phenomena 45 years ago.

"But the evidence has convinced me this sort of phenomena is genuine," he said.

He said he is aware that many serious scholars are not convinced psychic phenomena are real.

"We welcome serious criticism," he said. "Some phenomena may be only magic tricks. But the fact that some might be faked does not mean that the phenomena do not exist.

"Whether the observer believes or disbelieves is not important. The important thing is what actually happens and that we study it to understand it."

He said when Kiyota and 15-year-old Hiroto Yamashita attempt to demonstrate their abilities at an Aug. 10 and 11 workshop in Madison, there will be no assurance they will succeed.

"People who are expecting a sideshow should stay home," he said. "The boys may or may not be able to do anything. At any rate, we do not intend to put them on display. Our purpose is to study their abilities and learn more about them."

A *Capital Times* Feature Story

On August 8th, Jacquelyn Mitchard and Rich Righ, a *Capital Times* photographer, came out to the New Frontiers Center for a story about Professor Hasted and our Japanese guests. This article, reproduced in full through reduced in size, summarizes that visit.

The first story in the *State Journal* had appeared on July 30th and the *Capital Times* feature appeared August 9th while the private workshop for scientists and investigators was in progress. The morning of August 11th, when the public workshop was underway at the Howard Johnson's Motor Lodge in Madison, the *Wisconsin State Journal* printed a completely negative article (photocopied in the next chapter) under a six-column headline, "Spoon Bending's a Crooked Ploy, Scientist Says." The article, over Robyne Curry's by-line quoted Paul Kurtz, a philosophy professor at the State University of New York and chairman of the Committee for the Scientific Investigation of Claims of the Paranormal, as saying, "It's a hoax. . .It's a use of magical means." He was appalled that Madison "a city of sophisticated, literate people...and a great science center. . .would allow themselves to be taken in by psychic hucksters."

Kurtz had never met the two boys or seen the metal bending and thoughtography which others have witnessed and reported, yet he was willing to call the two boys "cheaters" because what they do does not fit his concept of reality. Honest criticism and differences of opinion are always in order, but that article was certainly an uncalled-for "low blow"

Can physics explain 'spoonbenders'?

By JACQUELYN MITCHARD
Capital Times Staff Writer

THE CAPITAL TIMES

MADISON, WIS.
AUG. 9, 1979 — 31

"I try to go where the people who can bend metal are," said Dr. John B. Hasted, a professor and researcher at London University and investigator into psychokinesis (the ability to use the mind to alter matter). "Coming here was easier than going to Japan."

Hasted is in Madison to observe the abilities of Msauaki Kiyota, 18, the son of a Tokyo restaurant operator who has been observed to project images onto film in sealed cameras and make cutlery loop the loop, apparently by concentration.

Kiyota, who appeared as part of an NBC documentary in 1977 "Exploring the Unknown," is here as the guest of Walter and Mary Jo Uphoff, psychic researchers and authors of "New Psychic Frontiers," who first met Kiyota on a trip to Japan in 1976.

Kiyota and Hiroto Yamashita, 15, who has demonstrated similar abilities, will participate in a two-day workshop on psychokinesis Friday and Saturday. Before Friday, however, psychiatrists, physicists and parapsychologists from all over the U.S. will descend on the New Frontiers Center at the Uphoffs' Oregon, Wis., home, for private consultations with Kiyota and Yamashita, both of whom have performed what Hasted termed "significant" acts of psychokinesis.

No relisher of things that go bump in the night, Hasted told The Capital Times he deals in observable effects. He has tested many children in Britain whose families have reported various "disturbances" in the home and found a half dozen whose abilities are consistent enough to warrant serious study.

Though Hasted says the field is too new for him to have "detailed physical theories" on the roots of psychokinesis, he believes the mathematical theory of quantum mechanics might hold a link. "We may end with looking at the possible importance the human mind's effect on matter has in scientific experimentation," he said.

Already, Hasted says, he has seen Kiyota contort metal in ways that are impossible by established theory. Metal, he said, is a good medium to use for such testing because it is "not easy to influence. One knows where the atoms are and how they are arranged. Change is readily detectible."

In a London taxi, after the taping of a British television program on psychic phenomenon, Hasted said Kiyota put a bend in a spoon that should have put sufficient strain on the metal to break it. But the spoon remained intact, its stem tightly looped just above the bowl. Hasted keeps the spoon encased in isenglas and carries it with him in his travels.

Hasted said Kiyota was frustrated and disappointed by his performance for the documentary and that the frustration may have set the stage for the phenomenon in the cab. "I often find that anger, or some other like motivation, is a factor in these things," he said.

When he tests his subjects — mainly children — Hasted implants resistive strain gauges (metal sensors) in keys or spoons. The gauges are electronically attached to a pen recorder so that any movement at all in the metal will be recorded on a paper roll much like that used in a lie-detector (polygraph) test.

He usually test subjects in their homes because children seem most comfortable in familiar surroundings. He does insist that he and his two colleagues have sole access to the materials and instruments to be used, carefully weighing and otherwise identifying spoons or other metals before tests begin "to make sure that the spoon that is bent is the same spoon and not one purchased in the same shop, though that would seem an unlikely possibility."

He first asks children to touch and bend the spoons, then stroke them lightly, then try to bend them without touching them at all. "When they can do that, it is the moment of truth for these kids," he said.

Analysis of crystals of metal after experiments has shown that metal benders have induced "dislocations" in the atoms that make up the structure though the subject had not touched or bent the metal in any way.

Magnified photographs of a spoon broken by Kiyota flipping and stroking it were compared with photos of a spoon broken by a machine. Physicists found significant differences in the molecular structure of the two breaks.

That is the meat of the kind of research Hasted is attempting. Though he has observed countless incidents of metal bending, it is only those which occur under controlled conditions he allows himself to "count," disregarding the others.

"From what I have seen of these two Japanese lads," he said, "they are genuine. They are not tricksters." He said even children with demonstrable psychic abilities have been known to "cheat" — have been observed through two-way mirrors in rooms where they believed themselves to be alone trying to use force to bend metal. "There is a great deal of pressure to succeed," he said.

Laboratory tests were run on Kiyota and Yamashita at a large Midwestern research institute earlier this week, but no results have as yet been forthcoming. Hasted is skeptical about the success rate of such experiments in which a potentially psychic child is asked to start "cold" and basically demonstrate on command.

But during the interview, Kiyota and Yamashita, who had been roused from a midday nap, were each given a spoon to try to bend. "At this rate, I'll be running out of spoons," said Mary Jo Uphoff, who had been donating cutlery all week and seeing it end up in strange shapes.

The spoon given to Kiyota was part of a set. After a few minutes of shy smiles and attempted chat with the photographers and some fiddling with the radio, Kiyota and Yamashita (who speak very little English) appeared more interested in going back to sleep than in psychic phenomenon.

But as the reporter and photographer made ready to leave, Kiyota bolted out of the house, placed a spoon with a tight loop in its stem in the reporters palm, shook hands and ran off to play with the Uphoff's collie dog.

Less than two minutes had elapsed since the reporter and photographer had left the room. During that time, Mrs. Uphoff and a friend had been the only ones in the room with Kiyota, who had remained on the sofa, apparently listening to the radio. The remaining spoons in the set were unbent, and Mrs. Uphoff identified the teaspoon as the one she had given Kiyota 30 minutes previously.

The boy had rubbed the spoon between his thumb and index finger and tossed it into the air several times. He had allowed it to lie beside him on the sofa for a few minutes.

Hasted pronounced it a "good bend," and said the eleventh hour occurrence was a classic example of what often happens when children with psychic abilities are asked to perform in front of spectators. When the pressure is off, even for a brief time, he said, the channels seem to open more readily.

Unlike Hasted, Kiyota believes the ability to bend metal and place psychic images on film comes from a force outside him and that he acts as a channel for that force. He has said he believed until he was about 10 when saw Israeli psychic Uri Geller on television, that the ability to bend metal was a common thing — something everyone had.

Hasted believes as many as one percent of the population may have the ability without realizing it.

Kiyota will attempt to demonstrate his ability at a lecture and workshop beginning at 7:30 p.m. Friday in room 3650 of the UW Humanities Building. A second workshop will begin at 9 a.m.

Saturday and continue until 10 p.m. in the University Room of the Howard Johnson Motor Lodge, 525 W. Johnson St.

The Friday session will cost $6 per person and the Saturday workshop will cost $30 per person. Information on registration is available by calling the New Frontiers Center at 835-3795.

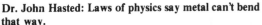

Dr. John Hasted: Laws of physics say metal can't bend that way.
Masuaki Kiyota *(left)* **concentrates on the spoon he later said he bent** *(right)* **by psychokinesis. His friend, Hiroto Yamashita,** *(lower right)* **was unsuccessful at this try at metal-bending, but has demonstrated the ability in other experiments.**
(Reproduced from *The Capital Times.* **Text and photos reduced and arranged to fit book pages.)**

Courtesy RICH RIGH/*The Capital Times*

125

at the integrity of two young lads whom Kurtz had never met. (To take the reader to primary sources, an article about Masuaki written by two members of Kurtz's Committee for the Scientific Investigation of Claims of the Paranormal is reproduced in full in the next chapter.) Prof. John B. Hasted, a physicist with top credentials and knowledgeable in the area of PK, had come all the way from London for experiments with the Japanese boys, but he was not even consulted before the attack on metal benders was printed.

When we started to write this book, I went to the **Wisconsin State Journal** and asked to met Robyne Curry, over whose by-line the article had appeared. I told her I would like to discuss an article she had written. She suggested that we go down to the cafeteria to talk. When I told her we were working on a manuscript for a book about PK, and that I make it a point to go to primary sources when possible, she said something to the effect that I had better talk with the city editor instead. "But you wrote the story," I said, "and I am merely interested in learning what I can about the circumstances that led to the story, who was consulted before writing the story, etc." I thought of the aphorism quoted at the end of the Introduction of this book, "Imagination takes over where information stops."

Miss Curry was friendly but would not, or could not, discuss the article. Was she afraid she might say the wrong thing? Was she under orders not to discuss the article? Had the article been written in a hurry and under pressure from one or more critics in the community who had objected to the article by Chuck Martin? Had there been no time to check on what I regarded as slanderous charges against two young lads whom neither she nor Kurtz had ever seen? I was at a loss to figure out the reporter's unwillingness to talk unless more had happened behind the scenes as a result of Martin's article than I had realized.

Miss Curry took me upstairs and asked me to be seated while she went to talk with Cliff Behnke, the City Editor. Three or four minutes later he came over to ask what I wanted. Apparently he had been told that we planned to write the story of our experiences with the Japanese psychics. I told him that I preferred to get information from primary sources and therefore had come to talk with the reporter who had written the article quoting Paul Kurtz. What did I want to know? he asked. I said I was curious as to how such a story had come to be written and who had been consulted before Kurtz' assertions were printed. Behnke replied, "We don't have to reveal our sources of information," to which I responded, "O.K. If that's your position, I will merely quote you as having said that."

I am aware of differences between objective and subjective "realities." I could not read Mr. Behnke's mind, but I got the distinct impression that here was a chapter of "history" which he would rather not have reviewed. I reminded him that Prof. Hasted was in the community at the time the article was written. Had anyone checked with people at the University before the article was published? I said it was grossly unfair to the two young men to quote charges from someone who had never met them, especially when there was no evidence to substantiate the charges. He replied something to the effect that after all, the **State Journal** had given them a favorable write-up earlier. That in no way justified printing unfounded charges against innocent persons, I said. I was so shocked by the response that my "imagination" took over again and I wondered how much of what we read in the press is the product of attempts to appease divergent points of view and yielding to pressures without regard for facts. As I left, I could not help wondering if Robyne Curry had actually written that article.

On August 12th, the **Wisconsin State Journal** carried another story about the boys, "Psychologist Sees Reason to Pursue Psychokinesis," (reproduced in full) which presented both "pro" and "con" viewpoints and quoted Dr. Maurice Pressman, a Philadelphia psychiatrist.

Psychologist sees reason to pursue psychokinesis

By Chuck Martin
Of The State Journal

Dr. Maurie Pressman said he did not know before this weekend whether persons who say they can alter objects by thought power are tricksters or genuine psychics.

Saturday the Philadelphia psychologist said he still isn't sure how persons bend spoons and create images on film apparently without physical force. But, he said, he believes he saw enough evidence at a workshop Friday and Saturday in Madison to convince him "there is enough there to investigate further."

"I've witnessed things in the last two days we do not understand," he said. "And they cannot be dismissed.

"It would be wrong to let our imaginations run away with the results. But it would be just as wrong to blot out the evidence and say it doesn't exist."

Pressman was one of about 90 persons who attended a two-day workshop in Madison to discuss psychokinesis, the ability to alter matter by use of the mind.

Two Japanese teen-agers who have said they can bend spoons and create images on film by thought power participated in the workshop. Pressman, 56, said he was impressed by what he saw Masuaki Kiyota, 17, and Hiroto Yamashita, 15, demonstrate.

Friday, Kiyota sat in a room in front of about 30 physicists, psychiatr-

ists, biologists and other interested persons. A Polaroid camera with lens removed and body sealed was placed in front of him. The camera was loaded with film bought earlier in the day in Madison.

Kiyota held the camera in his hands and said he was concentrating on producing images on the film. When he said he believed he had exposed the film, the eight photographs were removed from the camera.

All were exposed. No photograph exhibited a discernable image, however.

"The film was white," Pressman said. "It should have been black. Something happened."

Pressman said he doubted the demonstration was a trick.

"It was conducted under very controlled conditions," he said. "There were very qualified scientists present. For them to risk their credentials by being involved in anything fraudulent is just unimaginable."

Kiyota and Yamashita, who were examined at the Mayo Clinic in Rochester, Minn., earlier in the week, also bent several spoons during the workshop. Saturday, in front of observers, Kiyota held a spoon in hand and quickly flipped his wrist. When examined, the spoon exhibited a twist at the neck.

But Kiyota also failed to create images on film during a Thursday night attempt, and Yamashita failed to bend any spoons under observation

on Saturday.

Paul Kurtz, a philosophy professor at the State University of New York at Buffalo, said Friday in an interview published in The Wisconsin State Journal he believes spoon bending and image creation on film can only be done by physical manipulation.

"People who claim they can do such things are just magicians posing as psychics," he said.

Chairman of the Committee for the Scientific Investigation of Claims of the Paranormal, he said none of the psychic claims tested by his committee has held up under scientific scrutiny.

Kurtz did not attend the Madison workshop.

Pressman said he attended the workshop, in part, because of some of his professional experiences.

"In my work with hypnosis, intuition and dying patients I've been led to believe there may be something there we do not understand," he said.

The workshop was organized by Walter and Mary Jo Uphoff, Oregon, and Roger Severson, a University of Wisconsin-Madison educational psychology professor.

The Uphoffs, who invited Kiyota and Yamashita to come to the United States for the workshop, have written a book on psychic phenomena. The couple also has established a center on their farm for persons interested in psychic phenomona.

On August 13, the *Capital Times* carried the following story about the episode involving Prof. Szybalski (discussed in the previous chapter) and the Saturday workshop which Miss Mitchard had attended in part:

Psychic acts stir believers, skeptics

By JACQUELYN MITCHARD
Capital Times Staff Writer

8/13/79

The opportunity to witness genuine psychic phenomena doesn't come along very often. And when it did — last weekend in Madison — some witnesses were left wondering whether they'd seen it at all.

Psychic metal-bending has been called a phenomenon that happens outside the realm of science.

And apparently, it's doing its best to stay that way.

At the conclusion of a two-day workshop on "psychokinesis" (the ability to influence matter with the mind), two Japanese youths who were the subjects of the program agreed to demonstrate their ability to a group of five observers, including one reporter.

A spoon was looped in a double bend by Masuaki Kiyota, 17, whose psychic abilities have been widely studied and the subject of much controversy. But though Kiyota was in the room with the observers, at the moment when he said the bend took place he was seated about 10 feet from the main group. So though they saw it, no one in the group could pinpoint when and how the feat took place.

Since Kiyota, 17, and Yamashita, 15, came to Madison a week ago as the guests of psychic authors Mary Jo and Walter Uphoff, there has been a good deal of spoon-bending and some attempts to put psychic images on film.

There has also been a good deal of publicity — and it has divided those interested into three camps. There are those such as the Uphoffs, who believe in the boy's ability; those who call the feats nothing more than medicine show magic, such as philosophy professor Paul Kurtz of the State University of New York at Buffalo; and the greatest majority — those like the fellow from Missouri, who said, "Show me."

Professor John Hasted, a physicist and researcher into psychokinesis from London University, has done extensive tests on more than 1,000 youngsters and some adults in an attempt to ground psychokinesis (PK) in scientific terms. In Madison for the workshop, he said his research has shown the phenomenon to be a demonstrable reality. "What we are now about is a sociological exercise," he said, "— getting people to believe in what they see."

However, Kurtz, who is chairman of the Committee for the Scientific Investigation of Claims of the Paranormal — a group of some 70 scientists and consultants that attempts to act as a watchdog organization in the field — dismissed Kiyota's "spoonbending" as "a hoax." Kurtz, however, said he had had no direct contact with Kiyota, contrary to one newspaper report.

When Professor Waclaw Szybalski, a molecular geneticist at the University of Wisconsin and consultant to the committee Kurtz heads, attended the Friday night portion of the workshop, he submitted a spoon, which he had marked, for bending. Later, when attempts to bend it had proved unsuccessful, he asked to have the spoon returned, and said the two Japanese youths gave him a spoon that resembled his, but was not marked.

He insisted on having his own spoon, and followed the two to their auditorium seats to get it. There, he said he saw a briefcase full of hundreds of spoons, among which his was finally located. "If there was no fraud," he said, "there was the opportunity for it."

Kurtz has said that spoonbenders use sleight of hand to substitute a previously bent spoon that resembles the original. He has also said "magicians" use accomplices or distract the audience while using a concealed piece of metal with an aperture to bend spoons.

But Hasted, among others, has reported incidents in which Kiyota and Yamashita bent metal in such tight curves as to defy the laws of physics and the properties of the metals used — and within a matter of moments. He exhibited labeled examples of such spoons at the workshop.

In discussing the ephemeral quality of metal-bending feats, Hasted said the phenomenon often will not take place when there is pressure on the subject, or if the subject (usually a child) is in unfamiliar surroundings.

Hasted has said his experiments with metal strain detectors have indicated that Kiyota and Yamashita have genuine abilities. However, he said, almost all of the children he has tested — including the Japanese youths — have been known to try to "cheat" at least some part of the time during tests.

A fair percentage of bends are not induced by PK, he said, even among children who have shown strong ability. The pressure to be able to repeat a successful feat is great, he said, especially when the child is the subject of a media event or a laboratory test.

For this reason, "I am entirely opposed to these kinds of public demonstrations," he said. "The psychology of children makes the phenomenon difficult to pin down."

Though Kiyota and Yamashita said they were successful in about 80 percent of their attempts to bend metal, they were fatigued and did not feel "up to it" for most of the Saturday portion of the workshop, which was held from 9 a.m. until 6 p.m.

At about 4:30 p.m., Kiyota and Yamashita agreed to try to bend spoons for a group of five observers picked at random from the audience of some 75 in attendance, and including one reporter.

For the first half hour, the boys chatted with their interpreter and another young friend, and complained of weariness. Kiyota carried a handful of spoons around the room, always remaining within sight, but occasionally squatting down on the floor with his back to the observers.

After stroking and flipping the spoons for some time with no effect, and putting one into his pocket, Kiyota excused himself to go to the washroom and asked Yamashita to accompany him.

When he returned, he again picked up the spoons, and took a chair about ten feet from the group of observers, who were encouraged by his interpreter to act informal and not stare directly at him.

Within a few minutes, Kiyota tossed a spoon up into the air and when it landed, it was clearly bent at the stem — in two directions. An observer identified the spoon as one he had borrowed from the restaurant of the Howard Johnson Motel where the workshop was held. He had not, however, marked the spoon in any fashion before giving it to Kiyota.

Hasted said the frustration of feeling unable to perform could have sparked Kiyota to bend the spoon. But Kurtz said two of the researchers for his committee had studied Kiyota in London last summer during the preparation of a TV documentary and that the youth had been "unable to peform under controlled conditions" (meaning a properly lit room with observers present).

Uphoff later reported a second spoon was bent after the reporter left Saturday's conference.

128

The Media in General

There is no question that the media (the press, magazines, tabloids, radio and television) are devoting more space and time to unusual phenomena today than they formerly did. The treatment ranges all the way from full acceptance of the phenomena to "tongue-in-cheek" reporting and outright debunking. If there is discussion of a subject, the chances are better that the facts—whatever they are—will eventually emerge. Alternative modalities in healing are no longer shunned as much as they were even a decade ago. Reports about lost persons located with the help of psychics appear more frequently in the press. Experiments conducted at places like Stanford Research Institute, reported in Puthoff and Targ's book, *Mind Reach* (Delacorte Press, 1977) with an introduction by the renowned anthropologist Margaret Mead, help open the way for more serious examination of phenomena which have too long been dismissed as "nonsense."

Reader's Digest (August 1977) carried a six-page article entitled, "What Do We Really Know About Psychic Phenomena" by Laile E. Bartlett. The article was strongly protested by the Committee for the Scientific Investigation of Claims of the Paranormal (see Chapter IX). It concluded:

> People were aghast when Copernicus proclaimed that the earth circles the sun. But the new view won out.
>
> We may be at another such turning point today. In the words of Willis Harman of Stanford Research Institute: "Psychic research in the next few decades may be destined to have an impact comparable to the impact a few centuries ago of Galileo and Copernicus. I call it the Second Copernican Revolution.

Judging by the tone of the articles printed in *TIME* and *Newsweek* magazines, it appears that those in charge of editorial policy, at least in the early 1970's, were more skeptical at *TIME* than at *Newsweek*. The cover of *Time,* June 19, 1972, portrayed a weird black mask with only the eyes peering out and was captioned: "The Occult Revival—Satan Returns." Interest in witchcraft, tarot-cards, palmistry, reincarnation, astral projection and the Kabbala, *TIME* stated, had grown to the extent that "at Scribner's bookstore in Manhattan, books on the occult have completely taken over a counter that was once reserved for more traditional religious books." The 9-page feature, with four pages of color pictures, touched on a wide range of esoteric and far-out beliefs and practices and concluded with:

> *Perhaps the ideal solution would be to give the devil his due, whether as a symbolic reminder of evil or a real force to be conquered—but to separate him, once and for all, from "magic." Beyond all the charlatanism, there is a genuine realm of magic, a yet undiscovered territory between man and his universe. Perhaps it can once more be*

accepted as a legitimate pursuit of knowledge, no longer hedged in by bell, book and candle. Perhaps eventually, religion, science and magic could come mutually to respect and supplement one another. That is a fond vision, and one that is pinned to a fragile and perpetually unprovable faith: that the universe itself is a whole, with purpose and promise beneath its mystery.

The cover of the March 4, 1974 issue of **TIME** featured "The Psychics" and contained a 10-page article with 4 pages of color pictures including Dr. Thelma Moss, Ingo Swann, Dr. Elmer Green, Astronaut Edgar Mitchell, James Randi, the magician, Uri Geller and Cleve Backster—a diverse collection of investigators, psychics and debunkers. Reference is made to Prof. J. B. Rhine, Dr. Ian Stevenson, Dr. Montague Ullman, Dr. Gardner Murphy, anthropologist Margaret Mead, and Prof. Charles Tart. The thrust of the article is that there is no significant evidence for the paranormal, and a heavy reliance on statements of debunkers like James Randi, Martin Gardner and Charles Reynolds.

In all the reports about the Russian psychic, Nina Kulagina, we have read, never have we come across the assertion made by Gardner that she took the stage name "Ninel" (Lenin spelled backwards) or the charge that she is "a pretty, plump, dark-eyed little charlatan. . .caught cheating more than once by Soviet scientists." If such evidence exists, we would like to hear about it, but we cannot draw such conclusions without documentation. The article concludes:

> Some first-rate minds have been attracted to psychic phenomena: Freud, Einstein, Jung, Edison. The paranormal may exist against logic, against reason, against present evidence and beyond the standard criteria of empirical proof. . .Perhaps Geller and other magicians can indeed force metal to bend merely because they will it. Perhaps photographs can be projected by the mind. Perhaps plants think. Perhaps not. There is only one way to tell: by a thorough examination of the phenomena by those who do not express an *a priori* belief.

Although not explicitly stated, the writers apparently assume that a negative *a priori* belief will not interfere with establishing the evidence for psychic phenomena.

The same day as **TIME,** March 4, 1974, **Newsweek** ran a five-page article, with one page in color, entitled "Parapsychology: The Science of the Uncanny," citing the work of Lawrence LeShan, the Kirlians, Prof. William Tiller, Sister Justa Smith, Puthoff and Targ, whose work is well known in parapsychological circles. The work of W. J. Levy was also mentioned; he left the field later after he admitted "fudging" experimental data. One refrain from the debunkers was cited over and over: "the physicists are easiest to fool." If this is the correct view, why is the work of physicists taken so seriously in other areas of knowledge?

The New York Times (October 22, 1974) printed a feature story, "Physicists Test Telepathy in a 'Cheat-Proof' Setting." This was a report on experiments conducted with Uri Geller at the Stanford Research Institute, and on an article on parapsychology which appeared in the British science magazine, *Nature*. *The International Herald Tribune* (August 4, 1975) published an article entitled "Parapsychology: At the Point Where the Laughter Stops" by Al Martinez.

LOS ANGELES—Parapsychology, once ridiculed as a doctrine of the occult, is winning new interest among physical scientists.

They are beginning to feel, as one said, that "there is something else out there" in the realm of mind research. And for the first time, physicists are beginning to listen to psychics about what that something else might be.

Rocket engineers are talking to theologians about extrasensory perception (ESP) and clairvoyance.

Biochemists and physicians are studying faith healers. And conservative research institutions are experimenting with mind over matter.

Even the U.S. government, nervously aware of work being conducted in the Soviet Union, is beginning to worry about a parapsychology gap.

In the last two years, an estimated $200,000 worth of federal grants has gone into psychic research.

The National Aeronautics and Space Administration funded a Stanford University Research Institute study on ESP.

The Defense Department's Advanced Research Projects Agency paid for a translation of all available Soviet Literature on paranormal phenomena.

The National Institute of Mental health funded a study in dream research.

Rumors abound that the Central Intelligence Agency is already in the field.

Though the CIA will not confirm or deny this, researchers from New York to San Francisco insist that agency is indeed involved—for the obvious impact that mind-reading would have on intelligence gathering.

A University of Virginia scientist says CIA agents have approached him twice, wanting to know whether psychics could jam computers and radar screens, and whether people could be trained to leave their bodies.

Parapsychology is an ill-defined field that generally covers three basic categories: ESP (including telepathy, clairvoyance and precognition), psychokinesis (mind over matter), and survival (life after death and astral projection).

Until recently, studies of paranormal behavior were regarded as part of the lunatic fringe. Today, even such organizations as the American Institute of Electrical and Electronic Engineers are willing to take an interest in it.

Among the most determined exponents of research into paranormal behavior are laser physicists Russell Targ and Harold Puthoff, of the Stanford Research Institute.

Last year they conducted highly controlled experiments on Israeli psychic Uri Geller and dozens of "psychic non-superstars" that brought them worldwide attention and helped legitimize parapsychology.

The International Herald Tribune (April 18, 1975) ran a feature, "A Scientist on the Side of Uri Geller," quoting John B. Taylor, professor of applied mathematics at Kings College in London. Taylor, who has taught at the University of California/Berkeley, and at Rutgers University as well as in England, is both a physicist and a mathematician. His book, **Super Minds,** dealt with his research on Geller and about 50 English children. The article stated in part:

> . . .*Taylor says, in effect, that he eliminated—by controlling his experiments with extreme care—the possibility that Geller was cheating. He was left with the conclusion that Geller was indeed doing what he seemed to be doing: bending and twisting keys, spoons and other metal objects, and making broken watches run again—by remote control; by focusing his brain waves upon these objects. In short, Geller had demonstrated under rigid scientific control that parapsychological phenomena apparently do occur.*
>
> *Taylor, who is in his mid-40s, speaks with the wariness of a physical scientist trained to accept the evidence of his senses and to reject eveything else. "First," he says, I am convinced that Geller and others who bend metal are not cheating. . .It is conceivable, perhaps, that Geller is using forces unknown to science, the so-called 'psi' forces. . ."*

More Revealing

Taylor, it seems evident, was bowled over by his study of Geller. "One clear observation of Geller in action had an over-powering effect on me," he said. "I felt as if the whole framework with which I viewed the world had suddenly been destroyed. I seemed very naked, and vulnerable, surrounded by a hostile, incomprehensible universe. . ."

He goes on to talk about something even more revealing as an index of the Geller phenomenon. It is well known that many people refuse even to discuss the possibility of "supernatural" phenomena—poltergeists, metal-bending, UFOs or whatever; they feel "threatened" by such matters. According to Taylor, this extends even to some of his fellow scientists—"some of my colleagues even refused to attend demonstrations. That is an understandable position, but one that does not augur well for the future of science."

While admitting that he doesn't know exactly *how* Geller makes spoons bend and broken watches run again, Taylor has narrowed the possibilities: "What possible mechanisms are there for transmitting energy from the brain to the object [to be bent or otherwise manipulated]? Unless the mechanism is something new to science, it can only be one of four possibilities: gravity, radioactivity, nuclear force, or electromagnetic radiation. . .Of the four, only electromagnetic radiation (caused by the vibration of electrons or groups of electrons) seems to present a hopeful candidate. It can operate over considerable distances and a very wide range of wavelengths.

"[But] how could low-frequency radiation provide sufficient energy to bend metal? One possibility is that Geller and others like him do not radiate their energy at random but, like aerials, produce a directional signal. If they do, they may be able to focus the signal onto a small area.

To attempt a rough analogy: Taylor seems to be advancing a hypothesis of Geller as a broadcasting medium, transmitting to the object he has chosen to influence, i.e. to bend or twist. He tunes himself, in effect, to a certain frequency and makes a "closed circuit" broadcast. The receiving "station"—the spoon, knife, key, etc.—reacts in the manner noted.

Most Likely

"How then would the signal induce the metal to bend? The most likely explanation seems to be that it would affect tiny faults in the material, causing them to move and the specimen to be distorted and broken. . .

Alternatively, it is possible that the radiation causes the individual grains of metal to oscillate in sympathy and that the oscillation in turn affects the dislocation.

This detailed mechanism is not complete nor, perhaps, correct. Only further experiments will show this. . ."

Behind Taylor's restraint one can sense the shape of volcanic forces at work. It is what he does *not* say—checked by the double brake of British reserve and scientific caution—that makes one's own mind emulate a spoon in the grip of a Geller-type brainwave. Suppose, someone has suggested, that Geller—or one of the 50 English children found by Taylor to have similar powers—were to focus not on a spoon but on another kind of metal object? The directional fuse of a guided missile, say. Or the altimeter of an atomic bomber.

Taylor, whose imagination works as well as anyone else's, is adept at keeping it in check. As a scientist, he is accustomed to working within a framework of observable fact. But what if that framework begins to extend over thin air? Do you stop in your tracks, or do you move, very tentatively, into the void?*

The Observer for April 6, 1975 (British) had a long feature article entitled, "Uri Geller—a Phenomenon Explained—How a Leading Scientist Was Convinced Minds Can Bend Metal," and thirty-three months later, *The Times* of London headlined a story, "The Frightening Truth Society Dare Not Admit"—a preview of a book on

---

*Critics of the paranormal were elated when Taylor, several years later, retreated from the conclusions he had reached. What many outside of academia are not aware of, are the ways in which peer pressure can thwart innovative and unconventional exploration and research. Ridicule and isolation by colleagues can cause professional journals to 'go slow' on publishing research findings of academics who have ventured beyond the accepted concepts about politics, economics, paranormal phenomena, etc. and can also have a devastating effect on their careers.

parapsychology by Brain Inglis, titled *Natural and Supernatural.*

Matthew Manning, the young British psychic, was often referred to as the "Uri Geller of Great Britain," a label he understandably disliked; he also received extensive coverage by the media both in his own country and abroad. His first book, *The Link,* was translated into many languages and published in well over a dozen countries. He has also appeared on many radio and TV programs in England, the United States, Continental Europe, Japan, etc. The psychic feats of Jean-Pierre Girard, France, and Silvio Meyer, Switzerland, have received more attention in their native countries than abroad. Nina Kulagina and Alla Vinogradova have received attention in the Soviet press from time to time and in international journals such as the *Journal of Paraphysics.*

What are the probabilities that scientists in many countries, who have investigated psychic phenomena; the editors of newspapers, magazines and journals; and the producers of radio and TV programs, who have presented programs about paranormal events, have all been duped by tricksters? The next chapter will discuss those who still prefer to live with the belief that it is all deception and trickery.

X.   Those Who Say It's All Trickery—

In our judgement, knowledge and understanding will be augmented to the extent that society tolerates and encourages inquiry and debate and does not impose censorship on any area of human experience. In areas such as pyschic phenomena, unconventional healing, etc., it is understandable that divergent viewpoints should develop as a result of the kinds of experiences people have *had* or *not had,* and their view of what is "possible."

A letter from Kay Ranfone, Salem, NH, in *TIME* magazine for March 25, 1974, reflects the viewpoint we have developed during our years of exploring psychic phenomena:

> *Sir: I have an open mind about psychic phenomena, but let us not stop exploring new ideas and thoughts, even some of the most outlandish ones. If we had stopped in days of old and said majestically, "We know it all," life wouldn't be so much fun. The world would still be flat, the seas beset by monsters, and the moon would still be cheese.*

A Committee for the Scientific Investigation of Claims of the Paranormal was formed in Buffalo, New York in the Spring of 1976, some months after a statement, "Objections to Astrology," signed by 186 scientists, had been released. To our knowledge no mention was made of the number of scientists who were invited to sign the statement but had not, nor what a small percent of the scientific community they represented.

The Committee is now headed by Paul Kurtz, Professor of Philosophy at the State University of New York, Buffalo. When the Committee was first formed, Prof. Marcello Truzzi, a sociologist at Eastern Michigan University, was co-chairman, but he resigned in 1977 because he disagreed with the manner in which other members of the Committee wanted to conduct their crusade to debunk the paranormal.

A tally of the Committee's Fellows listed on its letterhead in 1977 included 3 astronomers, 7 psychologists, 8 science writers, 1 university provost, 8 philosophers, president of the American Humanist Association, 2 magicians, 2 statisticians, 1 parapsychologist, 1 author, and the senior editor of *TIME* magazine. Two years later, six names had been added and three removed from the list. The Committee's objectives, its officers and Fellows, as well as its list of scientific consultants, as published on the back cover of the Summer 1979 issue of

The Skeptical Inquirer, their official publication, are reproduced in the *Appendix.* This may help the reader to decide how to evaluate the Committee's pronouncements. [No one can claim that such disciplines as chemistry, physics, biology, and neurophysiology are over-represented on this committee for "scientific investigation."]

As an indication of the depth of the concern about the danger of the scientific pursuit being influenced by reports and films about psychic phenomena, we quote some excerpts from the Committee's press releases:

July 15, 1977

Because of the deep concern for what it terms "the uncritical acceptance or irrational beliefs" and "an alarming growth of anti-scientific attitude on the part of the general public," the Committee for the Scientific Investigation of Claims of the Paranormal has called an emergency meeting and press conference for Tuesday, August 9, 1977, at the Overseas Press Club in New York City. . ."

Of immediate concern is the resurgence of beliefs in pre-scientific forms of magic in many areas: psychokinesis, remote viewing, precognition, the psychics, UFOs, "chariots of the gods," astrology, faith healing, exorcism, astral projection, life after death, kirlian photography, pyramid power, psychic plants, sasquatches, and the Bermuda Triangle.

In the face of what it views as the incredulous acceptance of untested beliefs, the Committee and its supporters have expressed the fear that the general public is not sufficiently exposed to balanced scientific viewpoints. . .

In a continuing effort to counter the unsubstantiated claims in the area of the paranormal belief, the Committee, since its inception, has been interested in critical findings. . .

August 5, 1977

The Committee for the Scientific Investigation of Claims of the Paranormal, in a letter to Edward T. Thompson, editor-in-chief of Reader's Digest, has strongly criticized the magazine for publication of an article, "What Do We Really Know About Psychic Phenomena," in the August 1977 issue. . .

The Committee has scheduled a press conference for Tuesday, August 9th, at the Overseas Press Club, Biltmore Hotel, in New York City. Among other important matters, a statement detailing criticisms of the article by scientific spokesmen will be released at the press conference.

"The Committee. . .considers publication of the article. . .to be a serious act of journalistic imbalance which can be very harmful to gullible individuals among your readership.

"This biased article," the letter continues, "presents as fact a series of anecdotal and unsubstantiated 'psychic' experiences by individuals and pseudo-scientists. It also reports 'successful' experiments of various sorts, without acknowledging that virtually all. . .were subsequently proved to be inadequately controlled, inclusive, and in some cases, quite negative. . ."

*As justification for the Committee's concern, Kurtz said that following publication of this short—and critical—comment on the **Digest** article, he had received dozens of telephone calls from various part of the country from "obviously disturbed" individuals.*

"They professed to have all sorts of weird 'psychic' powers and sought my advice," Kurtz said.

"This is the kind of psychotic individual who can very easily suffer ill effects, sometimes harmful to others, when stimulated by the fallacious nature of irresponsible articles in influential publications," he concluded.

August 9, 1977

There has been a widespread growth in recent years in belief in the paranormal and the cults of unreason. This is a result in part because of a breakdown in communication between the scientific community and the general public. Science in general has been neither able nor willing to provide careful scientific examination of these claims, nor to explain the methods of findings of scientific inquiry. This has lead (sic) to a growth of anti-science and pseudo-science. Science fiction is often confused in various media with scientific fact, and the public is unable to distinguish between the tested and untested. We are virtually overwhelmed by pseudo-scientific pro-paranormal propaganda concerning alleged phenomena which have not been properly verified under rigorous controls.

*The mass media today are the most potent source of information for the American people. Television, radio, films, and the press pour a steady torrent of paranormal claims into the marketplace. Their presentations are often not based on hard evidence or scientific accuracy but on whether or not they will sell products. . .**The Geller Papers,** edited by Charles Panati, and **Mind Reach** by Targ and Puthoff are palmed off as true. Von Daniken's books, based on questionable data and interpretations have sold an estimated 34 million copies. Mass-circulation magazines such as **Reader's Digest** more and more ape the National Enquirer. . .*

We cannot abandon our commitment to science as a method of testing beliefs: when a society ignores all objective standards of knowledge, it opens the door to the possible development of ideological cults. A disturbing parallel is that the irrationalism of Nazi Germany was preceded by a vast growth of belief in the occult in the Weimar Republic. Some may consider excursions into the paranormal or occult as "harmless." But these primitive reversions may have far-reaching implications. There is always the danger that once irrationality grows it will spill over into other areas of society. The current retreat from reason may have unintended consequences for the future: in breaking down our critical judgement, it may also break down our resistance to new and unforeseen forms of tyranny. There is no guarantee that a society so infected by unreason will be resistant to the most virulent programs of dangerous sects. Such persistent propaganda may lead to psychic disorders, both in the individual and in the society. . .

Based on what they write or are quoted as saying, many of the debunkers of paranormal phenomena appear to believe they have a "corner on the truth." Terms like "nonsense," "fraud," "crackpot ideas," "hoax," "incredibly sloppy research," "tawdry," "shabby," "hocus-pocus," "screwball," "wishy-washy," "gullible," etc. are used freely and indiscriminately when they refer to psychics and parapsychological investigators. They seem to be sure that their views are closer to "reality" than those of the believers, or those who grant that there may be phenomena outside of currently accepted views of the scientific establishment which are not yet understood. At times they remind us of the aphorism: *The vigor with which an opinion is held is usually in inverse ratio to the amount of evidence which can be brought forward in its support.*

In the Fall 1978 issue of **The Skeptical Inquirer,** the CSICOP's official publication, Paul Kurtz reports that the Committee had "lodged a complaint against the NBC network and its affiliates for its broadcast of "Exploring the Unknown," a television 'special' on psychic phenomena. I regret to report that the Federal Communications Commission has rendered a preliminary decision rejecting our complaint. . ." He wrote further, ". . .although members of our Committee may differ about how to evaluate parapsychological research, we are all committed to the careful use of scientific methods and believe that the ultimate resolution must be based on the evidence." Unfortunately, articles written by the Committee's most active spokespersons in **The Humanist** magazine and **The Skeptical Inquirer** do not generally reflect that scientific attitude.

In the August 12, 1977 issue of **Science,** the publication of the American Association for the Advancement of Science, Nicholas Wade quotes Lee Nisbet, who was then executive editor of **The Humanist** and now executive director of CSICOP, in an editorial:

> The humanists believe there is a resurgence of belief in the far out which must be reined in. "It's a very dangerous phenomenon, dangerous to science, dangerous to the basic fabric of our society," said Nisbet.
>
> The rising tide of occultism is a symptom of the public's being "increasingly wishy-washy about the way it thinks about important issues. We feel it is the duty of the scientific community to show that these beliefs are utterly screwball," Nisbet declares.

An appeal by **The Humanist** for its survival fund (not the study of evidence for survival of death, but for the survival of the publication) prompted Theodore, Robert and W. Teed Rockwell to write a nine-page open letter to the readers, with seven pages of references and quotations cited from the publication, to point out that it was "trading away its rationalist birthright for a mess of rhetorical pottage."

"Our charge is that the evaluations published in these pages have abused the principles of rational discourse as often and as badly as the worst of these they seek to discredit," they wrote. Referring to a statement in the July/August 1976 issue of the magazine, " 'The scientific debunker's job may be compared to that of the trash collector. The fact that the garbage truck comes by today does not mean there won't be another load tomorrow', they wrote: A debunker is indeed like a trash collector, but a scientific investigator is not."

They point out that a lead article in that publication "explicitly lumps together for common criticism such disparate entities as Aikido, transcendental meditation, Jesus Christ, Mohammed, Mary Baker Eddy, encounter groups, yoga, organic gardening, Kirlian photography, and ESP" and that another article lumped together "all types of religious and occult beliefs under the sub-title: 'God-believers and believers in witches are closer than many of us realize...they have in effect rejected the use of logic and experience.' "

The Rockwells take issue with a statement in the May/June 1977 article which stated, "that a group of researchers 'are physicists to a man. Not, I hasten to add, that one has anything against physicists. It's just that they have an unfortunate tradition of being the biggest kinds of suckers when it comes to fraudulent psychic phenomena.' How can we apply such statements to the research in question—are we to conclude that NO physicist is competent to scientifically investigate paranormal phenomena?"

Under the heading *Faulty Logic,* the Rockwells say: "The critical test of a rationalist, once he is made to confront the issue, is whether his argument holds up...a researcher is criticized for lacking experience in the field, and elsewhere for being committed to it; the field is criticized for using physicists and for not using them; ESP is/is not a threat to science...a field is "disproved" by describing its primitive origins; scientists who believe in their work are not to be trusted; many famous scientists have been interested in psychical research, thus they are all 'suckers'."

After the feature article about Masuaki and Hiroto had appeared in *The Wisconsin State Journal* on July 30, 1979 (see previous chapter) someone may have suggested that the paper call Kurtz for comment because on August 11, the paper quoted Kurtz as saying that spoon bending "is a hoax" and "he said he tested Kiyota's claimed powers of 'thoughtography' with several other scientists in London last summer... "We know people who were involved in the Granada Television experiments in England in August 1978 (Prof. Hasted, Masuaki Kiyota, Prof. Miyauchi, and Elaine Morikawa) to be quite certain that Kurtz was not present during those experiments unless it was via astral travel. We also know that Kurtz had not met either of the two young Japanese psychics when he issued his statement about "psychic hucksters." The article from the *State Journal,* referred to in Chapter IX, is reproduced here in full.

Spoon bending's a crooked ploy, scientist says

By Robyne Curry
Of The State Journal

Claims of spoon bending and other feats of mental telepathy were dismissed as nothing more than psychic chicanery Friday by Paul Kurtz, a philosophy professor at the State University of New York at Buffalo.

"Spoon bending? It's a hoax. . . . It's a use of magical means," Kurtz said. "People who claim they can do such things are just magicians posing as psychics."

Kurtz is chairman of the Committee for the Scientific Investigation of Claims of the Paranormal. Begun in 1976, the 70-member group of scientists provides objective tests for claims of pscyhic ability and presents its findings to the public.

None of the psychic claims tested by the committee has yet held up under scientific scrutiny, Kurtz said.

Ten days ago The Wisconsin State Journal reported that two Japanese teen-agers claiming to bend spoons by psychokinesis (the ability to alter matter by use of the mind), had arrived in Madison and would try to demonstrate their abilities this weekend.

Masuaki Kiyota, 17, and Hiroto Yamashita, 15, are participants in a two-day workshop on psychokinesis that started Friday night at the University of Wisconsin-Madison.

Kiyota is the guest of Walter and Mary Jo Uphoff of Oregon. The couple has written a book on extrasensory perception and psychokinetic powers. They have also established a discussion and learning center on their farm for persons interested in psychic phenomena.

But Kurtz disputes Kiyota's abilities. He said he tested Kiyota's claimed powers of 'thoughtography' with several other scientists in London last summer. Thoughtography is the process of mentally transmitting a picture image on film without touching the camera.

Kurtz said Kiyota was unable to perform this feat under strict laboratory conditions. But when allowed to take the camera outside of the laboratory, Kiyota returned with a blurred image of Trafalgar Square on the film.

Kurtz said he was not prepared to say how Kiyota performed his trick but indicated that he probably used one of two common methods.

In the first method, a negative attached to a small round object is placed in front of the camera's shutter and the film is exposed. In the second, an existing photo is altered to appear fuzzy and then inserted into the camera.

Kurtz said spoon bending — or nail or key bending — commonly involves one of three sleight-of-hand operations

In one, the spoon bender uses an accomplice. Or he distracts the audience and bends the spoon while they are not looking. Or he bends a spoon beforehand and substitutes it for the original.

"Spoon bending is an old gag," Kurtz said. "The only way it can be done is by physical manipulation."

Although parapsychologists claim that psychokinesis is possible in influencing the roll of a die, Kurtz remains skeptical because tests of this claim have not been successfully duplicated.

Kurtz and his committee have studied the claims made by Uri Geller and thoughtographer Ted Serios. None have been proved. When a self-reported psychic predicted an accident under Niagara Falls involving several pre-school children last month, Kurtz and other committee members were present. This prediction was not substantiated either.

What precautions can be taken to guard against fraud?

Kurtz said anyone alleging psychokinetic powers should be fairly tested under controlled conditions. This means a properly lit room with observers all around. In addition, the subject should not be allowed to touch the object he claims he can alter.

Kurtz said a "psychic explosion" is taking place around the world. The United States predominates in this phenomenon, which Kurtz said is encouraged by media hype.

But, Kurtz said, the current psychic chicanery is a profitable business.

"I'm really appalled that Madison . . . a city of sophisticated, literate people . . . and a great science center . . . would allow themselves to be taken in by psychic hucksters."

140

The article quotes Kurtz as saying that his Committee "provides objective tests for claims of psychic abilities," yet if he told *The Wisconsin State Journal* that he tested Kiyota's abilities in London, as the article states, he did not tell the truth. If he did not tell them that, then the reporter took liberties in drawing inferences from what he may have said about other members of the Committee observing Kiyota in England in August, 1978. As a professor of philosophy who presumably has been trained in logic, Kurtz did not do credit to his profession if he is correctly quoted as saying "he was not prepared to say how Kiyota performed *his trick* [emphasis added] but indicated that he probably used one of two common methods." Had he seen Masuaki concentrate on Polaroid film that was supplied by others and loaded into a camera (in the case of the Nippon TV tests, into a light-tight box which had lens and shutter removed)and produced images without tripping the shutter, I suspect that even Paul Kurtz would not have offered such simplistic "explanations" for Masuaki's PK abilities.

We do not know whether or not Professor Kurtz studied physics, metallurgy, etc. before deciding to become a philosopher, but in any case, his saying that "Spoon bending is an old gag. The only way it can be done is by physical manipulation," hardly fits the last of the six stated objectives of the Committee: "not to reject claims on *a priori* grounds, antecedent to inquiry, but rather to examine them objectively and carefully." The very use of the words, "psychic chicanery" shows prejudice without due examination. If he meant to imply that those of us who took the initiative to bring the two young psychics to the U.S. did so to make money, he is also badly mistaken on that count for we advanced the money for plane fares, etc. and were happy to recover about 7/9ths of direct expenses involved, from contributions and registrations.

As more people have an opportunity to know sincere, talented young people like Masuaki and Hiroto, it will become difficult for Kurtz (and others) to categorize as "psychic hucksters" persons he has never investigated, simply because he cannot imagine the possibility of certain phenomena which occur outside his narrowly defined universe.

Certainly those unfamiliar with the evidence for psychokinesis who had seen the earlier story by Chuck Martin in the *Wisconsin State Journal,* must have been confused or bewildered to see a follow-up article so completely at variance with the first. What were they to believe. Had we been duped, or were we a party to perpetrating a hoax?

The *Skeptical Inquirier,* the official publication of the CSICOP, had carried a feature article in the Spring 1979 issue which speculated how Masuaki might have produced effects on film by trickery. Permission was granted to reproduce the article in full.

Television Tests of Masuaki Kiyota

Christopher Scott
and Michael Hutchinson

THE SKEPTICAL INQUIRER
Spring 1979

We were asked by Granada Television to participate in tests it was to conduct in London on August 8-10, 1978, with Masuaki Kiyota, a 16-year-old Japanese who had been featured in part of an NBC-TV program on the paranormal. It is claimed that Masuaki can project mental images onto unexposed film under very tight conditions.

Granada proposed to start the tests very informally under whatever conditions the young man desired. Further tests would be progressively more difficult, first of all under the control of Professor John Hasted in a laboratory at Birkbeck College, and finally under the skeptically tight conditions of the writers. We would therefore not be required to participate until the third day. In the meantime we were kept informed of progress.

Through a change in plans, the very first day was spent in the laboratory of Professor Hasted. Whatever the protocol, the results were negative. The monotony of the day was broken by the production of what Hasted hailed as a "whitey," a term invented by American parapsychologist Jule Eisenbud. This was a photograph which, when peeled, was completely white, whereas it should have been black, as Masuaki

---

Christopher Scott is a statistician, psychologist, and former Council member and research supervisor of the Society for Psychical Research. Michael Hutchinson is an amateur magician, investigator of the paranormal, and secretary of the UK branch of the CSICP.

---

works without operating the camera shutter. When Morris Smith, the technical representative from Polaroid, was asked for his comments, he pointed out that a light-sensitive diode—which had been used for the previous experiment—had been removed, leaving a hole through which light could pass. When the rest of the pictures from the pack were removed and peeled, they too were "whiteys," to no one's surprise.

At the start of the second day, Masuaki managed to produce a photograph of poor quality, with the foreground completely underexposed and the rest of the picture blurred. In the center was a grey "pole" which could have been Nelson's Column in London's Trafalgar Square, although it was not clear enough for anyone to be absolutely positive. A

The "Trafalgar Square" photo

building on the right showed up well enough to be compared with an original, if this could be identified. We later spent considerable time in and around Trafalgar Square but failed to find an angle from which the picture could have been taken. However, most people who saw the photograph initially thought that it *was* Trafalgar Square.

The second photograph, even poorer in quality, was said to show six guardsmen in file, from the right to the left. Questions were then raised

as to whose camera and film had been used for these shots. It transpired that both had been given to Masuaki the previous evening and had been with him overnight. How many shots had been left on the film was not known, but "Trafalgar Square" was on frame seven and the "Guardsmen" on frame eight. While the former could have been the result of a normal shutter release exposure without pulling the photograph from the camera, the latter could not. Morris Smith stated that it was not possible to tell if the film pack has been tampered with.

The rest of the day was spent conducting tests using a camera and film supplied by Morris Smith. The location was changed from the previous day's laboratory to a room in the White House Hotel—where the first two photographs were produced—and later to the local park. Relatively tight conditions produced no results. But once more, after being allowed to have a camera and film to himself—this time for a two-hour lunch break—Masuaki achieved some success. What actually happened was later to cause a fierce argument between the interpreter on one side and the television presenter and his director on the other.

The interpreter was an Anglo-American journalist named David Tharpe, who had lived for some years in Japan. He had written at least one article about Masuaki, had been present at the young psychic's home during some successful experiments, and had been proposed by Masuaki (or his advisers) as interpreter for the London trip.

In an interview at the end of the test, Tharpe said that the most interesting photograph taken during the two and a half days was the one taken after the lunch break on the second day. He said that the camera and the film had not left his sight or that of his girlfriend, a Japanese-American who had been in London for some days. She was not part of the "official" group from Japan, which consisted of Masuaki, Tharpe, and Professor T. Miyauchi, who is an expert on "nengraphy," which is Japanese for "thoughtography." He didn't take any part in the Granada experiments.

According to Tharpe, the first two photographs were black, but the third produced a picture. This "picture" looked like a black square partly washed out by a white circle, leaving two black corners in the shape of triangles. Tharpe said that Masuaki had asked him how to symbolize Switzerland. His answer had been, "By the Alps, or the Matterhorn," subsequently explaining that the shape of these was triangular. The photograph was therefore captioned "The Matterhorn."

The version given us by the producer on the morning of our arrival was more detailed. The session after lunch took place in the hotel room. Masuaki said he wanted to work without the film crew—there were too many observers around, he said—so the camera and lights were switched on by Gordon Burns, the program presenter. Also present were Jeremy Fox (the producer), David Tharpe, and his girlfriend. Granada suggested the use of another Polaroid camera, and a fresh film pack was loaded in front of the movie camera. But, said the producer, Masuaki wanted to use the camera that had been with him over lunch. He drew attention to this camera and the case that had held it. This was a small black case with a hinged lid, and was only just large enough for a Polaroid camera.

With both hands Masuaki placed the camera in the case and closed the lid. After several seconds, the producer told us, Masuaki took the camera from the case and produced the "Matterhorn" photograph. This was the first photograph, not the third as claimed by Tharpe, who also seems to have forgotten that, for no apparent reason, Masuaki had placed the camera in the case.

We have tried, without success, to find out what the developed movie film showed. However, the circumstances do not convince us that the photographs were evidence to prove the case for "thoughtography," for Masuaki could have operated the shutter release while placing or removing the camera from the case.

As previously mentioned, the afternoon brought no further results. Masuaki thought that he might be able to produce some photographs that evening if a small party were held in his room. This the television team arranged, and the party was held. But still Masuaki was unable to live up to his claims.

When we arrived on the third morning we were told that Masuaki had again been left with a camera and film overnight. It was confidently expected that—as on previous occasions—this would lead to an early success.

The first photograph to be peeled was black. But the second had a gray impression of the Eiffel Tower with a lamppost in the foreground and slightly to the right of the tower. After inspection, Morris Smith again said that there was no evidence to show whether or not the film pack had been tampered with. The serial number on the photo confirmed that the film was from the batch supplied by Polaroid for the tests. This had also been the case with the other "successes."

Further tests using fresh film were not successful. After about an hour a short break was called. While few people were paying attention,

Masuaki pulled a shot from the camera. On it were a number of vague light smudges running down the picture. These, it turned out, can be produced by pulling the film out of the camera in a jerky manner, as Morris Smith effectively demonstrated. Further tests using fresh film

Image of Bath Cathedral exposed onto Polaroid film by Mike Hutchinson without a camera, using a color transparency and a "pinhole projector."

were not successful.

Morris Smith told us that, while in theory it is possible to take a film pack to pieces, expose each frame to the light, and reassemble it, he wasn't exactly sure how. (Obviously this is not something that Polaroid needed to do.) The main problem is that complete darkness is necessary. The film is very fast (3000 ASA, compared to around 100 ASA for normal film) and even a "safe" light used in a conventional darkroom would fog the film. He and one of the writers (M.H.) decided to take the pack to pieces and reassemble it. M.H. tried to reassemble it with his eyes closed, but found that when trying to slide the final piece on, it fouled the film, and if he continued would have folded it back. Opening his eyes, he realized that this final piece need not be slid on but could be snapped in place without difficulty.

It still remained to be discovered how an impression could be made on each frame without showing signs of tampering. We knew that the film could be folded back without showing signs that it had been. Perhaps at this stage a contact print could be made. Alternatively, it might be possible to make a crude pinhole "projector" using a slide viewer. If pointed at the folded film, a quick press on the slide illumi-nator might create enough light to produce a poor quality picture.

To test this theory, M.H. carried out experiments in his apartment hallway. This was the darkest place he could find. Even so, a small amount of light came through glass panels at the top of five doors. This light was just enough to see by when his eyes became dark-adapted, but did not fog the film in any noticeable way.

The front lens of the slide viewer was covered with a piece of cardboard that had a hole in it made by a small darning needle. The pack was taken to pieces and the film was unfolded. One end of the film is fixed to the pack by a staple. Taking care not to tear the film from the staple, it was folded back with one hand. The other hand pointed the "projector" toward the film at a distance of six to eight inches. An exposure of two or three seconds is all that is needed. In this way, up to eight frames can be exposed.

In M.H.'s experiment the "projector" was hand-held. While this did not cause much "shake" on the prints, it did make it difficult to expose the full frame every time. However, it would be quite simple to make a small stand that would both steady and aim the projected image correctly.

The size of the subject on the print can be varied by altering the distance of the projected image. This means that sometimes only part of the original slide will be reproduced. The positioning of the main subject can also be altered by different angles of projection. For example, two of Masuaki's previous successes were aerial photographs of the Statue of Liberty. While the view and the shadows were identical, the Statue in one picture was in a different position of the frame.

These variations are to be expected when using a pinhole "projector." Similarly, variations of exposure also occur. Could it be that, after seeing the underexposed photographs of "Trafalgar Square" and the "Guardsmen," Masuaki decided to give a second or two extra to the "Eiffel Tower," which turned out to be overexposed?

Conclusions

Under fairly tight conditions Masuaki Kiyota was unable to fulfill his claim to project mental images onto film. The only time he achieved any success was after the film had been in his possession—and not under any control—for at least two hours.

Unfortunately, no steps were taken to ensure that the film pack could not be tampered with. In fairness to the television team, this only seems important with hindsight. Given the benefit of this report, we hope that future experimenters will either seal the pack or, preferably, prepare it in such a way that any signs of tampering would be obvious.

Finally, a few words of praise for the television team. They started the assignment believing in Masuaki and hoping for good results. Their initial enthusiasm and confidence gave way to understandable skepticism when it became evident that Masuaki couldn't perform under tight conditions as claimed. However, they didn't let this sway them in their professional approach, nor encourage them to loosen the controls. Whether the negative results will lead to a final program being broadcast remains to be seen. •

This article is a good example of how easy it is for someone to speculate about how something "might" have been done by trickery. No evidence is presented to demonstrate that cheating occurred, but the tone of the article implies that the effects could have been produced by cheating. Had Mr. Scott and Mr. Hutchinson, Prof. Hasted and ourselves all been present during all the waking hours that Masuaki was in London, it should have been possible to establish, at least with reasonable certainty, whether or not there was any evidence that trickery was used to produce the "Trafalgar Square" picture and the other effects reported.

Paragraph 6 states that a fierce argument took place between the interpreter, David Tharp, and the TV presenter and director, but the reader is given no clue as to what it was all about. We did learn from two persons who were present that Mr. Tharp was so offended by the treatment accorded young Kiyota that he refused to accept payment for his work as interpreter. We tried to get a first-hand report by writing to him at the last address we had for him but learned that he had moved.

We have many questions about this article but since we were not there, we are also in no position to more than speculate. In paragraph 12 we read: "We have tried without success, to find out what the developed movie film showed. However, circumstances do not convince us that the photographs were evidence to prove the case for 'thoughtography'." This is the first and only time a reference is made to a *movie* film; no mention is made about where they tried to find out what the film showed; yet the reader is expected to accept their word, with no elaboration of the "circumstances" referred to, that there was no evidence for paranormality.

After Prof. Hasted had read the article, he wrote the following letter to the editor of the **The Skeptical Inquirer:**

Dear Sir:

Scott and Hutchinson are misleading (or perhaps even attempting to hoax) your readership in the Spring 1979 issue by offering a picture of London's Albert Hall under the caption of "image of Bath Cathedral" (presumably the Cathedral at Wells, of the diocese of Bath and Wells). Other errors in the article include Hasted's hailing the production of a "whitey," only for the sales representatives of Polaroid to point (suggest) a hole in the camera. Scott and Hutchinson, who were not present, are not to know the several gross inaccuracies in that statement, which comes close to being legally actionable.

Morris Smith is supposed to have told Scott and Hutchinson that he wasn't exactly sure how a film pack can be taken to pieces, each frame being then exposed to light, and reassembled. But in fact he explained this in detail to Hasted, with a description of the traces of evidence that would remain and the statement that he had searched the pack for such traces and not found them. (Hasted has since searched other more recent Masuaki packs and found nothing.) This differs from Scott and Hutchinson's statement that Morris Smith twice said it was not possible to tell if the film pack had been tampered with. Hutchinson has more recently claimed to have found a method without leaving traces, but Polaroid have not investigated this claim to my knowledge.

Finally, journalist David Tharpe's claim that the camera and the film had not left his or his girl-friend's sight during the two-hour lunch break should not be dismissed. No doubt he will communicate, Sir, with you,

whose obedient servant I beg to remain,
JOHN HASTED

Presumably Morris Smith of Polaroid, had not supplied a camera with a hole in it. If it did, why was the first photograph referred to in paragraph 15, black? Statistically, what are the chances of producing a recognizable image of the Eiffel Tower by jerkily pulling the film? If there were the slightest suspicion about Masuaki using miniature images to produce "trick photos" why did not the CSICOP representatives and/or the TV staff insist on a thorough search of Masuaki's clothing and luggage to determine if he had brought with him (or had acquired since arriving in England) pictures which could explain the images produced under the circumstances that prevailed? Not to do so was a serious omission on their part, as far as establishing evidence—positive or negative—was concerned. Since they did not take such an obvious step, it makes it possible to conjecture to their heart's content after the event.

In paragraph 16 we read: "While few people were paying attention, Masuaki pulled a shot from the camera. On it were a number of very light smudges. . ." The reader is not told whether anyone from among those who **were** paying attention, saw him either trip, or not trip the shutter. If the shutter was not tripped, the film should have been black, whether it was pulled steadily or jerkily—that is, unless some PK energies were involved.

In paragraph 20, we read that up to 8 frames can be exposed in two or three seconds, but there is no mention of what the results should be. Should the same image appear on each frame, or should there be different images on some or all of the frames? The article contains much conjecture and few details, but demonstrates the authors' predilection to assume fraud, rather than considering the possibility that PK might explain the images that were produced.

The objectives and list of officers of the CSICOP is included in the *Appendix* so that readers can decide how to evaluate the objectives and the supporters of the Committee. We agree with the Committee's objectives and hope that with time they will move closer to the goals, such as the sixth: "not to reject claims on *a priori* grounds. . ." It is our impression that there are more philosophers, authors, pyschologists, editors and magicians listed as Fellows of the Committee, than persons from the basic sciences.

We had been invited to write an article about Masuaki Kiyota for *FATE* magazine in June 1978. The article appeared in the January 1980 issue and brought in response, a critical letter from Mike Hutchinson, the secretary of the British branch of CSICOP. Since most of the contents of that article are incorporated in this book, it is not reproduced here, but the paranormal photos of the Keio Plaza Hotel, which we saw Masuaki produce during the Alan Neuman filming and a picture of the hotel—for comparison—are reproduced at the end of the letters. It will be noted that the paranormal images appear as though taken from an aerial perspective, even though Masuaki was in his home ten miles away when the images were produced. The photo on the right shows the top of the hotel with the air-conditioning units on the roof, and the lower structures in the vicinity.

An Accusation of 'Fakery'—and a Reply

Source: *FATE*, May, 1980.

ACCUSATION OF FAKERY

Walter Uphoff's article "The Psychic Photography of Masuaki Kiyota" (January 1980 FATE) afforded me a certain amount of amusement.

The Granada Television Company's tests of Kiyota took place at the beginning of August 1978. Jeremy Fox of Granada TV invited Dr. Christopher Scott and me to represent the United Kingdom's branch of the Committee for the Scientific Investigation of Claims of the Paranormal. We were to design the final protocol.

As Scott and I reported in the Spring 1979 issue of *The Skeptical Inquirer* Kiyota was unable to produce images on film under anything approaching controlled conditions. He could only do so after having the camera and film in his possession either overnight or during the two-hour lunch break. This kind of production does not provide evidence to support Kiyota's claims — particularly in view of the experiments I subsequently conducted which show that "miracles" like Kiyota's can be faked within 10 minutes.

I therefore wonder at the conditions which existed on the occasion that Kiyota produced such wonders for Uphoff. At one stage he mentions "a dozen witnesses" and also "family members present." Were family members among the dozen witnesses? If so, Uphoff's supporting evidence is reduced, because family witnesses cannot be considered impartial.

Over what time period did the nengraphy take place? Uphoff reports that the Japanese boy worked with the camera "later that evening." In the meantime there must have been a lot of activity and excitement, what with the dozen witnesses, interviews to be done and spoons to be bent. What certainty is there that the camera and film had not been removed from the place where all this activity was taking place? Similar questions could be raised about the spoon bending.

And is Uphoff certain about the camera shutter being tripped? It is certainly not necessary to do so in nengraphy and Kiyota didn't need to do so during the tests in London. This point is important to show how observant Uphoff may have been.

I look forward to further tests of Masuaki Kiyota — but only if such tests are conducted and reported correctly. — *Mike Hutchinson, Secretary, British Branch CSICP, Loughton, Essex, U.K.*

THE AUTHOR REPLIES

Since I was invited to write the FATE article in June 1978, we have accumulated more evidence of Masuaki Kiyota's paranormal abilities. Mr. Hutchinson says that he is "interested in hearing of further tests . . . but only if [they are] conducted and reported correctly." If he is willing to examine all the available evidence I believe he will be convinced of Masuaki's psychokinetic abilities.

Space permits listing only some of the evidence:

(1) My wife Mary Jo and I spent March 20 to 26, 1979, in Tokyo investigating the PK abilities of Kiyota and 15-year-old Hiroto Yamashita. We now have a collection of twisted forks and spoons, paranormal images on Polaroid and on a movie film produced in a Canon 514 camera which had its lens and film compartment securely taped.

(2) Nippon Television Network (NTV) produced an hour-long documentary on Kiyota and Yamashita for nationwide viewing in Japan on July 5 and 12, 1979. Prof. Shegemi Sasaki, University of Electrocommunications, and Yutaka Fukuda, a professional photographer, were two of the consultants for the filming, part of which we witnessed at the Kiyota home.

(3) The boys' PK abilities so impressed us that we invited them to visit our home last summer. Prof. John B. Hasted, a physicist associated with Birkbeck College, University of London, came for a week to serve as resource person for a seminar in Madison, Wis., and a two-day workshop at our home in which professionals and academicians in physics, psychiatry, biophysics and bioengineering, electronics, biology and photography participated. The boys produced 27 additional paranormally twisted forks and spoons and numerous Polaroid shots.

(4) William E. Cox, a well-known parapsychologist and magician, observed the boys in San Francisco and wrote us on September 17: " . . . After you left Kiyota significantly affected a strain gauge for me, started my watch, scored well on quantitative PK and produced multiple effects on my own non-Polaroid film."

I can comprehend why spokesmen for CSICP are so highly selective of the bases for their conclusions only by assuming that their materialistic "nontheistic" theology permits considering no other explanation than deception. If Mr. Hutchinson would look at all the evidence, he could not assert that a "Polaroid whitey" (referred to in his *Skeptical Inquirer* article) could have been produced by a small hole in the camera, or infer from that that all unusual or paranormal effects are, or could be, trickery.

Professor Hasted wrote *The Skeptical Inquirer* on August 12, 1979, refuting Hutchinson's claim that Morris Smith, a technical representative for Polaroid, stated "that it was not possible to tell if the film pack had been tampered with" during the Granada TV experiments. Smith had explained to Hasted in detail how a film pack can be taken apart, exposed to light and reassembled. He also told Hasted he "found none of the traces of evidence he should have found" — contrary to Hutchinson's report.

The Skeptical Inquirer article includes a picture of "Trafalgar Square" produced by Masuaki. It is not a very clear picture but there are enough resemblances so that Hutchinson writes, " . . . Most people who saw the photograph initially thought that it *was* Trafalgar Square." He goes on to say that he spent considerable time around the square and "failed to find an angle from which the picture could have been taken." If he is indeed familiar with thought-ography he should realize that many of the pictures produced by Kiyota, Serios and Schwanholz are from a perspective that cannot be faked — unless one is in a helicopter or can fly. Pictures with unusual perspectives are some of the strongest evidence of paranormality and thus the most difficult for debunkers to deal with.

I bought Polaroid film on my way to the Kiyota home when we were in Japan in March 1979. On the evening of the 23rd we experimented with film after a metal-bending session. The first picture, a control, was black, then came two whities and at about 8:45 P.M. Masuaki produced a clearly recognizable image of the Statue of Liberty (see cut). Then Mr. Fukuda, Toru Ozaki and my wife Mary Jo took the camera about 100 meters down the street and after five minutes, pulled the next film — again without tripping the shutter. In the Kiyota home, three of us held hands with Masuaki as he concentrated on influencing the film. The resulting picture, ejected from the camera some distance away, turned out to be a double inverted image of the Statue of Liberty (see cut).

Hutchinson's polemics regarding the family members present are as wide of the mark as if I were to speculate whether the astronauts' trip to the moon could have been simulated with special photographic effects. What difference does it make whether the number of nonfamily witnesses was six, nine, 12 or 20? What is more important is whether the people present were objectively observing *whatever* occurred. Witnesses present included film producer Alan Neuman; Hollywood cameraman Bob Collins; Pamela deMaigret, writer and investigator; physicists Miyauchi and Harada, Fukuda, Toru Ozaki and me — as well as family members. Of course it's important to observe how cameras and film are handled, but to be so wedded to the notion that every hard-to-understand event must be trickery that no alternative explanation can be seriously considered will not advance our knowledge.

The nengraphy experiments monitored by Dr. Miyauchi took place about an hour after experiments with cutlery. Speculation that "there must have been a lot of activity and excitement" is not as relevant as who controlled the camera and the film before and during the experiment. It is not essential that Masuaki trip the shutter. What is significant is that he produced two aerial perspective photos of the Keio-Plaza Hotel 10 miles away. Mr. Hutchinson grants that tripping the shutter is not necessary in nengraphy. The Japanese TV documentary shows Masuaki affecting Polaroid film in a sealed cameralike box without shutter or lens.

Logic does not warrant a broad dismissal of all events as deception just because they do not fit a narrow concept of reality or because some magician can simulate some phenomena. Established concepts die slowly but they must give way when the evidence warrants. — *Walter H. Uphoff, Oregon, Wis.*

Note that the hotel, in the paranormals above, is narrower at the bottom.

I See By The Papers — Curtis Fuller

Publisher of *Fate* Magazine, May, 1980

QUOTE OF THE MONTH

The Newtonian framework, as was natural after 250 years, had been found too crude to accommodate the new observational knowledge which was being acquired. In default of a better framework it was still used, but definitions were strained to purposes for which they were never intended. We were in the position of a librarian whose books were still being arranged according to a subject scheme drawn up a hundred years ago, trying to find the right place for books on Hollywood, the Air Force, and detective novels.

— Sir Arthur Eddington
Eighth Annual Haldane Lecture

THERE HAS been a great deal of gossip and continuing concern about the unexpected attack on parapsychology made by Dr. John Wheeler, a respected theoretical physicist, at the Houston annual meeting of the American Association for the Advancement of Science. We have reported the attack in these columns, including Wheeler's personal attack on Dr. J. B. Rhine, and we have told you of Wheeler's demand that the AAAS remove the Parapsychology Association from membership. We also reported on Wheeler's apology to Dr. Rhine.

We will omit from this discussion the possibility that Wheeler's half-baked attack was orchestrated by ill-informed members of the Committee for the Scientific Investigation of Claims of the Paranormal who "used" Wheeler. The most important points in the whole fiasco, it seems to us, are why Wheeler launched the attack and exactly what his disagreement with his fellow panelists really is. We don't have an answer.

The story is this: Dr. Robert Jahn, dean of the school of Engineering at Princeton University, organized the Houston AAAS symposium on "The Role of Consciousness in the Physical World." Members of the symposium included Dr. Eugene Wigner, Nobel laureate in physics from Princeton, Charles Honorton of the Maimonides Medical Center, Dr. Harold Puthoff of Stanford Research Institute, Dr. Willis Harmon, also of SRI and president of the Institute of Noetic Sciences, and of course Wheeler.

In his opening remarks Dr. Jahn defined the basic problem as follows:

"The concept of a deterministic universe, which passively awaits human observations and utilization, has become progressively less tenable. The role of human consciousness as an active factor, not only in the perception of reality, but in its determination, needs to be deliberately addressed."

∞

MIND-BOGGLING

OBVIOUSLY Jahn thought that at the very least Wheeler would be a sympathetic speaker. A 1974 paper by Wheeler states what an increasing number of physicists believe — "according to this view the analysis of the physical world, pursued to sufficient depth, will lead back in some hidden way to man himself, to conscious mind, tied unexpectedly through the very acts of observation and participation to partnership in the foundation of the universe."

Wheeler's 1974 paper also states: "Each of us has his own catalogue of the great unknowns: three at the top of my own list are the mind, the universe and the quantum. I know of no area where the mystery is greater than it is in these three fields, or anywhere the linkage between observer and the system observed is stranger or any more suggestive of things hidden beyond present imagination."

Wheeler said in 1975, "Whatever it will prove to be, we can believe that (the solution) will somehow touch the tie between mind and matter, between oberver and observed."

But Wheeler now seems not only to have reversed his thinking but to have come to believe that all parapsychology experiments should be regarded as unscientific. From believing that the mind may have mystical qualities, Wheeler now has swung to insisting that it must be completely material — like a computer with electronic circuits or like a brain driven by chemical compounds.

THE MIND-BODY PROBLEM

OBVIOUSLY Dr. Wheeler has reverted to 19-Century materialism and rationalism. If he ever believed what he wrote in 1974 he no longer can face its implications as it applies to consciousness research and parapsychology.

Historically the mind-body problem is the basic mystery we deal with in FATE since its resolution determines how reality is to be viewed. The most widely held view among physical scientists is the one Dr. Wheeler now seems to espouse — namely, that all phenomena in mind and nature can be explained by physics and biology.

A second view, called "neutral monism," was put forth by Ernst Mach a century ago and argues that everything is mind and that the concept of nature itself is a construct of mind that can only be tested by experience. Mach held that nature cannot be known directly but only through a human observer.

Still a third view is the classical doctrine that physical and psychical events run on parallel courses without affecting each other.

However, Nobel laureate Wigner, a man more honored than Wheeler,

said, "The most obvious area not subject to the present laws of physics is that of life and consciousness and there is no path apparent yet leading to a common basis of physical and mental phenomena."

The "Consciousness People" are obviously trying to tell us that the mind not only is active in defining reality but that the mind actually influences reality.

This is where parapsychology enters the picture. The parapsychologists have been telling us for years that the mind can influence reality, not only directly as in psychokinesis but in its ability to apprehend events without known physical contact as in remote viewing (call it clairvoyance if you prefer). This is a completely different claim from the one that holds that the mind merely defines reality and that reality cannot exist without the perceptions of the mind.

RANDI SPUTTERS

OBSERVERS have expressed concern that the AAAS may be moved to kick the Parapsychology Association off its list of members. Wheeler even has difficulty believing that there is any such thing as parapsychology! Dr. Kenneth Boulding, new president of the AAAS, has stated that he favors keeping the association in the AAAS but still it is feared that as many as half of the AAAS membership doubts the wisdom of this. This attitude seems equivalent to denying that man has a right to investigate the strange mysteries of his own mind.

I regarded the fear of the AAAS terminating the Parapsychology Association's affiliation as paranoid imaginings until the January 25 issue of *Science,* the AAAS official journal, came across my desk. It contains a news article on James Randi, the bearded conjuror, repeating the myth that he has been trying to give away $10,000 for the past 15 years to anyone who can prove paranormal powers. Publication of this claptrap can only be regarded as a hostility toward parapsychology.

It seems incredible that *Science* should fall for the same publicity gag that Randi learned from Houdini, who invented it. The article conspicuously fails to mention that Randi himself determines the reality of the paranormal phenomena — he is policeman, judge, jury and prosecuting attorney. FATE has documented and published two lengthy case histories of times when Randi welshed on his offer.

How "amazing" that he continues to be believed and accepted by such a prestigious journal as *Science* — the same magazine that returned Velikovsky materials unopened and has refused to publish documented rebuttals on topics relating to parapsychology from respected researchers.

SCHOLARLY BELIEVERS

READERS of FATE may take heart, however. Issue No. 5 of the *Zetetic Scholar*, the scientific review edited by Prof. Marcello Truzzi, defected cofounder of the Committee for Scientific Investigation of Claims of the Paranormal, reported on a study conducted by Mahlon Wagner and Mary Monnet. Some of the details are based on a 1973 survey of 2100 scientists, 49 percent of whom responded to a questionnaire.

The Wagner-Monnet study shows that nine percent of the natural scientists in American colleges and universities believe ESP to be an established fact and another 45 percent believe it to be a "likely possibility." In the academic community as a whole 16 percent believe ESP to be established and 50 percent consider it a likely possiblility. Natural scientists were more skeptical than average and social scientists even more so.

The survey shows 1188 professors were favorably disposed toward parapsychology by a 2-to-1 ratio but only 38 percent felt positively about ESP in plants and animals. Professors in the natural and social sciences averaged 55 percent positive but in the arts, humanities and education, 77 percent were positive.

Least positive were psychologists — only 34 percent — and, in fact, 54 percent of them believe ESP to be an impossibility.

An accompanying table shows the relationship between the academic field of the respondents and their beliefs. The persons receiving the questionnaire were selected at random; the only requirement for the college selections was that the institution have at least 1000 students and more than 100 faculty members.

Relation between academic field and attitude toward ESP Academic Field

ESP is:	natural science No. %		social science No. %		humanities No. %		arts No. %		education No. %		Total No. %	
an established fact	28	9.5	23	9.6	47	22.2	54	30.9	40	16.4	192	16.5
likely possibility	134	45.6	112	46.9	108	50.9	84	48.0	141	57.8	579	49.7
merely an unknown	43	14.6	31	13.0	17	8.0	14	8.0	18	7.4	123	10.6
a remote possibility	81	27.6	48	20.1	31	14.6	20	11.4	43	17.6	223	19.2
an impossibility	8	2.7	25	10.5	9	4.2	3	1.7	2	0.8	47	4.0
Total	294	100.0	239	100.1	212	99.9	175	100.0	244	100.0	1164	100.0

$X^2(16) = 110.2, P < .0001$

Courtesy Mahlon Wagner, State University of New York at Oswego

XI. Additional Documentation and Evidence

Further evidence has so increased the probability of the existence of PK as a part of reality that we should get on with research. The list of those who are investigating PK, both pro and con, is too long to recount. Honest criticism from both sides should always be welcome and can do much to sharpen the reasoning to bring us closer to facts—whatever they may be.

Here are some names which will be encountered by the reader who wants to explore further: Hans Bender, E. Douglas Dean, Wilbur Franklin, John B. Hasted, Michael Hutchinson, Robert G. Jahn, Brian Josephson, Stanley Krippner, A. R. G. Owen, Soji Otani, Harold Puthoff, Shegemi Sasaki, Werner Schiebeler, Russell Targ, John Taylor, William Tiller, Marcello Truzzi. We will limit this chapter to citing the Human Dimensions Institute report on PK and some of the research reports received from Japan.

The HUMAN DIMENSIONS INSTITUTE, 4612 West Lake Road, Canandaigua, NY, 14424, was incorporated by the State of New York in the Fall of 1968 and received its tax-exempt status in May 1969. An impressive list of persons interested in the broader dimension of human potential make up the board of directors and Institute advisors. Readers are encouraged to subscribe to its publications and support its research. (New address: Rt. 1, Box 1420, Columbus, NC 28722.)

Robert Cantor, M.D., edited the monograph, *The Psychokinetic World of TOMORROW'S CHILDREN Today.* (Vol. 6, Nos. 3 and 4, 1979).($4 postpaid) It presents extensive information and evidence for psycho-kinetic metal bending (PKMB). Parts of this publication are produced here with permission.

In her introduction to *Tomorrow's Children—Today,* Jean Rindge,

---

Robert Cantor, *M.D. psychiatrist, F.R.C.P. (C), received Ph.D. degree, 1966 and M.D. in 1970 from Wayne State University, Michigan; Psychiatry Specialty from McMaster University, Hamilton, Ontario, 1974. He is a member of the Royal College of Physicians and Surgeons, Ontario; member of the Royal Society of Medicine (London), and the American Society of Clinical Hypnosis and the Biofeedback Society of America. He has been a consultant psychiatrist for ministries of the Ontario government, a consultant psychiatrist at White Oaks Village for emotionally and behaviorally disturbed children, and the Child and Adolescents Services branch of the Hamilton-Wentworth Regional Health Unit, Ontario.*

the editor, wrote:

In this International Year of the Child, it may be important to focus attention, not only upon the sorely disadvantaged children of the world, but also upon the handful of exceptional youngsters who may be the harbingers of our most creative possible tomorrows.

The possibilities of the future seldom emerge full-blown over night. Evolution sends out tentative tendrils whose flowering depends upon the salubrious sustenance of the holo-systemic environment. The unfolding holographic paradigm which is uniting science, philosophy and religion is confirming the age-old intuitions that every aspect of the universe contains and is contained by every other aspect (see HUMAN DIMENSIONS, Vol. 6, No. 1 & 2, double issue, "The Holographic Reality"). Without an interflowing supportive symbiosis and synergy, evolution's tender shoots rapidly become inhibited, warped or annihilated.

The tendrils of our tomorrows reside in our children—today. If adult prejudices, fears or insensitivity intervene, the "magic moment" of flowering may be lost for generations to come.

The psychokinetic metal-bending children are a case in point. Contrary to much accepted present opinion, the last nail has not been driven into the coffin of this phenomenon.

Although the international hoop-la over the quixotic young Israeli, Uri Geller—whose metal-bending claims by mind power are substantiated by competent researchers while others cry fraud—has died down, the pastime has not departed.

Although most of the hundreds—yea, thousands—of self-styled mimickers of Uri's "power" on both sides of the globe during the mid 70's have returned to mundane affairs, a few persons, especially children, are continuing to demonstrate unexplained talents quietly in their own homes or in the laboratories of a few dedicated researchers.

Let us not ignore this—whatever our prejudices or predilections. To do so may be a colossal error. What seems to be happening, no longer with fanfare or public acclaim, may be the acorn of a mightier oak than we yet have realized. If the psychokinetic bending of forks and spoons— granting for the moment its validity—seems a meaningless and futile syndrome, the significance is not. The potential implications of the power of mind over matter for good or for ill boggle the intellect and strain credulity. . .

Dr. Cantor wrote in his opening statement:

"We all evolve conceptual boundaries beyond which we are fearful or loathful to tread. Yet the unknown is a siren that beckons, however softly. By training I am a psychiatrist, an individual who from my youth has been accustomed to learning and working within the framework of 20th century science.

"I live my profession, having the daily opportunity to help via conventional techniques to intervene positively in the personal problems

of children and of their often despairing families. The state of our present knowledge has much to offer and properly implemented, can assist these needful persons. Yet no one would be so rash as to suggest that we have tapped more than a fraction of what there is to know.

"Although a professional works comfortably and creatively within the bounds of the "known," there often resides in the recesses of his mind, possibilities which fail to fit the accepted scheme of things."

Below is reproduced a photograph of four spoons contorted in unusual shapes by Julie Knowles, one of the young persons studied by Prof. John B. Hasted. Julie Knowles, now 19, was only 13 when she found she could replicate Uri Geller's metal-bending she had seen on TV. Fortunately for Julie, her family was pleased with her new-found ability and their supportive attitude has been encouraging to the shy girl when schoolmates and others were disdainful and even disapproving of of her talent.

Despite her retiring nature, Julie has been able to work in the presence of skeptics, if they are "open-minded and constructively critical." Prof. Hasted has given her a variety of PK tasks to perform and has continued to conduct experiments with her until the present.

At first she was physically and mentally exhausted by her efforts to bend objects, but she is now able to work for longer periods of time. PKMB makes her hungry and thirsty, however, and she often loses weight—at one time three pounds. Once she has directed attention to the object and rubbed it between her left thumb and forefinger, she can be detached and carry on a conversation while the metal-bending goes on.

As a psychiatrist, Dr. Cantor wanted to know how these gifted young people adapted and adjusted to their talents and the attention they

Some of Julie's spoons—the "world on a bender."

received (not all of it pleasant) on the part of their environment. He made two visits to Great Britain that provided some observations which are valuable in understanding the "children of tomorrow." Dr. Cantor reported (in part):

A. PHYSICAL BEHAVIOUR USED TO PRODUCE PKMB

A very clear pattern of working with the object to be bent emerges from our research. Initially, almost all the children rubbed the object. Some held the object with one hand and stroked with the other. Some rubbed the object between their finger and thumb, and others with their index finger alone. Some used their dominant hand and others their non-dominant hand. Some rubbed in various ways in order to achieve slightly different bends—away from the bender versus towards, tight-looped bends versus loose-looped bends, etc.

Initially everyone rubbed steadily, patiently, sometimes for as much as an hour before results were obtained. This tedious technique worked in that it achieved bending and familiarity with the process. After a period of some weeks (or sometimes months) over half the children discovered that constant rubbing was no longer necessary. They discovered that on a moderate number of occasions simply holding the object would suffice.

Interestingly enough, several of these children reported that they would have to revert to the rubbing techniques when observers arrived. It seems that rubbing provided further assistance in a more difficult atmosphere.

Once enough facility had been gained to bend the object simply by holding it, the children began to experiment with bending an object while having no physical contact with it. Many of them had recognized that it should be possible intentionally to bend such an object since some of the children had had experience with objects spontaneously bending in an unintentional fashion.

The most experienced and capable metal-benders are the ones who have had the greatest success with this non-touch technique. It appears that this approach allows for the expression of more detailed and creative form. Thus, it was via this method that Stephen N. produced a bracelet for this mother (out of three separate pieces of metal) and Peter M. produced a prolific number of wire and metal strip sculptures. . .

B. PSYCHOLOGICAL TECHNIQUES

Behind the outer veneer of physical activities lies the realm of conscious and unconscious psychological procedures which each child developed to facilitate results.

Initially, all the metal-benders "told" the object to bend, often repeating the phrase, "bend, bend, bend," for example, as one lad put it, "I say bend—politely but firmly." Over half the children reported becoming very stern toward the object and one young lady sheepishly confided in us that in a pinch she would go so far as to swear at the object to make it bend.

Although this apparently catalyzed the process, it also required faith or expectation that bending would occur. More than half learned that they could facilitate the results by firmly centering their emotional stance toward the task.

i) Letting Go

Much like putting a plane on automatic pilot, once the child had set up an intentional course of action, he often would "let go" of it at a conscious level and the process would proceed perfectly well at an unconscious level. The trained typist, pianist or automobile driver experiences the same process.

Typically the child would observe "Well, it just gets boring saying 'bend, bend, bend', so perhaps I would lay the spoon down and watch T.V. and then look down and discover it was bent. . ."

ii) The Role of Visualization

Five out of the twelve children mentally visualize the object bending. One boy imagines himself among the very atoms of the metal spoon and he watches the atoms move in the desired direction. The other four picture the object as it appears to them and then in their mind's eye watch it bend. (We have the impression that using this technique allows the child to create bends which more precisely produce the desired result, but we were unable solidly to confirm this.)

Although rather complex behavior patterns for producing PKMB emerged, we were struck by the general similarity among children with little or no contact with each other. This suggests the existence of a uniform underlying human potential rather than the fanciful imagination or self-delusion. . .

Mark H., one of the young PKMB children in Great Britain, had trouble with his watches. Dr. Cantor reports:

Mrs. H. reported that Mark's inability to wear watches always has been unusual. A good quality watch, which she purchased when he was six years old, would run for only a few weeks at a time and then invariably the balance would break. The jeweller repeatedly worked on the mechanism but the watch simply would not function in a satisfactory way. Mark has owned a number of watches since then, and it is not unusual for them to stop after being worn for only one or two weeks.

Mark's maternal grandmother, a lady known as a "psychic" in the community, used to wear a watch for decoration only because it would invariably break again whenever repaired. This apparent family trait raises interesting questions which need further exploration. The family noted that there had been a tendency for keys around the house to bend quite spontaneously since Mark was about ten years of age. No one could explain these events.

Sometime before he consciously began to bend metal, Mark had an embarrassing experience at a local swimming pool He left all of his belongings in the locker and locked it with the key, which he wore while he was swimming. When he came back to unlock the locker he found that the key was bent sideways and was quite useless. This caused quite a commotion when he went to the manager of the swimming pool to obtain another key.

Dr. Cantor, in contrast with many investigators who have been trying to prove whether or not children who bend spoons and other household cutlery are genuine, is interested in the human side of the phenomenon and the effect that the attention and controversy have on the children themselves. Uniqueness is not always valued in our society; it is known that talents and gifts which are misunderstood or disapproved are often suppressed and submerged in children.

In 1976, with the support of the Belk Research Foundation and several individuals, Dr. Cantor spent some time in England studying children who had been subjects of studies and experiments by Prof. John B. Hasted, a physicist at Birkbeck College, and Dr. John Taylor, professor of mathematics at King's College in London.

A dozen families who had metal-bending children (with siblings) were chosen to learn what family attitudes and other

Julie was able to rotate a balance straw under glass in an experiment for Dr. Hasted.

factors made it possible for these children to explore their unusual abilities. What were the effects of the research conducted with the children and the effects of the general climate of curiosity, disbelief and skepticism which they encountered? What were the reactions of the school personnel, other children, relatives, the community, etc. and how had these social groups affected the children? Did they feel they were, as Ingo Swann has said, "laboratory rats" exploited by the media and by sympathetic and skeptical investigators to prove or disprove the validity of the PK phenomenon?

Poltergeist activity, the curiosity of the press and other media were difficult to deal with. Parents worried about the effect of this attention on the children. The children, and to some extent the families, have experienced a sense of isolation because of the attitudes toward the children's metal bending, on the part of teachers and peers. In one case a child was transferred to another school.

The family backgrounds, as portrayed by Dr. Cantor, are absorbing to read about, although it is somewhat difficult to believe that the families adjusted as smoothly and easily to the experiences as he reports. What he found, as reported by Prof. Hasted and others, is that the ability of the young metal-benders to perform such feats is greatly affected by the attitudes of observers and those around them. Interest in the feat (or experiment), a comfortable familiar place, success in achieving, and of course, confidence or belief, are all important factors in their performance.

The metal-bending talents of the children took interesting turns. One boy found he could "will" strips of metal into artistic shapes. With the encouragement of his mother (who is an artist) and his father, who provided him with the metal strips, he created abstract "sculptures" of considerable artistic merit. Another boy learned to bend straightened paper clips into fanciful shapes. One little girl, although she was a successful spoon-bender, has been attracted to healing which became so demanding that she and her family endeavored to curtail and control the activity for the sake of the child's own health and the family's privacy. Metal-bending, exciting at first, can become boring and it is not surprising that some of the children abandoned it in favor of activities which were more satisfying.

Poltergeist occurrences of various kinds, particularly in the early period of metal-bending activity, were the common lot of most of these families. Objects moved, disappeared, and sometimes broke, exploded or shattered. One child found his bed turned 180 degrees when he awoke one morning. Some parents found the dislocations and disappearances of objects downright annoying, even though they came to understand that these occurred at unconscious levels in the presence of the children. Many of them could see potential for mischief in this ability which raised ethical questions as to whether or not it ought to be encouraged or accepted. Fortunately for the children and the families, they realized that this talent had some positive results: improvement in learning, development of confidence, increased creativity in music and art, and in one case, achievement in sports.

Metal-bending is but one facet of the PK ability. The children have experienced a variety of other phenomena: telepathy, precognition, auras, visions, clairvoyance, unexplainable voices and sounds, influence on electrical and mechanical apparatus, e.g. watches, TV sets, lights, etc.

The families were confronted with ethical questions about the positive vs. negative use of these "powers," which sometimes are out of conscious control, as in cases of spontaneous PK. Should money be accepted for healing or from the sale of objects created by PK as art, since the psychic talent which produced them appeared to come from "outside"? If it is conceded that psychic ability does come from some outside force or influence, what is it and what is the meaning of it? Are these questions only for scientists, or should philosophers and theologians also be discussing them?

Experiments in Japan

The first page [Plate 1] reproduced here from a research report published by PSI Research Committee, Denki-Tsushin University, Tokyo, provides an abstract in English of an investigation of the PK abilities of Masuaki Kiyota and Hiroto Yamashita.

| 論 文 | 非金属材料の曲げ変形に及ぼすPKの影響 |

（単純梁式支持の竹材と木材の場合）

Some Experimental Studies on Deformation Process of Noncrystalline Materials by Psychokinesis
(Simple Beam Bending Tests of Bamboo and Wooden Specimens)

佐々木 茂 美[*]　　小 林　　明[*]　　小 林 正 幸[*]
Shigemi Sasaki　　Akira Kobayashi　　Masayuki Kobayashi

越 智 保 雄[*]　　伊 藤 文 雄[*]
Yasuo Ochi　　Fumio Ito

Abstract

In the preceding paper, it was already confirmed that the deformation by PK (psychokinesis) had a relation with a degree of plastic deformation of polycrystalline metals (steel, Al).

In this paper, simple beam tests are carried out for bamboo and wooden specimens, being examples of noncrystalline materials.

(1) The deformation by PK depends on the possibility of mechanical deformation of tested materials, i.e. the deformation by PK produces frequently in the specimens at the conditions of being able to deform easily by mechanical force and the specimens are deformed without touching by fingers under such conditions.

(2) The deformation by PK consists of two components, i.e. elastic and permanent deformation. The bamboo specimens are deformed elastically for the most part in it, on the other hand, the wooden specimens are permanently.

(3) The frictional force at the supporting end of simple beam specimens is of help towards the deformation by PK.

§ 1. はしがき

金属材料を取扱った前報[1]からは、試験片の危険断面が力学的な力によって全面降伏した後で、しかも塑性変形による加工硬化が割合に少ない応力において、力としてのPK（psychokinesis念力）が顕著に現われ易いという結果が得られた。本報では、PKの性質究明[2][3]の基礎的な問題として、非金属材料としての

Mr.H.Yamashita, Mr.M.Kiyota

Photo. 1

158

We chose to reproduce part of this report because it deals with the effect of PK on non-metallic objects and shows that whatever the force is, it is not restricted to bending spoons.

The second page [Plate 11] shows charts (with English titles) which

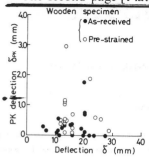

Fig.10 PK deflection δ_{PK} as a function of mechanical deflection δ of wooden specimens.

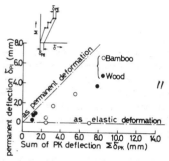

Fig.11 Relation between permanent deflection δ_{Pl} and sum of PK deflection $\Sigma\delta_{PK}$ of bamboo and wooden specimens.

//

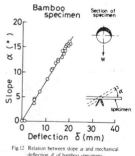

Fig.12 Relation between slope α and mechanical deflection δ of bamboo specimens.

竹材と木材の差異を求めるために，横軸にたわみ δ，縦軸に単純梁（試験片）の支持端における傾斜角 α をとって表示したところ，一例として Fig. 12，Fig. 13 が得られた。図より木材および竹材はともに弾性的である事がわかる。一方本報の場合のように試験片が弾性的であって，しかも δ_{PK} が弾性的な要素を多量に含む場合には，単純梁の支持端において，Fig. 14 に示す様に，式(4)の摩擦力 F を支える実験装置（本報の Fig. 1 の装置）が δ_{PK} としての PK 変形をより起こし易くすると考えられる。

$$F = \left(\frac{W + PK}{2}\right)\cos\alpha\cdot\mu \quad\cdots\cdots\cdots\cdots\cdots\cdots (4)$$

$$\mu = \tan\alpha_s \quad\cdots\cdots\cdots\cdots\cdots\cdots\cdots\cdots\cdots (5)$$

ただし，PK は念力の力による表示，α_S ＝臨界摩擦角，μ ＝摩擦係数である。換言すれば，F は PK を与える時には変形に対する抵抗として作用するが，PK を中止した時には，変形の戻りの抵抗となって δ_{PK} を維持させることになる。すなわち，支持端の摩擦力 F によって PK 変形の測定値 δ_{PK} が助けられる事になる。これを検討するために支持端の摩擦係数 μ を測定したところ，木材の場合には，$\mu = 0.31\sim0.34$，臨界摩擦角 $\alpha_S = 17\sim19°$，竹材の場合には，表皮部が下（引張側）の場合 $\mu = 0.14\sim0.18$，$\alpha_S = 8\sim10°$，表皮部が上（圧縮側）の場合 $\mu = 0.27\sim0.29$，$\alpha_S = 13\sim14°$ という結果が得られた。従って式(6)の場合，

$$\frac{W + PK}{2}\sin\alpha - \frac{W + PK}{2}\cos\alpha\cdot\mu \leqq 0 \quad\cdots\cdots\cdots (6)$$

換言すれば α が $\alpha \leqq \alpha_S$，または Fig. 12，Fig. 13 から，その α に対応する δ（あるいは M）の場合には，δ_{PK} を生じさせる事が極めて困難になるはずである。また μ のために M－δ 曲線の除荷の際の δ の減少が行なわれ難い現象が現われるはずである。実験結果は μ の存在が δ_{PK} 及び M－δ 曲線に影響を与えることを示している。

§5. むすび

PK 変形は金属の塑性変形の程度と密接な関係のあることが前報[1]で確かめられた。本報では，塑性変形の起らない非晶質材料の一例としての木材と竹材に対して検討を加えた。

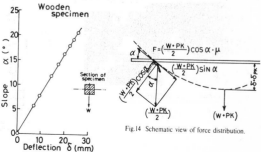

Wooden specimen

Section of specimen

Fig.14 Schematic view of force distribution.

$$F = \frac{W\cdot PK}{2}\cos\alpha\cdot\mu$$

$$\frac{(W\cdot PK)}{2}\sin\alpha$$

Fig.13 Relation between slope α and mechanical deflection δ of wooden specimens.

Plate 11

19

give some of the results of the tests. Plate III reproduces the first page of another research report by Professors Sasaki and Ochi, with pictures of the four young psychics who were subjects and a schematic diagram of the apparatus designed for their tests. This is followed by photographs

PKによる金属材料の変形現象について＊

佐々木茂美・越智保雄
（電通大ＰＳＩ研究会）

Some Experimental Studies on Deformation Process of Metals by Psychokinesis
by
Shigemi Sasaki and Yasuo Ochi
(PSI Research Committee, Denki-Tsushin Univ., Chofu, Tokyo)

〔Synopsis〕 To investigate the effects of PK(Psychokinesis) on the mechanical properties of metals, three kinds of test are performed for three kinds of test specimen by four boys who have special Psi ability.

After the weakest part of test specimens reaches to the general yield by the action of mechanical stress, and also when strain hardening by plastic deformation is relatively small, the plastic deformation by PK reaches to some maximum value.

1. はしがき

人の心の動きまたは意識が直接物に作用して種々の物理現象を起こすことを一般には，PK（Psycho Kinesisの略）または念力と称している。この種の研究としては，米国 Duke 大学におけるサイコロ投げに及ぼすＰＫの統計的科学的研究(1)，ＰＫの選択性，方向性，磁気作用，遮蔽効果などに関するソ連圏の研究(2)，ＰＫによる金属切断面の米国における科学的な観察(3)，ＰＫによる金属変形の英国の観察(4)などが報告されている。しかしながらＰＫが金属材料の強さに対してどの様な影響をもっているかという事に関しては，現在のところ充分には明らかではないように思える。そこで本報では，検討の第1段階として，超能力少年と言われる人達が心で念ずることによって金属材料を変形させる事が出来るかどうか，またその変形の特徴はどのようなものであるか等を実験的に検討する事にした。

本報で実験的に確められたＰＫ変形は，再現性のある客観的な観測結果であるとともに，機械工学（特に材料力学，材料強度学）の分野において今までに取扱った事の無い現象なので，ＰＫによる変形機構の解明および実用開発など今後の研究素材を提供する意味で，とりあえず実験結果のみを報告することにした。

Mr. M.Hirota

Mr. J.Sekiguchi

Mr. M.Kiyota   Mr. H.Yamashita

Photo.1

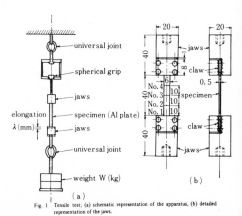

Fig. 1 Tensile test; (a) schematic representation of the apparatus, (b) detailed representation of the jaws.

＊ 本報の1部は超科学 vol. 1, No. 2（昭49）P. 2ならびにテレパシー vol. 9, No. 1（昭50）P. 16にて発表済

[Plate IV] showing the differences in metal specimens fractured by mechanical bending and PK. We hope some day the entire reports will be available in European languages, since Japanese is not widely read.

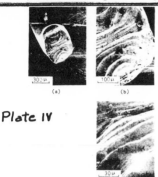

Plate IV

Photo. 2. Same specimen as Photo.1 at a location approximately 10 mm away fractured by ordinary mechanical bending fatigue. (a) Macrophotograph. (b) a portion of the lower right side of (a). (c) a slight left portion of the center of (a).

ＰＫ破断のphoto.1と物理的な疲労破断の方がphoto.2を比較すると、両者は似ているが、前者の方がストライエーション間隔がより狭いこと、より複雑な破断面であること。部分的により延性的なこと、及びより脆性的であること等の特徴を示している。

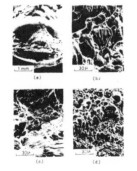

Photo. 3. SEM photographs of a fracture surface of a 13-Cr stainless steel spoon broken by PK in the presence of Mr.D. (a) Macrophotograph. (b) an upper portion of the center of (a). (c) a central portion of the left side of (a). (d) a lower portion of the center of (a).

photo.3はＤ少年による13クロムのステンレス鋼製スプーンのＰＫ破断面を示している。実験日は昭和52年8月24日の午後5時半頃、自宅応接室（洋間）に接した広い居間（じゅうたん敷き）の蛍光燈照明下で、超能力を持たない妹の見ている前で、曲がれと念じながら5〜10分の間に5回程スプーンを投げ

てＰＫ切断したものである。『明日は電通大のＰＫ実験日なので久し振りにやってみたら』と母に云われて、リラックスしながら、遊びの心算で投げたところ5回目で突然破断したと告げている。photo.3の(ａ)はＰＫ破断面全体のマクロ写真（30倍）、(ｂ)は写真中央の突出部（上部）よりもやや右寄り部分（1000倍）、(ｃ)は左端のほぼ中央部（1000倍）、(ｄ)は中央下部（1000倍）である。上述のphoto.1の場合と同様、場所により破壊形式が異っている。換言すれば、種々の模様が入り混じっている事が特徴的である。(1)スプーンの柄の表面近くのＰＫ破断面には、脆性破断を特徴づけるリバー状パターンが き裂の進行方向とほぼ直角の方向に顕著に存在している |(ａ)及び(ｂ)参照|。従ってその部分（スプーンの柄の表面）は塑性変形しておらず、また疲労破壊に特有な突出し、入り込み状の横方向の縞模様は見えない |(ａ)の上部の破断面に対して直角方向の奥行の面（柄の表面）がつるつるしている|。(2)スプーンの柄の裏面には疲労特有の突出し、入り込み状の横線模様がある。従って裏面近くの破断面には延性破壊特有のディンプルが見える |例えば(ｃ)及び(ｂ)の中央部|。(3)それらの部分にはストライエーション状模様も見えるが、photo.1の場合と同様、その間隔は極めて小である。

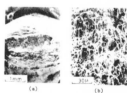

Photo. 4. Same specimen as Photo.3 at a location approximately 15 mm away fractured by ordinary mechanical bending fatigue. (a) Macrophotograph. (b) a portion of the center of (a).

photo.4はphoto.3のＰＫ破断面よりも約15mm離れたスプーンの柄の太い部分を、実験者が万力とペンチを用いて通常の速さではほぼ同じ程度に前後に繰返して折り曲げたところ19回目で疲労破断した場合の一例を示している。(1)スプーンの柄の表裏両面には、(ａ)の下側の柄の表面に示されている様に延性材料の曲げ塑性疲労特有の突出し、入り込み状の横縞模様が現れている。(2)ストライエーションは見えず(ｂ)のようなディンプル状模様が全面をおおっている。すなわち、延性的に破断している。

ＰＫ破断面のphoto.3と疲労破断面のphoto.4を比較した場合、前述のphoto.1〜2の場合と類似し

Next is a wiring diagram [Plate V] for the experimental apparatus used for nengraphy experiments conducted with Masuaki. This is

161

photo. 1 Mr.
Masuaki Kiyota

報のSPD出力に関しては2～3時間にわたって本実験が続行された。なお、本報の実験とは別に、2～3種類の他の実験が、其等とほぼ同一の実験日に清田、村沢、山下氏（アイウエオ順）によって行われているが、本報はSPDによる念場出力の確認を主目的としているのでそれ等にはふれないことにする。

2-1) 実験装置

実験装置の略図をFig. 1，ブリキ板製の缶の蓋を開けた時のSPD，発光ダイオードの配置状態をp-hoto. 2，その配線図をFig. 2に示した。

念写は、黒遮光紙を介して行なうのが通常なので、実験当初に於いては著者らも宮内－福田[1]らとほぼ同一の装置（黒遮光紙で漏光を防ぐ方式）を用いて本報の実験を行なったが、種々の問題点のあること

が判ったので、それを改良したのが上述のFig. 1～2，photo. 2の実験装置である。なおこの装置を作製したときの注意事項は次記である。
(1)結果に影響を与えると思われる物理的な要因を測定系の全体にわたって極力排除する。
(2)出来るだけ単純な実験装置である事。

実験装置の本体には、ブリキ板製の缶（市販品の浅田飴の空缶）を用い、その中にはシリコンフォトダイオードSPD-111，発光ダイオード（LED）TLR-106，金属及び炭素皮膜抵抗R₁及びR₂がFig. 2の様に結線してある。それ等はFig. 1，photo. 2に示す様にベークライト端子板（54×17×2 mm）の上

にハンダ付で固定された後、2個の3φ×12mmの丸小ネジによって缶本体に固定されている。缶の大きさは77φ×22mm、缶の蓋の厚みは0.24mm、缶の内面は黒色ラ

Photo. 2 Inside View of the darken box

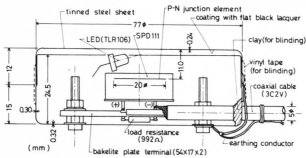

tinned steel sheet
P-N junction element
coating with flat black lacquer
LED(TLR106)
SPD 111
77φ
0.24
11.0
clay(for blinding)
vinyl tape (for blinding)
coaxial cable (3C2V)
12
24.5
20φ
15
(+)　(−)
5φ
0.30
0.32
load resistance (992Ω)
(mm)
bakelite plate terminal (54×17×2)
earthing conductor

Fig. 1. Experimental apparatus (darken box).

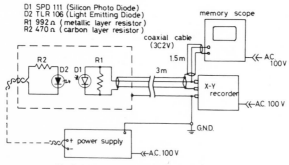

D1 SPD 111 (Silicon Photo Diode)
D2 TLR 106 (Light Emitting Diode)
R1 992 Ω (metallic layer resistor)
R2 470 Ω (carbon layer resistor)

memory scope
R2　D2　D1　R1
coaxial cable (3C2V)
1.5m
3m
AC 100V
X-Y recorder
AC. 100 V
G.ND.
+ power supply
AC.100 V

Fig. 2. Wiring diagram for experimental apparatus.

Plate V

4

followed by a report [Plate VI] in which Prof. Matsumi Suzuki, as experiment leader, and Yutaka Fukuda as reporter, give their findings related to the discovery of radio wave signals emitted by Masuaki and Hiroto during the Nippon TV filming sessions in 1979.

```
┌─────────────────────────────────────────┐
│  Radio wave oscillation phenomenon       │
│  Concerning the method of discovery and the │
│  result of the experiment.               │
└─────────────────────────────────────────┘
```

Plate VI

Experiment leader: Matsumi Suzuki
Experiment reporter: Yutaka Fukuda

1. In March of 1979, Nippon Television was making a film
   of Masuaki Kiyota's PK at his home.   I was present.

2. While making the film, one of the technician said he
   could hear noise Kiyota used his Nen(PK)powers.

3. After finishing making the video tape, we replayed
   the tape at the points where the noise had appeared several
   times.   When we increased the volume we all could hear
   a loud noise which sounded like the ignition of a car engine.

4. No motorbikes or cars were started or passed by when
   the filming was taking place.

5. At this point, Director Yamaguchi of NTV said he would
   ask Prof. Matsumi Suzuki to analyze the video tape.

6. According to Prof. Suzuki's analysis, it seemed possible
   that a radio wave was being emitted from Kiyota's body.

7. The following result were obtained from experiments
   performed in a sound-proof NTV studio.   Mr. Yamashita
   hiroto also took part.

8.

	KIYOTA	YAMASHITA
Fo	34.5MHz zone	21.0MHz zone
intensity	$\doteqdot$15db microV/m	$\doteqdot$150db microV/m
drift	$Fo^+_- \doteqdot$1 MHz	$Fo^+_- \doteqdot$1 MHz
	blocking,about 10sec	blocking,about 10sec
method of capsule	magnetic and static shielded room	
Radio	Colinse 501S	
	+X'tal comv.	RF Amp. 2stage
	RF Amp. 2stage	
Radio mode	SSB beat freq. Fo+ 1000 Hz	
out put	SP 16 ohms	
	pen-recorder(AF Amp. - Zo 50 ohms)	
Antenna	34.5MHz dipole	wier
Antena imp.	75 ohms	- - - - - -

....

Coil antenna	helmet type 13ch.
	antenna imp. 75ohms
	coil Q $\doteqdot$90
	Fo 34.5MHz

9. During this experiment as a means of producing PK, Kiyota concentrated on making nengraphs, and Yamashita, on bending spoons.

10. This experiment showed that radio wave oscillations were being emitted at a point 2 to 2.5 inches above the outside corner of the left eye of Mr. Kiyota.

Prof. Sasaki, on the faculty of the Department of Mechanical Engineering of the University of Electro-Communications, Tokyo, wrote us July 4, 1979: "Masuaki and Hiroto have special abilities of psychokinesis and are very interested to do some experiments. . .[with us]." He sent a dozen reprints of research reports on various aspects of PK. A few of the titles indicate the scope and extent of their investigations:

"The Effects of Psychokinesis (PK) on the Hardness of Pure Aluminum Plate. (The 1st Report: On the Hardening of Annealed Materials by PK)"

"Some Experimental Studies on Appearance of Nengraphy (Thoughtography) by Psychokinesis"

"Some Examinations of Supernormal Phenomena by Means of Silicon-Photo-Diode (SPD) during Nengraphy Process"

"Examinations of Paranormal Phenomena with PSI-Spots during Nengraphy (Thoughtography) Process by Means of TV-Vidicon-Tube"

A progress report on experiment Concerning the spontaneous appearance of light in a dark box.

by Tsutomu Miyauchi
Yutaka Fukuda

1. As indicated in fig.1.
   We remodelled a polaroid camera into a dark box by removing its focussing mechanism and shutter.
   We fixed the p-n junction surface of a silicon photo diode(SPD) in it so that it faced the emulsion surface of the film. We were careful to see that light did not leak in at any point.

2. As shown in fig. 2, we

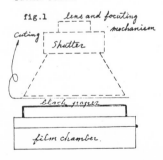

fig.1 lens and focuting mechanism
Cuting
Shutter
black paper
film chamber.

fig.2

connected the output terminal
of of the SPD to a micro ammeter with electric wire.

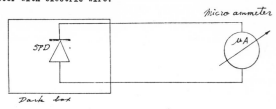

3.   The dark box was loadedwith polaroid film. When Masuaki
   Kiyota applied Nen(PK), the micro ammeter indicator moved.
      After development, sensitization of the emulsion surface
   of the emulsion surface of the polaroid film was observed.

4.   A transparency film on whitch a design had been drawn
   with bÍack ink was placed on the emulsion surface of the
   polaroid film in the dark box. The above experiment was
   performed. When the micro ammeter indicator moved, a figure just like the design appeard on the film. Five transparency films, each with a different identifying design
   were placed on top of each other touching the emulsion
   surface of the polaroid film. This experiment was carried
   out several times. Each time all of the designs appeared
   on the polaroid film.
      This is proof that light appears spontaneously above
   the five lagers of transparency film away from the surface
   of the transparency film whitch is touching the polaroid
   film.

   fig.3

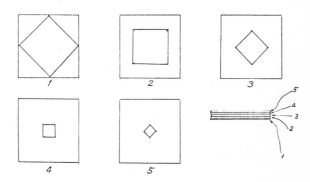

5.   The micro ammeter used in these experiments is a moving
   coil type and is a 100micro A/full scale. The coil resistance is 1000ohms.   In other to better record the moove-
   ment of the indicator in response to the change in input
   current, a small micro ammeter, 45mm in diameter, was used.

6.   As indicated in fig.4, the output terminal of the SPD
in the dark box and the input terminal of the electronic
pen-recorder were conected.   When Masuaki Kiyota applied
Nen(PK) to the dark box, a distinct exponential function
curve was recorded on the paper.

Very importantly, within this curve, recordings of a
reverse direction current were discovered here and there.

In other words, it is possible that occasionally, under
the influence of Nen(PK), The output current of the SPD
in the dark box reversed directions.   For this reason,
we feel the spontanious appearance of light takes place
behind the p-n junction of the SPD.

The electronic pen-recorder used in this experiment is
a 10mV/full scale.   The input impedance is 100k ohms.

fig.4

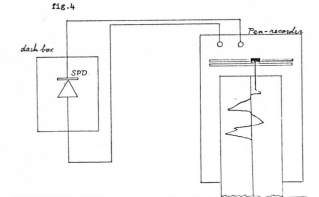

XII   Other Investigators and Psychics

By Mary Jo Uphoff

Although this book had dealt chiefly with the psychic abilities and experiences of Masuaki Kiyota and Hiroto Yamashita from Japan, they are only two of many who have come to public attention. We have no way of knowing how many hundreds or thousands of children, who having seen a performance by Uri Geller on television or heard about his metal-bending talents, have discovered that they, too, could replicate the feat.

Because he chose to demonstrate on the stage and on television and has been the subject of investigation in the U.S. and in Europe, Geller's controversial abilities are well known over a good part of the world. The publicity he received, even adverse or hostile, has probably helped swell audiences for his lectures and demonstrations. But the fact that he chose the stage and TV cloaked his psychic performances in the role of "show biz" incurred the hostility of some professional magicians and also aroused skepticism among some members of the scientific establishment who were inclined to "throw out the baby with the bathwater"—maintaining that even under stringent test conditions his psychic feats were suspect.

Geller, who was born in Israel and whose unusual abilities manifested in early childhood, began his public career while still in Israel and then, particularly after he came to the attention of Dr. Andrija Puharich, who persuaded him to come to the U.S., has had a decade of successful public appearances that included Western Europe, Japan and Australia. Following these appearances there were hundreds of reports of cutlery bent in the households of viewers and a host of reports of adults and children—but particularly children—who were successfully and enthusiastically bending spoons, forks and other items.

Uri Geller has been the subject of several books, one written by himself, and another by Dr. Puharich. Fantastic as some of the experiences reported about Geller may seem, the investigators who have pursued the study of PK have discovered that the same feats can be produced by others and the phenomena thus became more "believable." The stimulus provided by his career as a showman has uncovered some of these abilities in thousands of others in places where he has appeared and has led to serious research by investigators and scientists, not all of whom can be introduced here.

Matthew Manning, now in his mid-twenties, and one of the world's most gifted psychics, was at one time described as "England's Uri Geller," a designation he disliked. Matthew had the uncomfortable experience of persistent and disturbing poltergeist activities occurring about him in his pre-teen years. Once he discovered that he could allow his arm to be "controlled" in the production of automatic writing and drawing, the poltergeist activity ceased. During his most productive period of so-called "automatic art," he drew in the style of many famous artists: Durer, Picasso, Rowland, Beardsley and others. His ability to bend metal attracted attention to his psychic abilities but he soon gave it up, preferring to participate in tests and experiments conducted by scientists in Europe, Canada and the U.S., some of which are discussed elsewhere in this book. Some of the most intensive tests were conducted in Toronto in 1974 by a group of 21 scientists, including psychiatrists, physicists, physicians and parapsychologists—among them two Nobel prize winners—who reported the discovery of an unusual brain wave pattern called the "ramp function" which appeared when Matthew was performing a paranormal task, in this case, bending metal.

Matthew was our guest in November 1977 and again in 1979. During his first visit, Walter had arranged an interview on Channel 3 TV, Madison, Wisconsin. As they returned to the car, Walter shook the car keys out of the case and was astonished to find that part of the trunk key to his AMC Sportabout had "vanished." Although he knew about "dematerialization," it had never happened to him. Both keys were intact when he put them in his pocket on their way to the studio; there was no evidence of a sharp break in the key, nor had anything occurred to break it by force.

Later, at home, Matthew asked to see the keys. While we watched, he stroked the ignition key with his right index finger and the key bent before our eyes. (Photo, page 169.)

The small trunk compartment in the car was rarely used. Nine months later when Walter, for the first time since Matthew's visit, tried to open it with a duplicate key, the entire lock assembly fell apart, as shown in the photo.

On the last evening of Matthew's visit, while cleaning up after dinner, I noticed a teaspoon was somewhat bent. Laid on the dining table, it continued to bend almost imperceptibly, humping like an inchworm, while five of us watched. Then our son Charles, suggesting that we had

better check the silver, pulled open a drawer about 8 feet from Matthew and discovered one of our silver teaspoons twisted as shown in photo.

Like Geller, Matthew was for a time sensationalized and attacked in the press and by individuals seeking to make headlines. Matthew, who came to feel that his willingness to cooperate with those who wanted to test and investigate him was being exploited and uselessly repeated, has now established a healing center in England where he is finding satisfaction in the constructive use of his psychic gifts. He has written three books dealing with his own experiences: *The Link, In the Minds of Millions* and *Strangers Among Us.*

Silvio, another thoroughly studied psychic with remarkable ability to bend and break metal and other materials—and also to "repair" them—lives in Bern, Switzerland, Parapsychologists and other investigators, including the Institute for the Border Areas of Psychology at Freiburg, Germany, and the magician Rolf Mayr, have been convinced of his genuine psychic abilities.

A shy, retiring man of forty, who has had a severe speech impediment since childhood, Silvio prefers to follow his vocation of draftsman and to be out in the beautiful natural surroundings of mountains and lakes of his native country. Those who have studied him have concluded that his identity and ability to become "one" with his environment have an important role in his unusual talent. Silvio, as he prefers to be known, lives in two worlds; he has portrayed some of the "inhabitants" of other dimensions, which he claims to have communicated with and seen since childhood, in paintings which would be described by those who have had no acquaintance with this "other world" as bizarre and surrealistic. These paintings have been shown at several successful exhibitions.

Bernhard Waelti, who has studied and befriended Silvio since his discovery, has written a book about him, *Die Silvio Protokolle 1976-1977,* published in Switzerland.

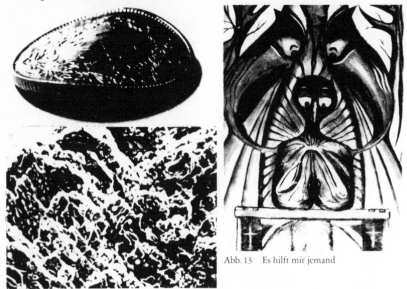

Abb. 13   Es hilft mir jemand

Photographs reproduced from a monograph by Bernhard Waelti, "Die Silvio-Protokolle-1976-1977" taken from *Zeitschrift fuer Parapsychologie u. Grenzgebiete der Psychologie. (Above)* A coin bent by Silvio by PK. *Lower left)* An electromicroscope photo of a section of metal broken by PK. *(Right)* One of the surrealistic paintings by Silvio, entitled "Es hilft mir jemand," (Someone is helping me.)

PK influence on film has been the contribution of **Ted Serios,** whose ability to project pictures onto unexposed film, has become known through his experiments with Dr. Jule Eisenbud of Denver, Colorado. Dr. Eisenbud summarized his experiments conducted with Ted, a Chicagoan, in the book, *The World of Ted Serios.*

Serios was able to impose on Polaroid film, targets concealed and unknown to him. He gave a spectacular demonstration during seven hours at the KOA-TV studio in Denver when he stared in the television camera and there emerged—not just Ted's features which first appeared—but a slowly developing street scene with a city bus and vehicles which gradually faded as the video camera rolled, whereupon the flabbergasted cameraman called it a day.

Ted, a colorful fellow who worked in a kind of frenzy of cigarette-smoking, beer-drinking hyperactivity, produced hundreds of pictures by a mental process termed "thoughtography"—projecting mental images on film, many of them under severely controlled conditions under the observation of teams of investigators. Then his "power" waned, except for occasional paranormal effects which did not equal his earlier productions. One of his last paranormal photos produced with Dr. Eisenbud was what appeared to be a billowing curtain, and Ted, with a psychic perspicacity, interpreted it as a winding down of the "curtain" on his thoughtography career. (This came at a time when Joseph, Richard and Fred Veilleux in Waterville, Maine, started producing paranormal photos. *New Psychic Frontiers,* pp. 55-59)

Italy has experienced what might be called an "outbreak" of "mini-Gellers" who are termed "Gellerini" since the appearance of Uri Geller there in the mid-seventies. These Gellerini are children between six years and the mid-teens; one of whom, a little girl, Lucia Allegretti, was presented on television by Dr. Piero Cassoli, one of the best known parapsychologists in Italy. Cassoli had been impressed with Lucia because she had not seen one of Geller's programs, but when her parents had been discussing the wonder of spoon-bending one evening, after hearing their friends talk about it, Lucia began stroking a spoon which bent before her astonished parents' eyes. However, Lucia who had bent spoons for some investigators, found appearing on television too stressful to be able to perform on that occasion.

Lucia's misadventure resulted in the discovery of the most talented subject Italian investigators have worked with to date: a 14-year-old boy, Orlando Bragante, who seeing Lucia on TV, proceeded to show his mother that he could do what Lucia could not.

Prof. Aldo Martelli and Dr. Ferdinando Bersani have conducted experiments with a number of these children under strictly controlled conditions. These have included PK effects (bending or breaking) by direct touch or handling of metal objects; PK effects on non-metalic objects with and without contact; telekinetic effects (from a distance) on objects; PK effect of warming or heating the object; and apporting or dematerializing objects.

One of their talented young subjects has bent metal objects sealed in plexiglass during his sleep. Many of the tests parallel the research findings of Prof. John Hasted, such as the effect of critical or skeptical observers on performance, the effects of "change of mood" on the occurrence of PK, etc.

PK abilities were intensively studied in Russia before the world heard about Uri Geller. **Nina Kulagina,** noted for her ability to move objects by mental power, worked in Russian laboratories with some of the country's famous parapsychologists until her health suffered severely from her efforts. Now an invalid, according to Gris and Dick, and having had a heart attack, her poor physical condition is thought due to the intense efforts she has made in the experiments conducted with her. She is credited with having stopped the heartbeat of a frog and has imposed burns on skin by intense mental concentration.

As a young girl, she demonstrated "dermaoptics" (fingertip sight); she was able to distinguish color by touch, but she was best known for her ability to mentally move objects (called telekinesis), an exertion which caused her blood pressure to rise markedly. Under laboratory conditions she has moved objects weighing up to a pound without touching them. She was also able to mark with letters and crosses, undeveloped film enclosed in envelopes by moving her eyes up and down "like a laser beam"—the same kind of term which Masuaki Kiyota has used to describe what he thinks he does when he puts images onto film.

Another Russian psychic, **Alla Vinogradova,** can move light objects back and forth, select one object from a group to move, while allowing the others to remain still. With practice she has become able to move objects weighing up to 200 grams. Her methods are somewhat different from Kulagina's. She can cause objects such as pingpong balls or plastic pens to spin and can start and stop them at will.

Vinogradova, a psychologist with the Research Institute of the Academy of Pedagogical Sciences, was intrigued by seeing a film of Kulagina's experiments and felt that she must also try to do the same. After a long period of practice she achieved success. Soviet parapsychologists have concluded that belief one can do the feat, and achieving success, even in a limited way, are very important factors in performing psychic feats.

Experiments in teaching metal bending by mental concentration (see the report by Mark Shafer in the *Appendix)* demonstrate that this ability is within the capabilities of many people, by no means all of them children, whose belief that it can be done seems to be of considerable help in the matter. Even more puzzling is the long distance effect of PK when clocks and watches start to run in homes of viewers, as has happened when Geller and Manning have appeared on television programs. Here the speculation that if one holds a disabled watch in the hand, the oil is warmed and allows cogs and gears to operate again, no longer holds true, for clocks which have hung on walls or have been stored in cupboards or simply laid on tables somewhere in the vicinity of the television set have begun to run.

Dr. Thelma Moss, in the Neuropsychiatric Institute at the University of California/Los Angeles, set up an experiment with one of her classes several years ago in which she invited her students to bring watches and clocks and other instruments, which were not in working order, to a session at which the class watched a 40-minute videotape of Uri Geller bending spoons and attempting to start watches. Clocks and watches started running—not all, of course—among them a wrist watch of Moss's which had not run for 12 years, and a TV set began functioning.

An incident like this leads to speculation whether or not Geller's activities were merely a stimulus to "program" the mental energies of a room full of excited people who were actually the agents who prodded the mechanical instruments into activity. Geller, to all appearances, believes that enthusiastic audiences do stimulate these occurences. Matthew Manning has indicated that the arousal of excitement in a paranormal event produces further phenomena, and under certain conditions there have been reports of PK activity in a household where no piece of metal was "safe" from intrusion. Orlando Bragante, at a movie with his mother, whispered to her that something which she would see later, was going on at home. What they encountered when they returned to their apartment was psychic mayhem. Bent and broken household items were everywhere. We have personally witnessed bursts of PK "output" on the part of Masuaki Kiyota. Ted Serios, when he was "hot" as he called it, turned out paranormal after paranormal picture.

The phenomenon can occur at conscious and unconscious levels, as we have also experienced, with or without direct contact, and at a distance. The notion of an "agent" providing or contributing to the occurrence of the phenomenon, in addition to the presence of the psychic, is worth consideration and may help to explain why the hostile or skeptical presence becomes an inhibiting factor in PK experiments on many occasions. Perhaps *attention* is a more accurate description of the PK-active state than *concentration*. Healers speak of it as "centering" or "focusing," and the paranormal voices on tape have told the listeners, "we think INTO you." The sense of ONE-NESS or identity with all things comes easier to children who do not yet have as strong a feeling of separateness or individuality as adults do, although it is not confined to the lack of individual identity in childhood. Is it alienation from the world of nature from which our race emerged which has brought about the denial of the interworking of our minds with matter? And only occasionally, when circumstances are right, is the evidence of "mind at work" encountered and called a "miracle"—or a trick?

The December 4, 1978 *Princeton Alumni Weekly* contained a delightful and provocative article by Robert G. Jahn, Dean of the University's Engineering School, recounting how he became involved in exploring psychic phenomena as a result of an electrical engineering student asking his permission to undertake an independent study of psychic phenomena (under his supervision) as background for skills in instrumentation and data processing.

When this unusual request came to him, Dean Jahn was noted for his work in advanced space propulsion systems, but being open-minded and intellectually curious, he agreed to join the exploratory venture.

Readers may be able to find the entire article in their library or get a copy from the *Princeton Alumni Weekly.* It will be worth more than whatever is charged. The 12-page article, with numerous references, is the work of a scientist who is truly free intellectually and in no hurry to come up with final answers. Here are excerpts from Dean Jahn's paper:

A PAW Special Report
Psychic Process, Energy Transfer and Things that Go Bump in the Night
By Robert G. Jahn '51

Two of the most celebrated joys of the academic lifestyle are the freedom to pursue any scholarly problem, no matter how irrelevant or far out it may seem at the time, and the impetus to do so provided by the perceptive, persistent, sometimes irreverent questions of the young students we are privileged to teach. Never in my career have these two benefits been more beautifully illustrated than in the case of the extraordinary topic of this report. Indeed, it is as much the flavor of light-hearted exploration of a very exotic field, hand-in-hand with an intelligent and dedicated undergraduate, as the substance of the field itself that I would like to share with you.

Late in the spring of 1977, an electrical engineering and computer science major came to me to ask whether she might undertake some independent work in psychic phenomena that would build upon her background and skills in instrumentation and data processing. Although I was well aware of the many times I have proudly spoken or written about the breadth and flexibility of the Princeton engineering curriculum, and the care with which we hand-tailor each undergraduate program to suit individual interests, the involvement of one of our students in psychic research seemed to me to strain even those generous guidelines.

In an attempt to table the issue, I asked, somewhat rhetorically, which faculty member could conceivably supervise this work, and with her characteristic bluntness, she responded that, obviously, I would. With the dilemma thus compounded, but no retreat path left, I provisionally agreed, pending the results of a full summer of background research in the field. This she undertook with considerable zest, digesting and reporting an enormous amount of literature in the process. Together and separately we visted numerous laboratories around the country, attended several professional meetings, had discussions with various people here and elsewhere, and started a few experiments of our own. As the following academic year began, we agreed the project was worth pursuing. . .

Dean Jahn next describes the design of experiments of two types—first, remote viewing and, second, the use of extremely sensitive interferometers and thermistors in the search for micro-psychokinetic phenomena. His paper then turns to a consideration of theoretical models.

174

Theoretical Models

Beyond the introduction of more sophisticated measuring and data-handling techniques, the second recent development which holds some hope of leading psychic research out of the dark ages is the growing interest of a number of theoretical and applied physicists in formulating models of the processes. We would need an entire article to represent any one of these models adequately. . .

Applications and Implications

If research like that outlined above is eventually successful in advancing our understanding of psychic phenomena from simply bemused observation to some capability for more regular and controlled practice, then a wide range of applications can be seriously considered, involving an equally wide range of personal and social impact. For example, one can readily extrapolate from the present abilities of those who apparently can perceive remote scenes with remarkable precision, identify equipment and documents in sealed rooms, describe geographical features of a location given merely its map coordinates, and even now are called upon by police and rescue units to locate lost persons or objects. The extent and effectiveness of such applications clearly depends on the number and competence of people who can be found or trained to perform such tasks, which again raises the fundamental issue of what degree of psychic capability is latent in the human race, and susceptible to orderly development.

With regard to applications of psychokinesis in particular, the prognosis is even more clouded, pending more definitive basic experiments and serviceable theoretical models. Disturbing negative applications, such as interference with delicate technological equipment, jump to mind—and have concerned various public and private agencies. More profound and significant, however, is the spectrum of potential personal applications whereby individuals might advantageously modify their immediate environment, and themselves, by this capacity. Already there is a small group of psycho-physiologists who feel that the early cognitive processes of control of body function—muscles, vision, blood flow, etc.—involve a significant component of trial-and-error self-PK, which by maturity has long since become routine and imperceptible. The practical distinction between this view and the more conventional models of infantile learning may not be of major consequence, but in matters of rehabilitation, some useful techniques might evolve. . .

Reflections

Where does all this leave us? At the start we promised a complex fabric of many implausible threads, and I think that has been fulfilled. Also sustained is our promise to advocate nothing, save possibly that we keep our eyes and minds and hearts open to this very new, yet very old, field. Certainly, the experiments are no more than suggestive, the models only vaguely promising, the applications and implications highly speculative. Ultimately, of course, the choice—and in a field such as this, it has to be a personal choice—must be between the assignment of all the inexplicable to mere chance, which is somehow bedazzling hyperromantic minds to delusion of order where there is none, or the acknowledgment of a legitimate, potentially coherent and useful, albeit very elusive, phenomenological domain.

Some 45 years ago, Albert Einstein confessed this same dilemma in his preface to Upton Sinclair's book **Mental Radio:**

> ...The results of the telepathic experiments carefully and plainly set forth in this book stand surely far beyond those which a mature investigator holds to be thinkable. On the other hand, it is out of the question in the case of so conscientious an observer and writer as Upton Sinclair that he is carrying on a conscious deception of the reading world; his good faith and dependability are not to be questioned...

One might turn to historical analogies for insight, for there are certainly many examples of original inexplicable phenomena gradually congealing into an established science and then into a useful technology. Take the field of electricity and magnetism mentioned earlier. At the same time the Greeks were consulting their Delphic Oracle, they were also rubbing amber to get static electrical effects, using lodestones to navigate their boats, and observing an occasional lightning bolt in the sky. They had no Maxwell's equations, not even a Coulomb's law, let alone television sets or hydroelectric generators. Those came much later.

Again at Princeton, the physicist Joseph Henry was repeatedly criticized by his peers for undertaking experiments that violated established scientific principles and common sense, yet we now live by many implementations of those same unreasonable ideas.

The choice between assignment of the mysteries to thoughtless chance, or to a more purposeful higher order, has occupied many thinkers and authors though the ages. One of my favorite opinions on the subject is voiced by Schiller's epic hero Wallenstein at the time of his impending tragic death:

> **Es gibt keinen Zufall; und was uns blindes Ohngefahr nur duenkt, gerade das steigt aus den tiefsten Quellen.** ("There is no such thing as chance; and that which seems to us blind accident, actually stems from the deepest source of all.")

Some day in the future the question may be posed whether it is proper and productive for a university such as Princeton to involve itself to any significant degree in so slippery, soggy, and suspect a field as psychic research, and there will doubtless be many opinions on this. My own is not at all fully formed, but there has hung on my wall for the past six years a statement which may have some relevance at that time:

> In the long history of civilization there are always strong pressures in favor of low-level sorts of conformity—pressures against unorthodoxy, individuality, and self-won responsibility. And all the while from left and from right aggressive voices proclaim that truth and virtue are theirs alone. But there is one place above all where it is (or should be) possible for men to think and act as their own reasoned judgment and best conscience dictate— namely, a university. Here it is that the willingness to think otherwise, to

dream, to question, and to dare should flourish.

If an utter stranger to our civilization should ask: "Where in your society can a person disagree with impunity with accepted practices, dogmas and doctrines?" the answer should be, "The universities. That is part of their being. Their role is to conserve the best of the past and to look forward from it. On both counts they are committed to freedom for the individual, the dignity of the human person, and tolerance toward dissent within broad and agreed upon limits."

This is signed by the U. S. Ambassador to India and president emeritus of Princeton University, the Honorable Robert F. Goheen '40.

At the very least, I do hope that you have enjoyed sharing our brief exposure to the psychic tapestry; that the colors have not been too garish for your taste, or the pattern too bizarre; and that some of you may now care to hold the cloth in your own hands, and attempt your own interpretation of its message.

Professor of Astronomy A. E. Roy at the University of Glasgow, Scotland, was quoted in an article in the *National Enquirer* (April 29, 1980) concerning the PK abilities of Robert Halpern. We wrote to him concerning the report and he responded in a letter, June 24, 1980, stating that the article was substantially correct and that he would not wish to change any of the statements made.

"I am well aware of the incredible skill of a stage magician, but Robert Halpern is a stage hypnotist and does not use any stage magician tricks in his profession. He does not make any professional use of this ostensible psychokinesis talent he has; in fact he seems rather puzzled by it. When I saw him with Alison Goodall, who brought him to my attention, we were careful to observe him throughout the two hours we spent with him. There seems no reason to doubt the evidence of our eyes, namely, that from a distance of about four feet he managed to rotate a matchbox through about 100° or that in the kitchen, from a distance of over 12 feet, he was able to slide a milk bottle a distance of about 12 inches or more across a table top.

"I hope to continue my investigation of Mr. Halpern perhaps under more stringent conditions, for I do believe that it is of great importance to study people with these ostensible talents."

"I know Professor Hasted and have been greatly interested in the work he is doing with metal bending. It seems to me that the more hard evidence we can collect about the possession by certain people of this psychokinetic ability, the more we will be able to understand what it is all about."

Investigators of Psychic Phenomena

Listing and describing briefly the work of all investigators of psychic phenomena today—not to mention those in earlier times—would be an impossible task. Presented here are names and addresses of some individuals and organizations in ten countries where outstanding work has been done. Anyone interested in more information can write to them directly. Since most investigators work with very limited budgets, any contribution toward postage and reprint costs is always appreciated. For a more detailed listing, the American Society for Psychical Research may be contacted, or refer to the appropriate section in *New Psychic Frontiers: Your Key to New Worlds* by Uphoff & Uphoff.

CANADA

New Horizons Research Foundation
P. O. Box 427, Station F, Toronto, Ontario M4Y 2L8
Prof. A.R.G. Owen, chairman of the Executive Council; Dr. Joel F. Whitton, psychiatrist, chairman of Research Committee; Iris M. Owen, secretary-treasurer; and others conduct research and publish findings related to PSI phenomena. They were part of a larger team who investigated Matthew Manning's psychic abilities in 1974.

Dr. Bernard Grad, Allan Memorial Institute, McGill University, Montreal, Canada

Prof. Duncan Blewett, Room C214, University of Saskatchewan, Regina, Saskatchewan S4S OA2 is investigating the extent to which the "psychic energies" of a group are greater than the sum of the energies of the same persons individually.

ENGLAND

The Society for Psychical Research, (Founded in 1882)
1 Adam and Eve Mews, London W8 6UG

The Paraphysical Laboratory, Downton, Wiltshire, England
Benson Herbert, the director, edits *The Journal of Parapsychics,* an international publication.

Prof. John B. Hasted, Dept. of Physics
Birkbeck College, University of London, Malet Street, London WE1E 7HX

Prof. Celia Green, Institute of Psychophysical Research, 118 Banbury Road, Oxford, England.

GERMANY

Prof. Dr. Hans Bender, Institute for the Border Areas of Psychology, 7800 Freiburg i. Br., Eichhalde 12.

Dr. Friedbert Karger, physicist, Plasma-Physik Institut, Garching bei Munich, Germany (BRD)

Prof. Dr. Werner Schiebeler, physicist and lecturer in parapsychology. Ravensburg Technical College, 7981 Ravensburg/Torkenweiler,

Torkelweg 2, Germany (BRD)

Prof. Dr. Alfred Stelter, physics and chemistry, Technical University, Dortmund, Germany. Home address: 46 Dortmund/ Holzen, Am Hang 64.

Deutsche Gesellschaft fuer Parapsychologie
2000 Hamburg 60, Fleminstr. 4, Germany (BRD)

Esotera, Postfach 167, 7800 Freiburg im Br., Germany (BRD), An excellent popular magazine dealing with psychic phenomena, reporting, events from all over the world. For those who read German.

HOLLAND

Prof. W. H. C. Tenhaeff, for many years headed the Parapsychology Institute at the University of Utrecht. He was the first full-time professor of parapsychology in Europe. He is best known for his extensive work with Gerard Croiset, Sr., and other paragnosts. **Dr. Martin Johnson,** Sweden, joined the Institute in 1974 to carry on research on parapsychology at Utrecht.

ITALY

Prof. Dr. Ferdinando Bersani, biophysicist, on the faculty of the medical school at the University of Bologna.

Prof. Aldo Martelli, chemist, on the pharmaceutical faculty of the University of Turin.

Dr. Piero Cassoli, parapsychologist, Bologna.

Associazionne Italiana Studi del Paranormale, Via Puggia 47 1, 16131 Genoa, Italy.

Directed by **Count Lelio Galateri.** The society has organized many conferences and television programs. ESOTERA published a series of reports in Nos. 1, 2 and 3, 1980 on psychic phenomena and research in Italy.

JAPAN

The International Association for Religion and Parapsychology, 4-11-7 Inokashira, Mitaka, Tokyo 181. Dr. Hiroshi Motoyama, director.

Japan Nengraphy Association, Dr. Tsutomu Miyauchi, managing director, Awiji-cho 2-25, Kannda, Chioda, Tokyo.

Mr. Yutaka Fukuda, professional photographer, D-61-202, Matsubara 4, Soka City, Saitamaken, Japan

University of Electro-Communications, Prof. Shegemi Sasaki, Dept. of Electrical Engineering, Chofu, Tokyo 122. (Prof. Sasaki is also with the PSI Institute of Japan)

Japan Association for Psichotronic Research, Toshika Nakaoka, president. Residence: 280   284-6 Anagawa-cho, Chiba-shi, Japan

Japan Society for Parapsychology, 26—14 Chun 4, Nakano, Tokyo 164. **Dr. Soji Otani,** psychologist

Dr. Matsumi Suzuki, Aeronautical Instruments Research Institute. (Worked with Nippon TV in producing the documentary on Kiyota and Yamashita.)

THE PHILIPPINES

Philippine Society for Psychical Research, Inc. Dr. Antonio Arneta, Jr., Director, 14th Street, Corner Atlanta, Port Area, Manila, P.I.

SWITZERLAND

Schweizer Parapsycholgische Gessellschaft, Dr. Hans Naegeli-Osjord, Frauenmunsterstr. 8, Zurich.

Schweizerische Vereinigung fuer Parapsychologie, Industriestr. 5, 2555 Bruegg b. Biel; Dr. Theodor Locher, director.

Prof. Alex Schneider, physicist, CH-9000 St. Gallen, Tannenstr. 1

U.S.S.R.

The leading researchers in the Soviet Union are named in the article by Larissa Vilenskaya in the *Appendix*.

UNITED STATES

American Society for Psychical Research
5 West 73rd Street, New York, NY 10023

William E. Cox, 20 Southbrook Drive, Rolla, MO 64501

Dr. Jule Eisenbud, 4634 East 6th Avenue, Denver CO 80220

Humanistic Psychology Institute, 325 Ninth Street, San Francisco, CA 94103, Dr. Stanley Krippner, Director.

Institute of Noetic Sciences (IONS), 600 Stockton Street, San Francisco, CA 94108, Brendan O'Reagan, Director of Research

McDonnell Laboratory for Psychic Research, Washington University, St. Louis, MO 63120, Dr. Peter Phillips, Director.

Mind Science Foundation, 102 W. Rector Street, San Antonio, TX 78216, William Braud, Ph.D., Research Associate.

Psychical Research Foundation, Duke Station, Durham, NC 27706, Dr. Wm. G. Roll, Director.

Stanford Research Institute, 333 Ravenswood Avenue, Menlo Park, CA 94025, Harold E. Puthoff and Russell Targ.

Washington Research Center, 3101 Washington Street, San Francisco, CA 94115, Henry S. Dakin.

XIII. Implications for Society

As is often the case when something new is discovered (although there is no concrete evidence that there is much that is really *new)* the implications are often only after-thoughts. Many still do not seem to comprehend the awesome implications of nuclear fission and fusion. Scientists probing and manipulating our genetic heritage are fascinated by what they have so far learned, but little attention has been given to the implications of this knowledge. Not all discoverers are like Nobel, the inventor of dynamite, who, realizing its power, hoped that it would be used for peaceful purposes.

The power represented by PK also has far-reaching implications. We already know that it has an important role in healing, whether labelled "faith," "spiritual," or "psychic" healing. The fact that it seems to present us with intimations of "help" or "enhancement" from what we call "other dimensions" is for some, even more mind-boggling to contemplate and even more controversial. Several strong psychics we have observed have learned that they can use their psychokinetic abilities to alleviate pain, repair damaged tissues and cure disease. Matthew Manning, the young British psychic discussed in Chapter XII, has ceased using his PK energy to bend metal, etc. for the satisfaction of parapsychological investigators and has turned to healing with considerable success. As mentioned in the interview with Prof. Hasted, he has observed that some of the children he has studied have also tried contact healing with some success. Masuaki Kiyota knows he can help alleviate pain. There are many others who can also do this.

Dr. Barbara Ivanova, a well-known Russian parapsychologist with whom we have corresponded for several years, reports the experiments she had conducted suggest that the energy which produces psychokinetic effects can be transferred from one individual to another, producing a healing effect. She has concluded that "living systems" have the ability to penetrate "through any screen," "at any distance" and that certain talented psychic-healers have the ability to "collect" and "resonate" these energies and to direct them.*

---

*Ivanova, Barbara, "Experimental and Training Work on some Group-Harmonizing Processes with Educating, Creativity-Heightening and Healing Results," a paper presented at the International Congress on Psychotronic Research, Tokyo, 1977.

Her experiences have led her to conclude that this energy can bring about physiological changes such as the normalization of blood pressure, dissolution of calcium in blood vessels, the decrease or disappearance of tumors, stoppage of hemorrhages, rapid or instantaneous coagulation of blood, and suppression of pain. Among the psychological effects she lists development of creativity, relief from tension and stress, increase in activity, increase in energy, improved optimistic attitudes, increased cheerfulness and will to live.

The social effects which could result from the foregoing, if better understood and practiced, could be far-reaching: reduction in illness and negative attitudes, improved family and personal relationships, and positive changes in personality. Greater harmony with the environment and sensitivity toward others would certainly contribute to the common good.

Obviously these are only isolated individual effects; they are indicative, however, of a far-reaching spiritual development, rehabilitation and growth. Such a transformation as indicated here would certainly be welcome in a world beset with severe political, economic and human problems.

A state of mind, according to Dr. Ivanova, creates an energy "field" which, if a group of persons are in harmony and accord, activates creative forces which work on the functions of the mind-body system and permeate the environment in a positive, vitalizing way. Several interesting examples of this come to mind: the Community of Findhorn has demonstrated this on a fairly large scale with the spectacular growth and hardiness of plants in the Northern region of Scotland where climatic conditions are decidedly inhospitable. In England, two healers, a father and daughter* are of the opinion that the healing energy they call the "healing wavelength," which they identify audibly as a highpitched musical tone, is responsible for the growth and exceptional beauty of their garden and their own heightened creativity in poetry and music.

It has been a number of years since Rev. Franklin Loehr wrote *The Power of Prayer on Plants,* and many individuals, school classes and researchers have experimented with "the power of thought" on plants, proving to their satisfaction that loving, prayerful thoughts are conducive to the health and growth of plant life. (Skeptics say this is simply the result of the exhalation of carbon dioxide in the presence of the plants.) The Green Thumb effect was a respected folk knowledge long before the experiments of Baxter, Sauvin and Vogel.

The Bells' awareness of their "healing wavelength" with the accompanying high-pitched tone leads one to speculate that there might

---

*Bell, Alan Fraser and Heather; Formsby, England, *The Healing Wavelength.*

be some connection with the high-pitched sound which was heard in the soundproof studio in which Nippon Television Network filmed the documentary about the two young Japanese psychics, Kiyota and Yamashita. The unexplainable sound tipped off the experimenters to the presence of an electrical wave which they found emanating from the left frontal lobe of the young psychics' brains.

Our mechanized, technological society probably may be not aware of how much truth there is in the ancient wisdom, "As a man thinks, so is he." We may well have lost our understanding of the effectiveness of thought in the molding and shaping of our lives and in the constructive use of our energies, and of the power of directed, concentrated thought, visualization and intent. Might not our understanding of PK and thought, limited as it is, point out new directions for education and rehabilitation as well as healing?

There are implications as well for war and peace which call for a judicious use of these energies. Although government investigation of these abilities is not generally in "the public domain," enough events have come to our attention to indicate that governments are not oblivious to the possible use of psychic energy for both war and peace, but obviously with greater interest in it as an instrument for warfare and "defense." We are familiar with events involving Matthew Manning, Uri Geller, Masuaki Kiyota and the mind-reach research at Stanford Research Institute which indicate that governments here and in England, Japan and Russia are not ignoring the inherent possibilities in PK phenomena, mind travel, "eyeless sight," telepathy, clairvoyance and hypnosis. The Toth* incident showed how carefully the Soviet Union guards parapsychological research. Many psychics have intuitive feelings that they must not use their talent for destructive purposes and have declined to participate in projects which are connected with defense or military preparations.

It is obvious that, to the extent recent discoveries about the mind and its psychic potential are accepted by medicine, psychology and psychiatry, developments and changes in these professions will be vast. New and different concepts of mind/body relationships and the capabilities of the mind and will are involved. The wholistic (holistic) development in medicine has begun moving in this direction at a much faster speed than we expected. It seems to portend a trend toward cooperative care and understanding between a number of the healing professions and away from the fragmentation of specialization, the direction in which these professions were moving.

---

*Robert C. Toth, a **Los Angeles Times** correspondent, was arrested and jailed in Moscow, June 1977, for accepting from a Russian some papers containing information about parapsychology research in the Soviet Union. He was later released.*

The acceptance of the power of mind over matter holds tremendous implications for education, particularly of young children. The recognition of the almost boundless potentials of the mind surely demands very different approaches to education than those presently employed. Above all, limitations should not be imposed on creativity; **much more needs to be learned about the role of visualization and** imagination and mental states in which learning, particularly intuitive learning, takes place. One of the most striking things to be learned from these occurrences of PK talent in children is that by imposing beliefs, we also set limitations on learning and achievement. It is obvious that metal bending activity in children is a product of their belief that it can be done and that disapproval and discouragement inhibit, if not actually obliterate it. Should we not ask ourselves whether adult and social attitudes generally limit many other areas of learning and performance?

—MJU

Some Further Implications

Time will tell to what extent the evidence of psychokinesis will be substantiated and the extent to which it will modify our view of life and of the universe and our relationship to it. At this point there is so much evidence for PK, in spite of the efforts of magicians to replicate such **phenomena with their skills of sleight-of-hand and deception, that the** implications are boundless. Whether the evidence is welcomed or feared has no bearing on the facts; such attitudes can only help to promote or retard its integration into a broader world view of reality.

Insofar as critics can, by selective use of evidence, point to instances of deception or inaccurate interpretation, when trying to dismiss the entire phenomenon of PK, they certainly can delay an acceptance of the concept as a part of our natural universe. Debunkers, by distortion and outright misrepresentation, can also confuse some and intimidate others who would like to know whatever is true. In the long run, the facts will prevail just as the flat-earth theory was replaced by the global concept and as our planet became one of many, instead of remaining the center around which the sun and moon revolved.

We hold no brief whatsoever for dishonesty on the part of either supporters or opponents of PK or any other phenomenon. Such efforts can obscure the facts, but not change them. We hope the first-hand and second-hand evidence we have presented in this book will contribute toward a serious on-going examination of the evidence for PK. Our purpose in writing this book was not to "make money" but to share observations and experiences with the hope that it will be a contribution toward creating a climate in which honesty and integrity in all aspects of life will be rewarded and where persons are not falsely accused of **trickery. Naturally, it is hoped there will be enough income to cover** costs so that investigations can continue. We hope that those who make a mission out of exposing fraud, a laudable objective, will honestly report the evidence they find and not seek to convict by inference, association or generalization.

I remember listening to our storage-battery-operated Atwater—Kent radio on our farm during my early teens (we had no electricity) and hearing Wilbur Glenn Voliva preach that the world was flat even though by that time most people in the United States at least, accepted the fact that it was round, even though it appeared flat. One of our neighbors agreed with Rev. Voliva and could not understand why I accepted my teacher's version instead. After all, didn't the sun rise in the east and set in the west, travelling around the earth once a day? I have often wondered how much different my world of reality would be today if I had stayed on the farm and not gone to the University.

Perhaps one of the reasons many persons, scientists and layman alike, have difficulty accepting concepts which don't fit their view of reality is because their training and experience have provided a model which is adequate and comfortable for them and they would rather not raise questions which would call for fundamental restructuring of their "world."

The evidence we have presented is this book does call for a serious reexamination of concepts which seem to be totally inadequate for the last decades of the twentieth century. Newer concepts will undoubtedly be advanced in years to come that will make what we have written obsolete.

What, How and Why?

Perhaps the greatest impediment to comprehending PK and its implications is that the rational mind tends too quickly to come up with "ultimate" and "final" answers. Many have a tendency to think in terms of "black and white," "yes" and "no." They have difficulty with "grey" and "maybe." They want their world neatly defined, whether it is accurate or not is not important for them, just so long as it is neat. That is why they tend to "pigeon-hole" (either accepting or rejecting) evidence depending on whether or not it fits into their belief system.

It took us a long time to come to that realization ourselves.

First, it is important to determine **WHAT** happened or what the situation is. There may be differences of opinion but on this point objective evidence can be accumulated:

1) Cutlery and other physical objects do exist which have been twisted or bent or misshapen.
2) Images and effects have been produced on photographic film, "which should not have been there," without exposure to light.
3) Persons are at times healed in parnormal and unexplicable ways after having been told that their condition is inoperable or terminal.

Before taking sides, determined to prove or disprove the authenticity of the event, our first step should be to ascertain **WHAT** occurred and to get as much evidence as possible about the circumstances surrounding the event. Then questions can be raised as to whether the phenomenon is genuinely paranormal or whether trickery or deception was used to produce the effect, or whether there was inaccurate observation. Had the spoon been twisted before it was given to the psychic? Was the health condition inaccurately diagnosed, or was there a "spontaneous remission"?

Then one can proceed to the question of **HOW** it might have happened. This question is more difficult to answer but needs to be addressed. It opens up many areas for speculation and it would be foolhardy to think anyone can come up with simple or final answers, but it is certainly worth the effort.

The question of **WHY** remains a mystery of the universe for our finite minds. We may come up with a variety of explanations but that does not mean they provide answers to the question of the ultimate **WHY**. We can use such terms as chemical reactions, electrical discharges, bioplasma, or God's plan, and even though that may satisfy us, it does not give us ultimate answers.

—WHU

In the previous chapter we reported on the work of some other investigators and psychics. In this chapter we quote what others have to say about the implications of PK, based on their knowledge of and/or experiences with the phenomenon, as seen from their vantage point.

The comments we received from several countries and various disciplines are recorded here in alphabetical order.

Prof. Dr. Hans Bender, has for years been the director of the Institut fuer Grenzegebiete der Psychologie u. Psychohygiene, Freiburg, Germany. His internationally-known institute has done much to gain wider acceptance of the paranormal and his research has been extensively reported in the European press and on television. He writes:

I am particularly interested in:

1. *Spontaneous phenomena: the problem of an extra-personal agency in poltergeist cases and haunted houses. I gave an outline of this aspect in my contribution to the symposium on "synchronicity" at the 22nd Parapsychological Association in Moranga, California, August 1979. ("Transcultural Uniformities in Poltergeist Events as Suggested for an Architypical Arrangement.")*

2. *Where the energy comes from for metal bending, etc.: I wonder if the hypothesis can be subject to experimentation that the "medium" gives only an information to the target in question (cutlery, bars,*

etc.) and that this information alters the comportment (behavior) of the molecules. This would mean that energy is produced by the object itself under the influence of "information" received by PK.

3. *Research on the influence of PK on living organisms: Pilot studies with Jean-Pierre Girard suggested that he can influence* coli bacteria *in a way that growth is suppressed. This could be of an eminent practical importance: PK—gifted healers could possibly stop the growth of cancer tissues, etc. We need gifted subjects and finances for research on a broad basis.*

Uri Geller, the young Israeli whose PK abilities were called to the attention of the Western world by Andrija Puharich, M.D. about a decade ago, and whose feats have been studied at Stanford Research Institute and witnessed by many thousands at public demonstrations and by millions on television, wrote:

"In the distant future PK will be a part of everyone's daily life. It will be a common place thing as using the telephone is now. Individuals will be able to influence matter with the power of their minds which will enable them to teleport objects to where they want them without lifting a finger. I would dare to say that they will also be able to teleport themselves therefore eliminating transportation vehicles such as airplanes, cars, trains, ships, etc. The human mind will be more highly developed and powerful enough through generating PK, allowing doctors in the medical field to be able to stop diseases, illnesses, etc. or even totally preventing them from happening. The progress to be made by PK is limitless. It will only make this world a better place to live in. And hopefully as years pass people will allow the force of PK to enter their minds expanding the horizons of the future."

Marshall F. Gilula, M.D., a psychiatrist and neurologist, heads Life Energies Research Institute in Coconut Grove, Florida. From May 14 to July 22, 1978 he was in Moscow on an American-Soviet biofeedback study, a project approved in 1975 by the John E. Fogarty International Center for Advanced Study in the Health Sciences (NIH), under the U.S.-U.S.S.R. Individual Health Exchange Program.

This phenomenon is merely a reflection of how fast evolution (including molecular-genetic effects) is going. Groups of these individuals may reflect very special molecular-genetic mutations or other quite specific training of latent abilities. The majority of PK phenomena may well reflect an overall elevation from a planetary viewpoint. These "lower psychic" abilities are cousins to clairvoyance, clairaudience, and a host of other so-called extrasensory abilities which merely REFLECT, in peripheral fashion, what is going on in the central inner portion of the being.

PK may also be described as an ability which can be learned by social imitation **period** *if the learner has a sufficiently susceptible nervous system (from a developmental point of view) and if the learner has been raised in a psycho-social setting which does not view PK as abnormal or unpermissable behavior.*

M. J. Martin, M.D., Chairman of the Department of Psychiatry and Psychology at the Mayo Clinic, Rochester, Minnesota, arranged for some tests of Masuaki Kiyota and Hiroto Yamashita while they were our guests in 1979.

It seems that every thinking person has questions concerning unknown phenomena. Since psychokinesis has not been satisfactorily proved from the scientific standpoint, it remains an unknown phenomenon. The innate curiosity of people for the better understanding of unknown conditions will continue to cause ongoing interest in this subjct. It is implied that there is a power that is not clearly explained in the production of the metal bending phenomenon. A better understanding of this power might result in a better understanding of the working of the the human mind. An understanding of the intricacies of the human mind is in its infancy. Much is to be learned and perhaps a better understanding of psychokinesis would be one more piece of the jig-saw puzzle in the understanding of the complexities of the mind. It is apparent that continued research is necessary in this interest that fascinates both believers and skeptics alike.

Jeffrey Mishlove, Ph.D., author of ***The Roots of Consciousness: Psychic Liberation Through History, Science and Experience*** (Random House 1975), was the first American to receive a Ph.D. in parapsychology. He works with the Washington Research Center, San Francisco, and teaches at John F. Kennedy University, Orinda, California.

Psychic abilities seem to be distributed normally throughout the population like other natural talents such as musical or athletic talents. Of course, when a young child shows musical or athletic promise, we have an extensive and integrated system of family support, peer support, role models, training, and institutional encouragement. This is not yet the case with psychokinetic talents.

It is my hope that within the next fifty years, we will develop extensive cultural programs for the cultivation of psychic abilities and their practical application in areas of benefit to humanity—medical healing and diagnosis, locating oil and minerals, archeology, crime detection and prevention, business forecasting, weather forecasting and control.

I believe that if humanity survives, such a development is inevitable. The interesting question for me is whether it will happen in our lifetime.

Dr. Tsutomu Miyauchi, Tokyo, a physicist who is also an official in the Japan Nengraphy Association, has worked with young Japanese psychics for a number of years, investigating their ability to paranormally influence film by PK. It was Dr. Miyauchi who made the arrangements to film Masuaki Kiyota when we first met the family while Alan Neuman was making the film, "Exploring the Unknown" in October 1976.

> *I am completely convinced of Masuaki Kiyota's PK abilities after conducting over 200 experiments during a period of three years. Hiroto Yamashita has demonstrated similar abilities. At this point we are speculating that this may be an "inverse energy." It is a well-known fact that photographic film turns black when non-exposed film is exposed to the energy of light from outside. We have found that an already exposed· photographic film returns to a non-exposed condition when exposed to this inverse energy. A heat-holding substance becomes cold when exposed to this inverse energy. If our study of this phenomenon completely supports our speculations, it will mean that concepts of physiology will have to be drastically altered.*

Dr. med. Hans Naegeli, a psychiatrist and parapsychologist in Zurich, Switzerland, had personally investigated and filmed psychic surgery in the Philippines and worked with many parapsychologists in Europe. He is a leader in the Swiss Parapsychological Association and author of *Die Logurgie in den Philippinen* (Otto Reichl Verlag, Remagen, Germany 1977) and many articles on the paranormal.

> *The phenomena of Materialization, Psychokinesis and Psychoplastic* prove that mind is over matter. Matter is a form of energy. Energy in physics cannot disappear but only change. So the energy of the mind does not disappear but only changes. This is the most striking evidence for immortality!*

> **Psychokinesis should be limited to movement, a change of place. When a change of form or aggregate occurs by mental means, I call that Psychoplastic.*

> *All spiritual healing and psychic surgery (Logurgia) is based on the concept of psychoplastic, whether chemical, physical or biological. The phenomenon requires a change of consciousness of the healer, reaching higher dimensions. Every psychic-healing is based on the harmonization of the "subtle" body.*

Dr. Werner Schiebeler is professor of physics and electronics at the Fachhochschule fuer Technik in Ravensburg, German. He has, for many years, taught courses on parapsychology for adults and is a frequent contributor to parapsychology journals in Europe. The Institute for Scientific Films at Goettingen, Germany, commissioned him, together with Dr. Hans Naegeli, Prof. B. Kirchgaessner and Katharina Nager to produce a film on psychic surgery in the Philippines. The film, made in 1973, was awarded first prize by an

Italian film society.

> *Telekinesis and psychokinesis show that there are possibilities for influencing matter and transferring energies, unfamiliar in today's physics and not likely to be fully understood for a long time. Precise research on the dynamics of PK should contribute significantly toward expanding the theoretical structure of physics.*
>
> *It is possible in that in the development of theories of parapsychology, when studying parapsychological phenomena, a situation will develop similar to that which exists in present-day physics; namely that theories or models are developed which may appear parallel or contradictory, such as the corpuscular vs. wave theory of light. It should be possible to formulate a unified theory broad enough to incorporate everything that happens in nature.*

Alex Schneider, Prof. Diplom. Ing. ETH, of St. Gallen, Switzerland, has been investigating unusual phenomena for a long time. We first met him at the 1968 Parapsychological Association convention in Freiburg, Germany, and then at the home of Dr. Konstantin Raudive in nearby Bad Krozingen. He has been interested in the entire field of parapsychology and has lectured frequently at conferences on the implications of the electronic taped voice phenomenon.

> *If we want to learn something about the characteristics of PK, we must follow the approach of scientists and undertake basic experiments such as Professor Hasted has done, even though some critics consider such investigations as "metal-bending" banal. Only then will we be able to establish whether the phenomena of energy and information transfer can be adequately explained within the present-day theories of physics. A study of para-phenomena could provide the stimulus and support for developing a better and more comprehensive view of the universe.*
>
> *When looking beyond the "banal" effects of metal-bending to its broader implications, it could have world-wide implications. The age-old question of Body/Soul, which scientists and philosophers have dealt with for centuries can be approached from a new perspective if we find that there is an independent psyche beyond the physical brain. Then phenomena such as paranormal healing, materialization, thoughtography, etc. will be better understood.*

Mark G. Shafer, School of Social Sciences, University of California, Irvine, has videotaped many sessions with mental-benders. A paper about these experiments, prepared especially for our workshops on PK, is presented in full in the *Appendix.*

> *The existence of PK phenomena implies that there exists a fundamental connection between human consciousness and the physical universe currently unrecognized by present psychological and physical theory. The presence of the PK anomaly acts as a stimulus for re-formulation of current theories to account for the anomalous occurrence. PK research thus implies that a revision of **both** psychological and physical theory is*

*forthcoming, though **when** is unclear and not implied. **What** that theoretical revision will be and what implications it will contain is likewise moot, especially given the present sparseness of findings on PK phenomena. What seems one of the most likely possibilities to me, however, is that we may realize that we play a larger part in **creation** of reality than we imagine now, whether it be physical health, environmental conditions, or personal and interpersonal experience.*

Prof. Mulford Q. Sibley has for years been professor of political science at the University of Minnesota. He has accumulated extensive data on the paranormal through the years and teaches a course in parapsychology at the University. He is the general editor of a series on **Psychic Explorations** published by Dillion Press, Minneapolis, and authored one of the series, **Life After Death?**

I have observed some of the work of Kiyota and Yamashita and have read much of Dr. Robert Cantor's book on British psycho-kinetic children. My comments are based on these experiences, against the background of a strong interest in and teaching of psychical phenomena.

It seems to me that there is a strong presumption of genuine PK ability in these cases—of "mind over matter." What is more, certain types of PK phenomena seem to go together in given persons—healing and metal-bending, for example; or metal bending and thoughtography. I tend to believe that all of us have these capacities in a measure, although in a few of us it is almost at "genius" level.

But we really don't have definite, clear-cut answers to many of the questions we might pose. For example,

"What tends to 'trigger' discovery of the powers?"

"Is there a correlation between certain personality types and PK capacities?"

"Is the factor of age an important one? Is there a tendency for PK capacity to be concentrated in the young? Does it 'fade' as the person grows older (somewhat like fading memories of alleged previous incarnations)?"

"To what degree can we train a person's PK capacities?"

For centuries we have strongly suspected PK abilities in certain persons. Now we are subjecting those abilities to more systematic testing. I would hope that we might conceivably open up the possibilities for much greater knowledge of mental and spiritual healing, to cite only one field. Both scientifically and philosophically one of our great unsolved issues is what we have called the "mind-body" problem. Studies of PK metal benders, healers, and thoughtographers should help cast new light on this ancient puzzle. From the viewpoint of Physics, it should be obvious that metal bending PK could be of enormous interest.

It just could be that we are on the verge of new discoveries which will be of great significance not only for parapsychology but also for more 'normal' or orthodox science as well.

Alfred Stelter, Ph.D. teaches physics and chemistry at Dortmund Technical University, Germany. He has studied parapsychology and written books and articles on the subject, and travelled extensively in the United States, Europe, Russia, Asia and the Pacific Islands.

Last October 21 I had occasion to participate, together with a Swiss biophysicist, in a discussion of paraphysical phenomena. During the discussion, the handle of a pewter pitcher became detached at the top and straightened out with no one near it. I took the pitcher and noted that the handle was pliable and could easily be bent back and forth. I have worked in laboratories long enough to be thoroughly familiar with the physical properties of pewter. I know that this metal is brittle and should normally break rather than bend. The handle was later bent back to its normal position where it hardened and has remained that way. When one witnesses PK effects, where there is no chance of trickery, one's view of reality is naturally expanded.

F. A. Popp, a German biophysicist, appears to have established the fact that electromagnetic waves play a decisive role in the life process of plants. When we remind ourselves that the Lasar principle is known to man only for several decades but that nature very likely used that same principle for millions of years in the development of living cell aggregates, we should not be so certain that we have all the answers.

Prof. William A. Tiller, Department of Materials Science and Engineering, Stanford University, is undoubtedly one of the foremost investigators of new frontiers of knowledge. He has published extensively on radionics and radiasthesia, on "the Varieties of Healing Experiences," "Energy Fields and the Human Body," "Corona Discharge Photography," "The Positive and Negative Space-Time Frames as Conjugate Systems," etc. He has travelled extensively, including a trip to the Soviet Union and a sabbatical year in England. He is a much sought-after speaker for health and New Age conferences.

1. *Human mental intention is a force, at some level of the universe, which is capable of significantly perturbing the stability state of material systems at the physical level.*

2. *Other energies function in the universe than those presently acknowledged by conventional science.*

3. *The universe is much richer in structure than presently acknowledged by the prevailing "world view."*

4. *Humans have capacities far beyond those acknowledged by prevailing sentiment.*

Larissa Vilenskaya, Israel, is both a parapsychologist and a healer. She emigrated from the Soviet Union in 1979 where she had been involved with a number of other investigators of the paranormal. In response to our invitation to submit a brief statement on PK, she sent to us an article (with photos) about research in PK in the U.S.S.R. which we are happy to include in the *Appendix* of this book.

Implications for Healing and Psychiatry

The statements from Dr. Hans Bender, Dr. Marshall Gilula, Dr. Hans Naegeli, and Professors Schiebeler and Stelter all stress the potential value of PK in healing.

The body-mind split that, to a large extent, still separates physicians who deal with the body and those who deal with the mind is less wide since the writings of Dr. John Schindler on EEI* (emotionally-induced illness) became widely published in the Fifties. The term, 'psychosomatic' is now used to label many health problems; there is more emphasis on holistic health which, for some, includes the use of psychics and healers.

In December 1979, William Singer, professor of ethnopsychiatry at Oakland University, Rochester, Michigan spent $6,000 personally to bring Juan Blanche, a Filipino psychic healer, and two of his assistants to the United States to perform "psychic surgery" under scientific observation. The results were encouraging enough that associate professor of medical anthropology, Kate Ankenbrandt, who has chosen "psychic surgery" as her topic for a Ph.D. dissertation, is taking the initiative to raise funds for bringing Blanche back for a second series of demonstration sessions. (Those interested in supporting that project or getting more information about it can write to Prof. William Singer, Oakland University, Rochester, Michigan, 48063.)

Reports of paranormal healing come from all over the world. Maurice Barbanell, editor of *Psychic News,* London, recently sent an article from a French publication, *Nice-Matin,* which reported that *Tass,* the official Soviet news agency, released a story about a psychic healer, Vladimir Safonov, a retired building engineer. He was reported to have the "extraordinary gift" of diagnosing and treating illnesses, *Tass* said, by running his hands about four inches above the body to detect past and present ailments. Safonov, whose abilities Soviet scientists are trying to explain, also diagnoses by photos. The engineer believes that humans have a "bioenergetic field" around them which alters according to the physical state and that somehow he can transfer to them some of his "bioenergy."

The story of Arigo, "the surgeon of the rusty knife," a Brazilian

---

*Schindler, John, M.D., **How to Live 365 Days a Year,** Prentice-Hall, 1954.

psychic who performed many amazing feats of healing, has been written by John Fuller, Dr. Andrija Puharich and others and has appeared in books and publications throughout the world.

David St. Clair's book, *Psychic Healers: True Stories of America's Most Unusual Healers* (Doubleday, 1974) tells about eleven unusual healers and the varied ways in which they work.

During our travels we have been fortunate to observe well-known healers in several part of the world, to talk with patients treated by them—in some cases to be successfully treated ourselves—and to record the events on film and tape. Persons who have never had such an experience understandably may have difficulty integrating such a statement into their views of reality. People tend to call something that is not understood a miracle—that is, if they do not dismiss it as trickery or deception. In medicine, the terms "spontaneous remission" and "inaccurate diagnosis" are substituted. For myself, miracles are a matter of defining reality in terms broad enough to encompass what we may not understand—considering "miracles" a part of the nature of a much greater, more magnificent universe than we have learned about so far. Certainly there are dimensions beyond our limited five senses. How much more restricted would our views of the universe be if we had no microscopes or telescopes?

We have witnessed Olga Worrall, the well-known healer from Baltimore, Maryland; Harry Edwards, George Chapman, John Cain and Rose and Peter Gladden of England; Gerard Croiset, Sr., of Utrecht, Holland; Dr. Hiroshi Motoyama, in Tokyo, Japan; Vergilio Guiterres, Max Piodos, Josefina Sison, David Oligane, Eleuterio Terte, and Neives Jimenes (a co-worker of Tony Agpaoa) all of the Philippines, work with people who sought relief from pain or illnesses which did not yield to conventional treatment. Walter was successfully treated by Vergilio Guiterres in the Philippines for a severe bursitus condition in his left shoulder; Mary Jo had a poorly attached ligament of the ankle, which was unlikely to be improved by surgery, "repaired." Walter witnessed Rev. Harold Plume, who was described in St. Clair's book, penetrate bodies with an apparently "elongated finger" to heal persons seeking help and personally experienced the phenomenon—an experience he cannot even now fully comprehend.

With the aid of electron microscopes and more sensitive monitoring and measuring equipment, scientists have learned much about life processes, health, energy and matter—mysteries only a short time ago. More and more people, including physicians who treat illnesses of the body, and psychiatrists, who deal with the illnesses of "the mind," are willing to look at other approaches to healing today. To what extent these alternative modalities will supplement and/or replace present practices only time will tell. The concept that we should strive for maximum wellness in body, mind and spirit rather than functioning below our highest potential, is growing—as evidenced by the numbers who are becoming interested in preventive care, better nutrition, changed life styles, a clean environment and alternative modalities of treatment. To the extent that psychics are willing to work with practitioners of the healing arts, and to the extent that those who practice conventional medicine are willing to examine the results of unconventional treatment, we can expect to come closer to developing methods which incorporate whatever works—whatever offers the best promise for success and the least risk.

Space permits citing only one example of such working together;

Matthew Manning, Linton, England, one of the most gifted young psychics we have come to know very well during the last six years, decided several years ago to channel his PK ability (bending metal, automatic writing, etc.) into healing—with considerable success. Between January 9 and 26, 1978, Matthew participated in a series of experiments with Dr. John Kmetz, a physiologist who was at that time director of research at the Science Unlimited Foundation in San Antonio, Texas. These experiments were part of a larger series of tests arranged by Dr. William Braud, experimental psychologist and research associate with the Mind Science Foundation in the same city.

Almost two years later, January 2, 1980, *The National Enquirer* carried a feature story, "Psychic Healer Destroys Cancer Cells With Mind Power in Scientific Tests," reporting how Matthew was able, in repeated tests, to dislodge cancer cells from the side of a plastic flask by "mind power" when he held it in his hands for 10 to 20 minutes and also when concentrating on it from another room.

Dr. Kmetz is quoted as saying, "If psychic healers can somehow affect how these cells are growing, they should be able to use the same effect on people directly."

Brief news items can never adequately relate the whole story and to some extent we are hampered also by limitations of space, but here are additional details:

According to Matthew Manning, the experiment was designed to measure whether he could influence the death rate of cancer cells by PK. Kemtz told a TV interviewer in San Antonio, while Matthew still was in the city, about the experiments and explained that ". . .the flask itself has a negative charge; the cells on the other hand, have a positive charge on their cell surface. This positive-negative attraction maintains the cells, then, on the surface of the flask. The individuals that I've been working with can apparently disrupt this charge on the surface of the cell and thus cause the cells to float free into the medium in which the cells have been grown. . .the magnetic field is not necessarily being disrupted. What one is disrupting is the charge on the surface of the cell. In order for the cell to have this charge it must be maintained as an active metabolising cell. If he can somehow disrupt the metabolism of the cell and thus cause it to decrease for some reason or other, then you can decrease the charge which is on the surface of the cell and cause the cell to float free. . ."

According to Manning, "it was quite clear that Kmetz believed he was observing a paranormal effect at the time of the tests." When Manning was back in the U.S. two months later, he telephoned John Kmetz, April 15th, to find out how the report on the experiments was progressing. "He was still very enthusiastic about the work and was keen to have it replicated elsewhere." He repeated his intention of submitting his report, which he claimed to be writing at the time, to *Science* magazine.

Manning waited for months to see Kmetz' findings published. Then he heard that he was writing an article for *The Skeptical Inquirer*. After a year Matthew wrote to Mr. G. W. Church, a supporter of the foundation where Kmetz had worked, saying in part: "I do get very exasperated with researchers who waste my unpaid time on work that never gets reported. . ." He got a reply from Gary Heseltine, a research associate which said, in part: "A couple of days after your departure last year, it was found that larger numbers of cells could be dislodged by a *light* finger tap or by properly agitating the flask. Thus the conclusion that a paranormal influence was involved cannot be drawn because of the manner in which the experiments was concluded. . ."*

"If the discovery had been made 'a couple of days' after I left Texas," Matthew wondered, ". . .why did Kmetz maintain his belief in the experiment to the point of suggesting that he would submit his report for publication in *Science, two months later?*"And, of course, this did not explain how Matthew had influenced the death rate of cancer cells from a distance.

The December 1979 issue of *The Journal of the Society for Psychical Research*** carried an article by Dr. Braud, Gary Davis and Robert Wood, entitled "Experiments with Matthew Manning." It reported experiments in which Matthew was able to influence the behavior of gerbils and small knife fish (*Gymnous carapo)* by PK, as well as the rate of haemolysis of human blood. It was this latter experiment which caused Braud to write:

> *"We have had the privilege of observing first-hand the experiments of Dr. John Kmetz of the Science Unlimited Research Foundation in San Antonio. Cervical cancer cells are cultured in specially prepared plastic flasks. "Healthy" cancer cells adhere to the plastic surface of the flask by*

---

* Private communication, January 22, 1979.

**Journal of the Society for Psychical Research, 1 Adam and Eve Mews, London. W8 6UG.

means of an electrostatic force. Changes in metabolism, the injury, or the death of the cells disturbs their normal positive charge, causing them to lose their attraction to the negatively charged flask wall and slough off into the surrounding fluid medium. Microscopic counts of the number of cells in the medium provide measure of the "state of health" of the cultures. M. M. was able to exert quite dramatic influences upon these cancer cells cultures, ranging in magnitude from 200 to 1,200 per cent changes, compared with appropriate controls. Most of these effects followed M.M's "laying on of hands" on the experimental flask for a 20 min. period. However, strong effects also occurred when M. M. never touched the flask, but attempted to influence the cultures at a distance, while confined in an electrically shielded room.

Dr. Kmetz' willingness to talk for publication almost two years after the experiments, after he had apparently changed his mind about the significance of the tests, and then reversed himself again, illustrates the pressures the "scientifically trained" mind is often under to "stay afloat" within a skeptical environment.

When Matthew Manning was at our home in September 1979, he was anticipating working with a physician in London, in an experiment involving 30 leukemia patients. Ten were to receive no attention from Matthew; he was to go through the motions of treating the second group of ten; and to exert "healing effort" on the third group. The experiment was called off in favor of a less traumatic experiment involving non-life threatening ailments. As the results of such experiments are made known, we will learn more about the extent to which PK can play a role in healing.

Implications for War and Peace

Most discoveries and inventions have potential for both contructive and destructive use. Although some have hailed the splitting of the atom as a boon to Mankind and as a deterrent to war (because nuclear war is presumably too horrible to contemplate), the proliferation of nuclear technology has created a veritable nightmare for the inhabitants of Planet Earth.

Although psychokinesis is not as well understood as nuclear fission is at this time, what is known about it suggests that it is potentially at least as important a "genie out of the bottle" as nuclear energy but, as far as we know, does not have the same lethal properties of radioactive bombs and waste materials. It is obvious that this little understood power of PK is not being ignored by the super-powers in their desperate drive to achieve or maintain military superiority—even though the public is certainly not privy to all that is going on in this area either in the United States or in the Soviet Union.

Our hope is that Mankind will somehow assert itself and tell the heads of their governments that war is not the answer to the differences in ideologies and political and economic systems, and that the outmoded concept of the nation-state keeps us from recognizing that we are all on the same "boat" (Planet Earth). When a ship springs a leak, its crew and passengers quickly forget other issues and concentrate on keeping the ship afloat. It is high time that the military, economic and political leaders of all countries recognize that they, as well as those they send to war, will be doomed if the ultimate weapons are unleashed.

The amazing ability to influence matter by PK, to twist metal, scramble magnetic tape, etc. have such far-reaching implications that it is understandable, though regretable, that the military mentality, no matter in what country, should think that this power might be utilized as part of their arsenal.

The Colorado Daily at the University of Colorado carried the following article October 14, 1976.

Pentagon researching psychic defense

(ZNS) Will mind-reading become just another military weapon? *Science Digest* magazine reports that the Pentagon is actively looking into the possibility that Extra Sensory Perception could become a major component of arms of the future, and is going so far as to fund a number of private psychic research projects.

According to the magazine, several branches of the defense department are interested in scientific studies into "astral projection" which indicate that the human mind can leave the body and witness events taking place in other parts of the world.

Reported experiments at Stanford Research Institute in Menlo Park, and at the University of California at Davis indicate that it might even be normal for most individuals to possess psychic powers.

The Navy is reportedly interested in what is called "remote viewing," which is defined as the ability to spot or monitor potential military targets anywhere on earth using only clairvoyance.

Science Digest states that military researchers are also interested in reports that certain psychics, like Israeli silverware curler Uri Geller, can use their mental powers to bend objects or even to erase magnetic tapes.

If a person could in fact erase tapes through mental processes, it follows that this gift would enable the individual to wipe out entire defense systems which are coordinated by computers using magnetic tape.

But these types of psychic powers could have their drawbacks, says Berkeley Ph.D. candidate in parapsychology Jeffrey Mishlove, who believes that anyone with the ability to jam up computer systems through the use of mental magic "would probably have to be destroyed." Mishlove adds, however, that "if this hypothetical psychic were truly talented, death probably wouldn't even stop him."

Three and a half years earlier, *TIME* magazine, March 12, 1973, in an article entitled, "The Magician and the Think Tank," reported that the U. S. Department of Defense had sent three investigators to Stanford Research Institute of California to observe tests conducted with Uri Geller by Dr. Harold Puthoff and Dr. Russell Targ. Those sent by the Department of Defense included Ray Hyman, a psychology professor at the University of Oregon, who was later to become one of the articulate members of CSICOP; George Lawrence, Department of Defense, projects manager for the Advanced Research Projects Agency (AFPA); and Robert Van de Castle, a University of Virginia psychologist and researcher in parapsychology. Hyman and Lawrence were not impressed, while Van de Castle said that Geller was an interesting subject for further study.

Having seen frequent news items about research in parapsychology at Stanford Research Institute, we wrote our Congressman, Robert Kastenmeier, asking if he could get any information on the amount of funding awarded to SRI for research in paranormal phenomena. His reply, the pertinent part of which is reproduced here, indicates that records kept by the four agencies mentioned in the letter are either incredibly vague, or they are not telling the Congressman the whole story.

BOB KASTENMEIER
2D DISTRICT, WISCONSIN

2232 HOUSE OFFICE BUILDING
PHONE: AREA CODE 202, 225-2906

HOME OFFICE:
SUITE 505
119 MONONA AVENUE
MADISON, WISCONSIN 53703
PHONE: AREA CODE 608, 264-5206

COMMITTEE ON
JUDICIARY

CHAIRMAN, SUBCOMMITTEE ON
COURTS, CIVIL LIBERTIES AND
THE ADMINISTRATION OF JUSTICE
SUBCOMMITTEE ON CRIME

COMMITTEE ON
INTERIOR AND INSULAR AFFAIRS

SUBCOMMITTEES ON:
NATIONAL PARKS AND
INSULAR AFFAIRS

Congress of the United States
House of Representatives
Washington, D.C. 20515

March 25, 1980

Mr. Walter H. Uphoff
Route 1
Oregon, Wisconsin 53575

Dear Mr. Uphoff:

. . . .
Regarding Stanford Research Institute's research in parapsychology and/or psychic phenomena, the digging did not produce much here. It was suggested that possible contracts may have gone out from National Science Foundation, National Institutes of Health, the Department of Defense, or the National Academy of Sciences. However, each one queried said that the print-outs on their outside contracts were not specific enough to tell just what the research involved.

A call to the local office of SRI elicited the suggestion that it was probable that such research was classified, and would generally not be open to public inspection.

. . . .

Sincerely,

ROBERT W. KASTENMEIER
Member of Congress

RWK:ac

The report he got from the Washington office of SRI indicated *"that it was probable that such research was classified,"* [emphasis added]— this seven years after *TIME* magazine tried to minimize the potential significance of research on psychic abilities. This does not surprise us because there is abundant evidence that similar investigations are going on in the Soviet Union. What does disturb us is that the leaders of both nations are still so immature as to think that weapons solve problems.

Our correspondence with Masuaki Kiyota and his father has continued since Masuaki and Hiroto Yamashita were our guests during the summer of 1970. On November 21, 1979, Masuaki wrote:

> *"I was experimented for my psychic power by Prof. Otani who teaches psychology at the Defense Academy...and of course Prof. Sasaki of the* **University of Electro-Communications also keeps on experimenting...** *I am experimented from the outside of myself and the inside of myself..."*

On December 12, 1979, Masuaki's father wrote:

> *"Lately, Prof. Otani's group of the Defense Academy—the military college in Japan—began to study PK with Masuaki. On last experiment in the hospital attached to this college, Masuaki could project Nengraphy and twist spoons, while he was hooked up with electroencephalographic machines. And then, the electroenchephalogram readings showed the unusual concentration of mind. This test was not the one experimented at NTV by Dr. Matsumi Suzuki—the test demonstrate electric waves emitting from the head—but the same electroencephalographic test as the Mayo Medical Center had tried. I also want to inform you that Prof. Otani's study is not aimed at the military use.*

> *"The very extraordinary twisted fork which Masuaki had succeeded in twisting in your country and brought back with him to show me, surprised me so much. Masuaki's PK, I think will still continue to evolve powerfully.*

> *"On November 30 and on December 7, Masuaki spoke through the* **radio—each 30-minute programs entitled 'Challenge the Unknown'. In** *this program he changed sound frequencies with PK and surprised the people attending to this program..."*

On January 28, 1980, he wrote again:

> *"Lately Masuaki reversed the North of a compass to the South—The* **North showed the South. And their directions are still reversed. One of** *these days, Masuaki is to go to the Defense Academy, and to stay for two days at the hospital or some other place attached to the college, and to work together with Prof. Otani's group..."*

Since I felt that Masuaki had been maligned by Mike Hutchinson— first in the article in *The Skeptical Inquirer* and then in his letter to

FATE magazine, (Chapter X), I sent a copy of the Hutchinson letter to Masuaki for his information.

Masuaki replied in a letter dated February 1, 1980:

"I read Mr. Mike Hutchinson's letter, I felt very sad. I wish a perfect polygraph to be invented soon. Then the truth that I haven't made a trick will speak for itself. And I will be able to have those who have called me a liar compensate for their statements in order to reestablish my impaired reputation. As technological improvement is quite remarkable, so a perfect polygraph will be invented in a near future.

"When I read his letter I thought of a tick. Mr. Hutchinson is a man who believes only abilities which he has. A tick has no eyes, no ears and no nose. How can I make a tick understand the sense of sight, smell and hearing!. . .

"Prof. Otani's group of the Defense Academy succeeded again in the experiments with me. . .This time many U.S. military officers (who had cameras) witnessed the experiments.

Masuaki reported on tests at the medical center attached to the Defense Academy which "showed me to be normal, not a liar or an insane." He expressed regret that Mr. Hutchinson is unfamiliar with extensive experiments that have been conducted in Japan over the past six years and added:

"The progress of psychic field does need eminent scientists and outstanding research methods. (Most experimental failures resulted from the incompetency of workers who didn't know how to deal with psychics and psychic phenomena. For example, they demand a subject to do a thing which is quite beyond his capability—to bend or twist a thick iron bar, and so on.) Workers should know psychic properties. At the same time we need strong psychics who can stand the strain of controlled conditions of the experiments. I consider myself one of them.

". . .We believe in the existence of Napoleon or Lincoln as a historical great figure or the roundness of the earth. But we only know these facts from our education. I suppose one of the causes (reasons) that many people don't believe in psychic phenomenon is their lack of psychic knowledge. From now on we must direct our efforts to the advancement of parapsychology. . ."

In a postscript to the letter he added:

"So the professors who are experimenting with me and I am sure that to deny the existence of my psychic power forever is the same that to announce their own ignorance to people. I know whether I am a trick(st)er or not a trick(st)er better than any other people in this world."

Masuaki wrote again on March 3, 1980:

". . .You asked me the names of the staffs of Prof. Otani's group (which consists of professor, physician, psychologist, nurse and so on, but I know only the names of Prof. Otani and a psychotherapist, Kasahara.

*The number of the members attached to that experiment was about 20 persons that included U.S. military officers. What I know about that experiment is that I was hooked up with many cords, and then I twisted or cut spoons, or exposed simultaneously six or eight films of a camera (whose battery was removed in order not to start a shutter), and that I was tested by various polygraphs and machines. These experimental scenes were videotaped. And a student (who is not a psychic) of the Defense Academy was tested under the same conditions as I was done— just to compare a psychic with a non-psychic. **And U.S. military officers took many photographs of these scenes with their cameras.**"* [Emphasis added.]

He added that in another experiment, Prof. Otani discovered changes in Masuaki's blood occurred while he was demonstrating PK but that for the present, Prof. Otani intends to keep this discovery a secret and has declined to accept magazine interviews.

"Prof. Otani has established a new experimental method to recognize PK from the physiological point of view. He can do so while he sees a polygraph. And on this experiment, I needn't to twist a spoon or project Nengraphy. In these experiments are the hardest ones that I have ever experienced as I receive pressure both physically and mentally. Once I am hooked up with cords, I can't move an inch at least three hours. And I feel a great deal of pain whenever my blood is extracted from a vein of my arm by a needle. But I will bear up and do everything in my power for the better progress of society and science. . ."

Here we would like to raise a question too often overlooked or ignored by the scientific community which wants to measure and quantify everything to try to fit it into a conceptual materialist framework. May it be that such a framework is too small to encompass the psychic dimensions involved in psychokinesis, and that personal experiences are likely to yield more meaning than card guessing or blood tests? Up to a point it is desirable to try to replicate phenomena in a laboratory setting, but eventually more effort and study should be devoted to learning how psychic energies can be used to enhance the quality of our lives.

Sheila Ostrander and Lynn Schroeder's book, **Psychic Discoveries Behind the Iron Curtain** (Prentice Hall), first published in 1970, did much to call attention to parapsychological research in the Soviet Union and other Eastern countries. It contains reports that should be examined in the light of what is now being learned about psychic phenomena and not be taken lightly just because it was written by two journalists, rather than by "scientists."

In 1978 another book, written for the general public by Henry Gris and William Dick, was published by Prentice Hall, entitled **The New Soviet Psychic Discoveries.** We have seen reports about Soviet parapsychological research in Benson Herbert's **Journal of**

Paraphysics, published at Downton, England. We have also corresponded with Dr. Barbara Ivanova, one of Russia's more outspoken parapsychologists. We understand that she was relieved of her official duties when she chose, some years ago, not to get involved in secret research. She is referred to as "the stormy petrel" of Soviet PSI in the Gris and Dick book. They quote her as saying:

". . .I combine more areas of parapsychology than any of my colleagues. For instance I practice telekinesis, but I am also a clairvoyant. I am a telepathist and I also heal by long distance. I am a medium. I have ESP. I regress people and I talk to animals. And I don't let myself be bugged."

When they asked her about being a "witch," she replied, "I am glad I am living in the twentieth century this time. I was burned at the stake twice in previous lives."

In the field of parapsychology one often finds that what persons believe privately is not quite the same as what they express publicly. In the Soviet Union, where materialism reflects the predominant or official view of life, investigators of the psychic seem more inclined to explain non-materialistic phenomena in terms such as "bioenergy." In Germany a polarization has developed between *animism* (energies of the person's subconscious) and *spiritism* (which attributes the phenomena to intervention or assistance from other dimensions). Until recently many parapsychologists in the United States have also been more comfortable when conducting card guessing experiments, etc. than when speculating about the likelihood of help from "beyond the grave" or other dimensions.

Late responses to the question about "Implications of PK" came from Fred H. Mansbridge, Alexandria, Virginia, and Dr. Stanley Krippner, San Francisco.

Mansbridge wrote, (in part) "As a practicing psychic and one who is interested in the scientific exploration of psychical phenomena. . .the results of metal bending and the scientific verification of molecular structure change in the metal. . .prove that there is some unexplained force in the Universe that can obviously be captured and brought into the physical body, transmuted or transformed and eventually used for healing, etc."

Krippner speculates that PK may have practical applications in the field of healing but because of its unpredictability, will have to be an adjunct to orthodox treatment.

Should some of our readers feel the urge to attempt experiments with PK themselves, the experience of a member of Mensa's special interest group in Psi, Gerri Howard, will be of interest and caution. The excerpt from the publication *PSI-M* (March 1980) is reprinted by permission:

In looking back over. . .past months of trying to arrive at a step-by-step process for mind-over-matter AT WILL, I find myself both elated and discouraged. Elated because I have finally achieved some measure of success; I now know that it is within my ability to affect matter by pure thought. However, I have encountered side effects that I am not presently equipped to control. I can see no alternative but to discontinue any further attempts until such time as I become better equipped in my knowledge of this field.

Experiment process and results were as follows:

Purpose: To arrive at a correct process for telepathic manipulation of matter at will.

Condition: I felt good, relaxed, calm, secure, "well, here goes nothing" attitude.

Target: Largest cymbal in the set with a set of drums.

Desired Results: Turn the largest cymbal with a spinning motion.

Process: I relaxed my body and mind in stages by counting method, 25 to 1. Instructed myself that correct process/ability was contained within my own knowledge, whether or not I was consciously aware of it. Symbolically visualized 'knowledge' as a staircase; began descending steps one at a time, while focussing all energy/ability on the cymbal.

Results Obtained: As desired. I cannot recall exactly which 'step' I was on when I noticed white pulsating light moving and growing around cymbal (Step 7, 8, 9). There was a faint trail of this light in my direction as if it were coming from me. I intensified thought: "I would like the cymbal to turn-spin-turn-spin—". Some point here I was very startled (to be honest, frightened!) out of what I was doing. IT WAS SPINNING! THE CYMBAL WAS REALLY SPINNING! I thought: "What have I done?! How do I make it stop? Can I control it? Stop! [The Sorcerer's Apprentice effect?]

Note: In after-thought, I feel I was not so wise in trying this; all's well, but I can't help wondering if it just might have turned out differently.

Other Observations: The following is a list of events that occurred directly after:

1. The bulb in the light fixture nearest to me burst.
2. For a couple of days, each time I got within a few feet of a lamp, it would go out. If it were not 'on', it could not be turned on. Upon checking I found that in every case, the bulb had been unscrewed. This effect occurred only when I was present. Also it seemed to affect anything like a light bulb, e.g. jar tops, music boxes, etc., etc.
3. During the night I experienced several 'seizure-like' feelings, more severe than I have ever encountered. Also, marked emotional ups and downs.
4. I normally have great rapport with animals but our dog seems to be threatened by me.

Because of these difficulties, I'm discontinuing further testing at this time.

APPENDIX

ON PK AND RELATED SUBJECTS' RESEARCH IN THE U.S.S.R.

By Larissa Vilenskaya (Israel)

In the summer of 1978, at the U.S.S.R. Academy of Sciences Institute of Radioengineering and Electronics many PK experiments were run with Nina Kulagina as a subject. Below are descriptions of several observations and experiments performed with her.

1) The movement of objects without contact with them.

These experiments were repeatedly performed in a variety of ways. An official document was drawn up attesting to the fact that Kulagina's telekinetic abilities were real and that those present witnessed the existence of this phenomenon. This document was signed by Academicians Vladimir Kotelnikov, Yury Kobzarev, Tikhonov, Kikoin and others.

Shortly after this, the Director of the Institute of Psychology received, in answer to his inquiry, a letter from academician Yury Kobzarev. "I am persuaded," he wrote, "that the phenomena demonstrated by Nina S. Kulagina ("Telekinesis," i.e. movement of objects without contact with them), Rosa A. Kuleshova (reading without assistance of eyes), and L. Korabelnikova (recognition of Zener cards concealed in envelopes made of millimeter-thick carton) are by no means tricks but rather the existence of a manifestation of unusual capabilities in man. My conviction is based upon the results of experiments that were specially set up, and it is shared by many people including a group of professors and academicians. I believe that, as long as the physical and physiological bases of these and other phenomena, labeled as "parapsychology," remain unexplained, it is useless to study their psychological aspects." Signed, Yu. B. Kobzarev, 7 August, 1978.

2) Production of burns.

A lab assistant, with eyes blindfolded, lay on a couch having previously bared a part of the surface of his back. First several persons approached him and stretched their hands over the bare flesh on his back but he felt no sensation whatsoever, when Kulagina put her hand over the same area and began her ministration, he soon felt a sharp burning sensation. The leader of the experimental team, Yury Gulyaev, Corresponding Member of the U.S.S.R. Academy of Sciences, decided to check his hypothesis about the presence of an ultraviolet component in the radiation emitted by Kulagina. He took a piece of ordinary glass and placed it between Kulagina's hand and the back of the man lying on the couch at which point the burning sensation immediately ceased. When the ordinary glass was exchanged for a piece of quartz glass, which allows the passage of ultraviolet rays, the burning sensation was maintained although neither Kulagina nor the lab assistant (still lying blindfolded on the couch) were aware of how one piece of glass might have differed

Larissa Vilenskaya concentrating before starting a healing.

from the other.

3) Effect on an acoustic microphone and a piezoelectric recorder.

It seemed that in Kulagina's biofield there existed an ultrasonic component; measurements taken revealed that the amplitude of her ultrasonic signal in relation to noise (from the apparatus) was of an order of 100 decibels.

4) Experiments at the U.S.S.R. Academy of Sciences' Institute of Chemical Physics.

Kulagina was given a sealed test tube containing two reagents which normally begin to react at a temperature of 70° C. When she held this test tube, wrapped in black paper, for four minutes and tried to effect an influence on the reagents inside it, apparently one half of the reagents began to react (at a room temperature). The experimenters proposed that the result of this experiment could also depend on the action of ultrasonic frequencies radiated by Kulagina.

The radiation of ultrasound was observed in yet another PK medium, Elvira Shevchuk from Kalinin, who demonstrated the movement of a wooden rod and kept it in a state of instable equilibrium, one of its tips just touching the floor (see photo), the other raised and wobbling in the air.

Academician Migdal and Academician Kobzarev also carried out instrumental research on the biofield of a healer Dzhuna Davitashvily from Tbilisi. She has documents attesting to the fact that, after 15 treatments, her healing cured stomach ulcers, duodenal ulcers, and esophagal ulcers. Mrs. Barbara Ivanova, parapsychologist from Moscow, began to work on similar problems in 1971, training her own faculties and then training her students in healing processes. Their combined results in therapy were: "Normalization of blood pressure; dissolution of calcium in bones and vessels; amelioration of general heart and vessel conditions; decrease or disappearance of certain tumors, sometimes immediately; cessation of hemorrahages of small wounds; anaesthesia of almost any type of pain—generally when the pain

(Left) Barbara Ivanova with patients. *(Right)* Vladimir Safanov healing a patient.

disappears so does the cause; as with patients with certain types of ulcers."

In an experiment performed at the Institute of General and Pedagogical Psychology in Moscow, a healer Vladimir Safonov was asked to affect at a distance a subject located in another room. At the same time a reogram (measuring the volume of blood in blood vessels of the brain) was registered for the subject. It appeared that observed changes in the subject's reogram took place only when Safonov acted on certain centers in the subject's brain during which he had recourse to an action much stronger than that usually used by him in the process of healing. This led, when the session was over, to the subject's feeling so dizzy that he could hardly stand upright (after a short time this feeling went away). Noting this result, Safonov categorically refused to continue such experiments when the experimenters insisted that he do so.

*   *   *

On 9 October 1979, the Soviet newspaper "Sovetskaya Rossiya" published a note on the work of the psychiatrist Gennady Krokhalev under the title "Thought Photography" and the subtitle, "How an Idle Fiction Tried to Become a Scientific Discovery." The article took up experiments on the photography of successive visual forms and hallucinations successfully performed by a psychiatrist in the Ural Mountains.

The whole note is laced with phrases such as "pseudoscientific," "sensations," "anti-scientific ideas," "speculations," and "premeditated lies." It contains everything that distinguishes an article of this type: citations taken out of context, open manipulation of the essence of the scientific research, and insults directed to the researchers. However, it seemed that the note's author was most of all disquieted not by the scientific or "anti-scientific" character of Gennedy Krokhalev's research

207

as much as his publication of this research in Western press. "Even three years ago," the note reads, "the *International Journal of Paraphysics* (there is such a one) published in English an article by L. Vilenskaya with the pretentious headline "Experiments in Psi-Photography in the Soviet Union." A good half of it was devoted to Krokhalev...Something about him has already been published in Japan, and according to him an article has been promised in Australia. Evidently it will be something akin to the article in the journal **Psi**, issued in Hamburg, on the pages of which an interview with Krokhalev appeared two years ago."*

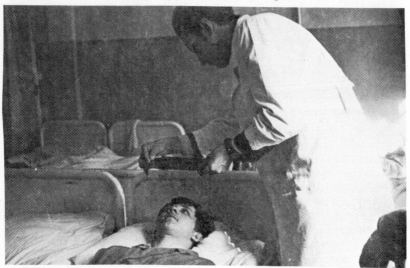

Gennady Krokhalev in a experiment in which he attempts to influence film in a black envelope—without a camera.

In Russia, "organisational conclusions," are usually made on account of such articles; researchers are fired from their jobs, prevented from publishing and submitted to repressive measures. The journalist, Vladimir Bogatyrev, has already been incarcerated for publishing an article on the experiments of the Perm psychiatrist in a popular magazine.* Professor Vassily Banshchikov, who worked with Krokhalev on the theoretical bases of the results of his experiments, has already declined co-authorship. What lurks behind all this: the desires of the Soviets to hide their serious interest in these problems or vengeance

---

Interview with G. Krokhalev by Barbara Ivanova.

**I should like to call attention to the fact that in 1973 the parapsychologist, healer and lecturer, Barbara Ivanova, was fired from her job at the Moscow State Institute for International Relations. She was dismissed by blackmail and threats, with infringing Soviet labor laws. She has, since that time, remained without employ, as has the top researcher of the Kirlian effect, Victor Adamenko, a Candidate of Technical Sciences (degree equivalent to the American Ph.D.).*

Boris Yermolaev holding match box suspended in air.

towards any scientist who refuses to carry out his research in a direction acceptable to the authorities and decides to make his results available to the world community? This question is all the more interesting in that a short while ago experiments on the photography of visual forms were carried out (secretly) by the Moscow Scientific-Research Institute for Optico-Physical Measurements and may be continuing to this day. Official research is being done on a series of other problems pertaining to Parapsychology.

For example, according to Mr. Avraham Shifrin (Israel), some time ago experiments with psychics were carried out (in a laboratory in Zykh peninsula near Baku) who were able to use a psychokinetic skill to break the tip of a spinal column at a distance. But most of all official parapsychology in the U.S.S.R. is interested in the study of the nature of bioenergy and the construction of devices to amplify and generate bio-fields and psi-fields for action on human beings with the aim of altering their mental states and controlling their behavior. It should be noted that the Moscow film director, Boris Yermolaev, who was able to "levitate" (to hold "suspended") in the air various objects between his hands (see photo) about three years ago was invited to a secret laboratory in an area outside Moscow and, for period of ten days, various experiments were performed with him, the aim of which was to clarify the nature of Pk phenomena.

PK IMPLICATIONS
(Some Types of Bioenergy Influence upon Living and Non-Living Objects)

1. Bio-influence upon (photo) film (Dr. Gennady Sergeev, U.S.S.R.[1] photos of after-images and hallucinations and their implication for diagnostics of

mental disorders. (Dr. Gennady Krohkalev, U.S.S.R.[2]).

2. Intensification of the sedimentation of suspensions and colloidal solutions. (Dr. T. G. Neeme, Estonia, U.S.S.R. [3]). Purification of water by means of bio-energy (Engineer Robert Pavlita, Chechoslovakia). Influence of the operator's emotional state upon thickness of (membrane) layer in the process of electrolytic production of thin layers (membrane) in radioengineering (research in a laboratory at Department of Cybernetics Moscow physico-engineering Institute).

3. Influence of the psycho-physiological state of the laboratory worker upon the distribution of physico-mechanical parameters of certain products consisting of concrete (research in the laboratory of Biotechnical Problems at the Kirov Polytechnical Institute[4]).

4. Intensification of chemical reactions (research at the U.S.S.R. Academcy of Sciences' Institute of Chemical Physics).

5. Bio-influence upon water properties, changing of surface tension of water.[5]

6. Distant influence on physical apparatus. Changing of properties of certain alloys.[6],[7].

7. Influence upon the germination of seeds and the growth of plants with the psychic energy[8], [9].

8. Human bio-influence upon electrical properties of plants.[10],[11].

9. Bio-influence upon animals (for instance, acceleration or slowing down the activity of mice—experiments by Dr. Sergey Speranksy, U.S.S.R.).

10. Bio-field influence upon the psycho-physiological and physical state of human being[12], [13], [14].

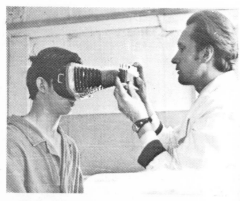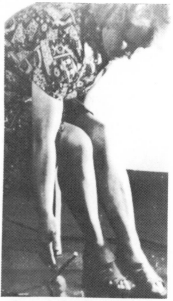

(Above) An experiment designed to influence film via light-proof bellows. *(Right)* Elvira Shevchuk raising one end of a wooden dowel without touching it.

References

1. G. A. Sergeev, Biorhythms and Biosphere. Moscow *Znanie,* 1976 (in Russian).
2. L. Vilenskaya, Experimental Psi-Photography in the Soviet Union. *International Journal of Paraphysics,* vol. 10, No. 3, 1976, pp. 68-70.
3. T. G. Neeme, in *Proceedings First International Congress Psychotronics Research, Prague, June 1973.*
4. V. Loginov, PK on Concrete. *International Journal of Paraphysics,* Vol. 9, Nos. 4/5, 1975, pp. 105-106. (From "Action of Psychic Energy" in *Soviet Engineer,* publ. in Kirov, U.S.S.R., No. 25, 1975).
5. R. Miller, Methods of Detecting and Measuring Healing Energies. In: *Future Science* (Life Energies and the Physics of Paranormal Phenomena), ed. by J. White and S. Krippner; Garden City, New York; Doubleday & Co., Inc., 1977, pp. 431-444.
6. H. Puthoff, R. Targ, Psychic Research and Modern Physics, In *Psychic Exploration—A Challenge for Science,* by Edgar D. Mitchell, Ed. by J. White, New York, Putnam, 1974, pp. 524-542.
7. E. Byrd, Uri Geller's Influence on the Metal Alloy Nitinol, (Naval Surface Weapons Center, White Oak Laboratory). In: *The Geller Papers (Scientific Observations on the Paranormal Powers of URI GELLER),* Ed. by Ch. Panati, Houghton Mifflin Company, Boston, 1976, pp. 67-73.
8. A. S. Roman, Psychoenergetic activity and its inward and outward manifestation. In: *Psychic Self-Regulation,* Issue 2, Alma Ata, 1974, pp. 301-311. (In Russian).
9. L. Vilenskaya, A Scientific Approach to Some Aspects of Psychic Healing, *International Journal of Paraphysics,* Vol. 10, No. 3, 1976, pp. 74-80.
10. M. Vogel, Man—Plant Communication. In: *Psychic Exploration—A Challenge for Science,* by Edgar D. Mitchell, Ed. by J. White, New York, Putnam, 1974, pp. 289-312.
11. N.A. Akimova, G. I. Angushev, V. N. Pushkin et al. Electrophisiological reaction of plant upon changing psychological state of man. In: *VII Nauchno-Technichesky Seminar 'Kontrol sostoyaniay cheloveka-operatora',* Moscow, 1975, pp. 74-77. (In Russian).
12. L. Vilenskaya, Interconnection of Psychotronic Phenomena: Paranormal Diagnostics, Healing and Dermo-Optics. In: *Third International Congress on Psychotronic Research,* Tokyo, June 27-July 2, 1977, Part 2, 1977, pp. 528-532.
13. B. Ivanova, Experimental and Training Work on Some Group (mass)-Harmonizing Processes with Educating, Creativity-heightening and Healing Results. In: *Third International Congress on Psychotronic Research,* Tokyo, June 27-July 2, 1977, Part 2, 1977, pp. 463-471.
14. B. Ivanova, Experimental and Training Work on Some Group (mass)-*Paraphysics,* Vol. 12, Nos. 1/2, 1978, pp. 20-21.

ON THE RECENT JAPANESE CLAIMS OF PSYCHIC PHOTOGRAPHY AND METAL BENDING
W. E. Cox (FRNM)[1]

The subject of this study is a 17-year-old Japanese boy, Masuaki Kiyota (M.K.). He first was reported in this country by *The National Enquirer* magazine, and later for an "Exploring the Unknown" telecast aired in October 1977.[2] His own discovery of certain PK abilities reportedly had occurred by the time he was 10, but their rarity was not known to him until a few years later when he observed Uri Geller perform on Japanese television. M.K.'s own claimed effects in that country included both metal bending and paraphotography. For the latter, both a Polaroid and motion picture camera had been used.

Paranormal pictures reportedly have been under supervision of different Japanese research scientists. Outstanding products show the "Tokyo Tower," hotels and other buildings (some of which are reproduced in *Fate* Magazine for January 1980,[3] often within specially protected cameras). The present report is of a later study, however, one which I personally conducted in August 1979 for the purpose of investigating these claims. As I am interested in all PK effects, metal bending also was one of my objectives, together with quantitative studies of both PK and ESP. They were sufficiently successful to warrant this brief report.

M.K. and another Japanese boy named Hiroto Yamashita (H.Y.), age 15, were brought to this country by Walter Uphoff, the author (with his wife) of

---

[1] *W. Edward Cox is both a semi-professional magician and a parapsychologist. He was a subscriber to the old* Sphinx *as early as 1932 and is a member of the Society of American Magicians and (formerly) of the International Brotherhood of Magicians. Professionally he is a Field Research Associate on the staff of the Institute of Parapsychology (Foundation for Research on the Nature of Man), Durham, North Carolina, a voting member of the American Society for Psychical Research, a member of the British Society (SPR), the Parapsychological Association, the American Society of Dowsers, etc. and is on the board of the Indian Foundation for Parapsychology.*

[2] *Here are several details for the purpose of completeness which has no bearing on the accuracy of the experiments reported by Mr. Cox. I accompanied Alan Neuman, a Hollywood producer and his filming crew to the Philippines and Japan in September-October 1976. In Tokyo I contacted Dr. Hiroshi Motoyama's Institute and through him met the physicists; Dr. Toshiaki Harada and Dr. Tsutomu Miyauchi who arranged for me to meet the Kiyota family. There Alan Neuman filmed both metal bending and thoughtography. A segment showing Masuaki projecting an image of the Tokyo Tower onto polaroid film (reported earlier) was shown in the 90-minute program, "Exploring the Unknown" narrated by Burt Lancaster, October 30, 1977.*

The second edition of our book, **New Psychic Frontiers,** *had already appeared in August 1977. In the March 14, 1978 issue of* **The National Enquirer,** *John Cooke reported their experiments with Masuaki who produced images on their polaroid camera film. (WHU)*

[3] *This article was written by Walter H. Uphoff 18 months prior to its appearance—on the invitation of the editor.*

New Psychic Frontiers—Your Key to New Worlds (New York: Sam Weiser, 1977.[4]) The Uphoffs recently had witnessed some of their effects in Tokyo, including a variety of cutlery which became twisted or otherwise bent. Particularly noteworthy is M.K.'s earlier successes in producing pictures showing the Statue of Liberty and other structures with considerably clarity, done in Tokyo, with a reporter's camera in 1978.

Both boys were requested [invited] to come to America last summer, and appeared at a workshop on "PK and its effect on metal and film" held at the Uphoffs' New Frontiers Center in Wisconsin. No reports of controlled tests from that appearence have become available[5]; however, the two were brought to California by the Uphoffs, by the Institute for Noetic Sciences, and the Washington (Street) Research Center (WRC), of San Francisco. Immediately following the 1979 PA Convention I had the opportunity to observe them at the WRC. Also present that afternoon, but only for a few hours, were Jule Eisenbud, Robert Van de Castle, (Harold) Puthoff and Russell Targ, in addition to the staff and other members of the WRC.

Although both boys claim similar parapsycho-physical abilities, practically all the effects which I observed during most of three days with them were by M.K. only, on August 17-19. For the first experiment I already had prepared a strip of regular 35 mm, Plus-X Pan. camera film, folded in three layers, each at least 2½ inches long. This had been covered with cardboard and stuffed into a discarded Polaroid film pack, which then was well sealed. At the WRC I simply secured it by rubber bands to the bottom exterior of a Polaroid Land camera with which the boys were experimenting when I arrived. This light-proof case remained in position the rest of the day while various mental efforts were made to produce paranormal pictures in the camera itself. The latter were all failures, as were two previous exposures, making a total of six "blackies," only. My pack was removed, but again attached during the following morning in the same manner. Later on, it was placed beside a strain gauge, during a different experiment which will be described shortly. I do not know which boy handled the camera at any particular time, but this made no difference since my film was not Polaroid.

Let me now jump to ten days later, when this film was professionally developed in Missouri. The negative revealed two exceptional anomalies, or so it appears to me.

Metal Bendings

On my second day at the WRC a buffet breakfast was provided, during which one or two pieces of inexpensive silverware were claimed to have been seen by others present to have bent or twisted after being thrown across the kitchen. Although I had observed the general situation, wherein M.K. informally was seated on the kitchen floor, I could have no control over effects, nor did anyone else, hence these will be omitted. It is appropriate to add,

[4] *Publisher: Colin Smythe Ltd., Gerrards Cross, England. Samuel Weiser, 740 Broadway, New York, is an American distributor.*

[5] *This book, **Mind Over Matter**, reporting on both controlled experiments and anecdotal observations, was written to make that information available.*

however, that the claim was made that stroboscopic pictures have been taken of such a flung spoon in the actual process of bending; and I have seen such pictures in a Japanese magazine.

During our noon meal, however, the situation was more appropriate. This was held at the residence of the WRC's Director Mr. H.S. Dakin. He and I and four others sat with the Uphoffs and both boys at a formal dining table, and I provided a heavy tablespoon of German silver. The handle was 3/32" thick, and 5/32" wide at its narrowest point. This one was too heavy for me to bend by hand, even with the aid of a pair of pliers. This spoon suffered a 183° twist, approximately, during that occasion, under the following conditions: I handed M.K. the spoon (unencased) at his table seat and asked him to bend it during the meal if he could. I occasionally observed him to be fondling it, but was paying more attention to a discourse with Uphoff during most of the meal so could not watch M.K. much of the time—nor was that necessary, I felt, considering the strength of this spoon and the presence of other diners. When we all rose to leave, M.K. entered the small study near the dining room, and there looked at a piece of computer equipment with which he had been fascinated earlier at WRC. He was out of my own sight only briefly. I looked for the spoon on the table but did not see it. When I asked M.K. for it, he nonchalantly produced it from his pants pocket. (Later he told me that twists occasionally did occur therein and without his knowledge. I did not ask if this one did.)

The spoon was now bent 183°, immediately beneath the bowl at its narrowest point. Space had not afforded his concealment in the doorless study; and I failed to find any earmarks of fraud, considering the toughness of this spoon.* These also were sought in a conversation that day, and during a trip to the airport next morning with the two boys, Stanley Krippner (S.K.) and H.S.D.

I should add that while awaiting the plane, there was an adroit move made by S.K. of interest here. While driving back from the airport, he mentioned having given M.K. a soft metal key of his, to toy with enroute, and at the airport. While waiting for the plane, he engineered their casual movement up to a wall, which would have given M.K. an easy chance to press the key against the wall and so to succeed in producing a bend, if he had a mind to, with effortlessness and dispatch. None was so produced or attempted.

Additional tests with M.K. and H.Y.

On August 19, an effort was made at bending a standard tensile strain gauge while it was enclosed by a protective plastic box. This happened to be available at WRC, attached to a chart recorder (Beckman, Type RS, 2 Channel). The most sensitive setting was used, for approximately 90 minutes. Most of the time M.K. was the subject. He would sit with his hand stroking the plastic box, but

---

In a series of controlled experiments by this researcher, now in progress with J. T. Richards of Rolla, MO., superior evidences of metal bending have been obtained in securely sealed containers. These include fine wires, pipe-cleaners, tinfoil, a spoon handle, and also various closures of safety pins, among other RSPK effects.

not touching the strain gauge. I observed him most of the time. Significant movement of the pen was only infrequent (of course): but on occasion the following movements were registered, which I cannot account for my normal means. (See Table 1)

Table 1

Some Measurements of Apparent Static-PK (PK-ST) upon a Beckman Chart Recorder (Type RS, 2 Channel), using a Standard Tensile Strain Gauge

Col. 1	Col. 2
Control tests by W.E.C., showing representative samples of degrees of pressure.	M.K's experimental tests, with gauge protected by plastic cover, showing the time* and degree of strain, via PK-ST

Col. 1:

1. Downward (-) and then upward (+) finger-pressure of approximately –1 oz. and +1 oz. respectively.

    3 cm. swing to left, and then
    3 cm. swing to right

2. –0.7 oz. downward:

    –2 cm. to left

3. +0.3 oz. upward:

    + 1 cm. to right

Sample Chart Recordings (non-PK)

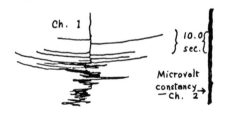

Col. 2:

Minutes into the session (see note*)	Direction and extent of each deviation (Left = –; Right = +)
24.3	–1.5 cm to +1.4 cm
38.2	+0.5 cm.
50.25	+3.0 cm.
50.3	–0.8 cm.
50.4	+3.3 cm.
50.7	–2.1 cm. to +3.0 cm.
50.75	+1.2 cm.
52.3	–0.2 cm.
56.5	–3.4 cm. to +2.9 cm.
62.25	+3.0 cm.
62.4	–2.3 cm. to +2.3 cm.
62.6	–1.2 cm. to +2.2 cm.
62.61	–3.9 cm. to +1.4 cm.
62.7	–3.7 cm.

*The first 24" and final 30" showed little or no reactions. There also were brief periods when H.Y. replaced M.K. (with no indicated reactions), or when there was a break. These are not shown.

Rest periods were interspersed during which no record was made. After nearly 25 minutes of no movements, the first of 14 deviations on either or both sides of the centerline appeared. Six of these showed instantly consecutive deviations on both sides, all beginning on the left, which hypothetically would have required PK pressure down and then promptly up at the movable end of the strain gauge. Of the remaining 8, 5 went only to the left, and 3 to the right.

It should be noted that H.Y. was subject for less than a fourth of the 90 minutes, and that in none of his irregular periods were there any deviations produced on the chart. The only value judgement which might be placed on this experiment—and tentatively on M.K.'s paraphotography and metal-bending—is that collectively they seem to show "signs of psi." Accordingly further research with strain gauges and M.K. is warranted. I have so advised Dr. S. Otani, our PA member in Tokyo.

Standard Statistical Tests

Conventional PK and ESP tests with dice and cards, or their equivalent, are quite likely to yield useful information when a static-PK sensitive is available. During this opportunity I used 6 coins, repeatedly thrown from a cup onto a soft blanket by M.K. and H.Y. Results were within chance for H.Y., but for M.K. there were 41 hits in the first half, or 5 above chance, and only 28 in the second, for a difference of 13, which is significant at the .02 level (*post hoc*). A continuation of this series was not found convenient. In ESP tests, neither subject did very well—nor am I aware of any ESP claims previously made by or for either or them.

A Special Watch Test

The concluding experiment was in a restaurant, where I had walked with the boys on their last evening there. My target object was an inexpensive Ingraham pocket watch which had been jammed with tinfoil projecting into the balance wheel from a glued position on the barrel spring plate. The aim was to lift this up by PK. The back was tight, and also sealed with sealing wax by myself in 1977.

The two boys had not seen this before, yet five minutes after I handed it to M.K. and he briefly to H.Y. he laid it on the table and mentioned that it was ticking. It was. I wondered in what condition the foil had bent during the past two years, if at all, and so decided to consider this test as something of a preliminary one, hoping that they would repeat it. On breaking the seal and opening it I found that the tinfoil had been lifted up sufficiently to allow the balance wheel to move back and forth under it. Even though I did not observe M.K. engage in excessive shaking of the watch, it was conceivable that shaking could have thrust the foil upward, hence a repeat test was definitely advisable.

I secured the foil in its place, replaced the tightly-fitting back, then shook it vigorously as a check against suspicions of inadequate confinement. It lay on the table for a few minutes, stationed between myself and M.K., and he too shook it briefly while holding it for a moment.

I do not recall whether both boys handled the watch this time, but once again it began to tick and M.K. called my attention to the fact. This was in less than three minutes. When I opened the back I once again found the tinfoil lifted out of the way of the balance wheel, even though this time I had firmly pushed it into position upon the plate so as to obstruct the balance wheel, in the intended manner.*

Since M.K. thrust out the foil without moving the regulator arm (which was itself a second target objective, and would have disturbed the foil), the significance of the entire watch-starting accomplishments by M.K. is reduced, as it is within conceivability that a vigorous revolving motion of the watch might have made the balance wheel spokes dislodge the obstructing foil. (I favor the PK-ST hypothesis, however, due to my own difficulty in starting it by shaking. M.K. alleged to me that he "often" had started defective watches.)

Some Concluding Observations

A brief comparison of M.K. and two or three similar sensitives may be profitable in concluding this report. Here we appear to have a predominantly fast metal bender. In contrast there have been slow, gradual bendings of keys and cutlery by Uri Geller, or of thick metal bars by Jean-Pierre Girard, both of whom have twice produced this while I myself held the target objects. (*JP* 1974, and *SERPA* 1977, Vols. 38 & 41)

Also, M.K.'s paraphotographic procedure differs from that of Ted Serios', even though their products are quite similar. Quantitative PK tests with both have shown very suggestive evidence as well.

It may be that by comparing a much larger array of past reputed physical sensitives in the general literature we can benefit more than has been realized to date about the nature of static PK. Such a history is in fact available (in manuscript), and a *Journal of Parapsychology* abstract is now in press.

For an account of Geller's starting my own specially prepared watch, see "Note on some experiments with Uri Geller," in the Journal of Parapsychology, Vol. 38, 1974, pp. 408-11.

(The next three paragraphs and the following page deal with W. E. Cox's experiment with a concealed 35 mm unexposed film piece.)

The Test with Film

These findings would seem to imply specifically, a down-through paraphotographic effect while under seal. Some control tests on layers of unexposed film, using pinpoints of light later revealed the following: a spot of light 4 mm. in dia. was produced upon the first of four layers, while its penetration produced spots of 3, 2 and 1 mm., approx., on the lower layers. The 4:3 ratio for the top two accords with the reduction of the white "base" of the paranormal image from 1.0 width to 0.7 cm. A less intense second spot of light also was produced, and this failed to register on the second layer of film probably because all undeveloped negatives are moderately opaque.

The novel relations found in the foregoing do not appear to exist for the wide, angular shaft of light at G, which is assumed on this basis to have been non-paranormal.

A further note is that the protuberance one centimeter from the bottom in A will juxtapose with the one at E, when the film is folded at F1, as if a penetration caused both. Presumably, therefore, the intriguing "/⚊" effect at E would have appeared more sharply (instead of less sharply) at A also, had not some light probably entered one and desensitized the roll at this point when first it was being loaded into the camera for conventional use.

Non-Polaroid film (W.E.C.'s Pan-X) housed in a plate film container:

Two arguments against normal cause of the image at B (1) I alone use this camera. On this roll nothing had been filmed prior to frame No. 1 (sideview of Dr. Eisenbud) and No 1-A (another man). (2) The image is much too close to the factory-cut left end of the roll.

There was some accidental light leakage when I packed this short segment of film. This is shown along most of the bottom edge, and by the two vertical spikes where this film strip was folded, at F1 and F2, as well as at C where another slight crease had been made and then smoothed out.

Special notes on symmetry which imply a down-through paraphotographic effect:

Due to the fact that the negative was twice folded (as a "Z"), A and B rested against D and E, with sensitive surfaces together, and this pair rested against G, with their non-sensitive surfaces together.

The photo-energetic which produced image B penetrated to D, but insufficiently to more than duplicate some of the base. The angles of incidence are exactly equal, and so are their distances from the fold at F1. The oval on top, being relatively bright, did penetrate with most of the base, although too weakly to be seen in this print. It is fairly visible on the negative, and its exact location is shown ($\bigcirc$) nearly a centimeter above D.

The following symmetries are of interest, relative to the fold, F1. (1) The oval top of both B and D are exactly the same distance from a point on F1 (25 mm.) (2) Two pairs of parallel lines have been drawn (white, dashed) to intersect the edges of the ovals at B and D, beginning from what appears to be two linear effects at A and two linear effects more conspicuously evident at E. (3) The latter two themselves also are parallel "extensions of" the drawn lines, a centimeter or more in length; and (4) both the former and latter intersect the fold F1 at exactly the same points.

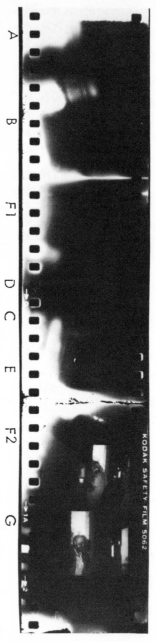

PARANORMAL METAL BENDING
IN A SEMI-FORMAL SMALL GROUP*
by Mark G. Shafer**

This paper summarizes 3 years exploratory research on paranormal metal bending by selected persons from Southern California. Methodology and results are presented that indicate the occurrence in a semi-formal small group of apparent psychokinesis (PK) under increasingly controlled conditions. Factors associated with the functioning of the small group and occurrence of the phenomenon are discussed. Suggestions for future research, particularly that oriented toward enhancement of, as well as observation and measurement of macro-PK events (directly observable PK), are proffered on the basis of experience from this research.

Subjects

From 1976 to 1978 thirteen people participated as subjects in the research, joining the ongoing program at different times and for varying lengths of time. Participation was voluntary and by invitation of the experimenter (E), the author, only.

Participants were Caucasian and tended to be from the middle socio-economic class. Males who participated were 12, 13, about 23, 28, about 38, and about 40 years of age; females participating were 12, 14, 18, 20, about 34, about 35, and about 36 years of age. Only 2 of the adults (males) had college degrees. None of the participants appeared to be significantly different from other psychological norms for the general population except in regard to a belief system incorporating psychic phenomena.

All participants maintained a positive belief in the existence of PK and all claimed to have produced macro-PK phenomena themselves. These claims usually referred to the bending of cutlery either without touching or by using PK to soften it so it required significantly less force to bend than usual. It was on the basis of these claims that persons were invited to participate in the research. Potential participants were brought to the attention of E either through self-announcement at one of E's public lectures on parapsychology, or through acquaintances familiar with E's research who told E of the person in question who was then contacted.

Participants all claimed to have noted the capacity for PK after hearing of, or seeing a demonstration of apparently genuine paranormal metal bending either in person or on television. Each later tried similar PK feats and at some point met with what they took to be success. Some continued to practice after this in an effort to enhance the ability while others then desisted from any further involvement with PK. Most participants noted having at least one significant

---

*This research was discussed by the author at the psychokinesis workshop sessions of both the 20th and 21st Annual Conventions of the Parapsychological Association.

**The author wishes to thank Robert Morris, Stanley Krippner, and Ron Hawke for suggestions and assistance with this research.

person in their past who professed a belief in psychic phenomena and who influenced their thinking about psi, and most currently believed other members of their family also had macro-PK ability.

Participants were told that no report of the research was to be leaked to any public press until after a scientific report or paper had been published on the research. Neither were they to use participation in the research for the purpose of gaining public notoriety until after such a report had been issued. All were cautioned about the damage to credibility that would result should any participant "go public" prior to scientific publication. This was openly embraced by all participants as a wise and desirable course of action and the best means for securing evidence for their PK ability.

Meetings

Research sessions were held once a week in a large room in the laboratory building of the Social Sciences Complex of the University of California, Irvine. Sessions lasted approximtely 1½ hours and were held in the evenings. During each session a small variety of PK tasks would be attempted, each many times by the individuals present. A video recording system was used in most meetings to videotape various attempts.

The atmosphere of meetings was purposive as well as congenial. Participants sat around the room on chairs or comfortable couches, forming a rough circle about 15 to 20 feet in diameter. After the opening of the session PK targets were presented to participants in their seats by E, or chosen freely from an assortment placed on the floor in the middle of the circle. Normally a substantial amount of social conversation accompanied PK attempts.

Sessions began formally when a circle was formed with the chairs and everyone joined hands, shut their eyes and visualized brilliant light passing counterclockwise around the circle through the linked hands. This opening ritual lasted about 5 minutes and was believed to enhance subsequent PK attempts. It did seem to have a relaxing effect and to remind everyone of the purpose of meeting—to exhibit PK.

Following this the first PK tasks were attempted. These were chosen so that it was actually possible to perform them without using PK at all. They entailed trying to bend rather flimsy cutlery by softening it through PK while holding it in one hand, then using the free hand to apply outside physical force to bend it. No attempt was made to assess whether this bending involved PK or not; everyone maintained publicly that it did. After successful bends were being produced in this fashion by most participants, sturdier cutlery and more difficult PK tasks were introduced. This usually occurred after about 5 minutes. The more difficult PK tasks eventually involved a variety of targets, some to be bent without physical contact and others to be bent under specified contraints. These, and results with them are described in following sections.

It was possible to maintain fairly well-controlled conditions during meetings because participants were enlisted as "experimenters" as well as "subjects" for the research. The goal of the research was specified clearly to all, "to gather unequivocable evidence for the existence of macro-PK." During sessions persons were asked to monitor each other to assure that the highest quality evidence for PK was being produced. A cohesive attitude was developed and encouraged: "we against the skeptics." When suggestions were made to a participant about how to improve the evidentiality of his/her PK attempts, willing cooperation resulted.

Participants were taught how to use the video camera and were given opportunities to be "cameraman" and record live research footage. The video recording equipment was turned on as soon as the evening's PK attempts began. A monitor was displayed so that participants could see exactly what image was being recorded by the camera. This proved to be excellent feedback for participants as they strove and encouraged others to strive to present the best visual "angles" of their PK attempts, to maximize evidentiality from the observer's standpoint. The person playing cameraman was commonly adamant about proper angles, more so than E sometimes, as s/he strove to obtain the best evidence possible. Being cameraman often made the participants more aware of how to exhibit their own PK attempts in a more evidential way.

Early Observations

All participants claimed to be able to bend spoons (also forks) psychokinetically by holding them in one hand and rubbing the neck between bowl and stem until the metal softened, at which point a bend or twist would be attempted with the other hand using physical force. Occasionally the effortlessness with which a spoon was thus twisted or bent was startling, involving no more than a quick, light flip of the wrist. At other times the effort seemed about equal to that required to bend the spoon non-paranormaly.

Practically none of the research meetings during the first year brought success at any PK tasks other than these routine bends-with-force. The early observations all related to this kind of bending, and are highlighted below. Results from later meetings and from other kinds of PK attempts are presented in the next section.

One of the earliest observations concerned the way a person knew *when* a spoon had been "psychokinetically softened" and was ready to bend: either this became evident as a result of periodic testing of the spoon by exerting a small force on it "to see if it was ready to go," or through feeling the spoon become slippery beneath the grasp as if suddenly coated with mercury, at which point it was reportedly soft. The soft condition was reported to last only a fraction of a second or so and it was only then that the spoon was easily bendable. Not all the participants reported feeling the "slippery" sensation and those feeling it did not feel it all the time. No one reported detecting the readiness of a spoon to bend by the presence of other sensations in the hands, arms, or body.

Sometimes a participant could bend a spoon 45 seconds after having received it and sometimes not for 45 minutes. The average time seemed to be about 5 minutes. Bending also seemed to occur more quickly and easily in sessions that met on the night of the full moon; participants expected that this might be so and this probably was the cause.

Various Mental Techniques Used

Participants used various mental techniques for bending. One involved the imaging of the neck of the spoon softened like putty while trying to bend it. Another involved repeated mental issuance of a command to the spoon to bend. A third technique, and the most prevalent, was to conceive the idea of what was desired to take place—the paranormal softening and bending of the spoon—and then to begin rubbing and ignore the idea while engaging in conversation with others. Often conversations were interrupted as a speaker discovered a spoon ready to bend, at which point full attention was turned to the spoon. Bends also seemed to be performed semi-consciously without a break in the flow of conversation during bending. Each participant seemed to use different methods at different times, sometimes mixing them, often during a single session or single trial.

The spoons, if touched immediately after having been bent, were only slightly warmer than room temperature, about as warm as a spoon held in a closed fist for about 5 minutes. Many spoons and forks were bent and twisted so as to be quite mangled in appearance involving very complex loops, twists, and bends. The physically stronger participants were as a rule able to cause the physically more difficult and involved bends though occasional exceptions occurred.

Silver-plated spoons were bent more easily and quickly than stainless seel spoons. Participants believed that they should be more easily bendable which was rapidly communicated to new participants because of the silver content (and not because these spoons were slightly more pliable than stainless steel). It was only occasionally that forks and even knives were bent, the favorite target being spoons. Brass keys could also be bent, these sometimes one-handedly by pushing the thin section down with the thumb.

Eventually very heavy gauge spoons, knives, and forks were introduced and these too were bent though usually not to as great a degree as lighter weight cutlery. There were many bends exerted on this heavier cutlery by women and children that E could not duplicate using the greatest of his physical strength.

Observed Differences Between Physical Force and PK

The most interesting early result was the difference noted between what happened when E asked one of the physically stronger participants to bend cutlery using normal physical force versus what happened during "psychokinetic" bends. The obvious exertion and physical tension in the muscles of hands, arms, and chest were absent in psychokinetic attempts as were impressions left in the hand where the cutlery was held. Even more significant was what happened to the physically bent cutlery: either the item broke or ruptures appeared on the surface in the area of the bend quite visible to the naked eye. On closer examination microcracks in the same area resulted in a visible roughening of the surface texture. None of this was present on similar cutlery bent "with PK" where the surface of the metal in the area of bends remained intact and shiny even on items bent to a degree considerably greater than the physically bent items. This same disparity showed between spoons bent physically by a non-participant claiming no PK ability and "psychokinetically" bent cutlery. These latter results were in the main responsible for extension of the research into the second and third years, and later results.

Later Results

It was clear that to begin to determine whether PK might be occurring in research sessions tighter controls and different targets needed to be employed.

As an example, either normal physical contact with the target or the target area of a system could be prohibited, or targets whose physical properties seemed to exclude the possibility of bending without fracture under normal, short duration conditions could be used (after Hasted, 1976). Gradually tasks and targets of these types were introduced and results reported below obtained. Unfortunately none of the results except one, the final one discussed, was caught on videotape due to the rarity and suddenness with which target events occurred, the group situation, the practice of not filming one particular person exclusively for an entire session, and frequent malfunctioning of the video equipment.

In one task participants were asked to hold a spoon in one hand and to concentrate on but not touch the juncture between bowl and stem to "soften" it there via PK so the bowl would droop over of its own weight. With no physical force being used to push the bowl over it was felt this would provide much stronger evidence of PK. Two instances of "droop-overs" were reported which were observed by other participants though not observed by E. The bowls were observed to droop over slowly toward the floor over approximately a 30-second period, stopping after having bent downward about 45°.

PK at a Distance

A target system frequently used involved a spoon clamped to a table by the stem, from the protruding bowl of which was hung a weight of approximately 5 lbs. Participants were asked to concentrate on but not touch the spoon, to soften the junction between bowl and stem through PK so that once soft the weight would do the work of bending which the free hand normally did. Here success would again provide the better evidence of PK as the agent could not apply direct physical force to the spoon. One instance of a bend with this target system was noted while E was talking in an adjoining room with the participant concentrating on the setup which neither could see. (Occasionally E would conduct private interviews with individual participants in an anteroom of the regular meeting room.) The other participants were left unobserved by E in the room where the target was located and none claimed to have touched it or approached it before or after the bend took place, or claimed to see the spoon in the process of bending. The participant concentrating on the setup was observed to scrunch his face in mid-sentence and to mention immediately thereafter that E should check the target. The spoon was discovered then to be bent at a 90° angle downward, pointing straight to the floor. Such spoon-with-weight targets were never observed to bend spontaneously due to the five-pound weight alone. At no other time during the research was that participant's facial behavior observed to reoccur.

Ordinary hack saw blades were used as bending-with-touching targets because of their brittleness which was believed to prevent their being permanently bendable without fracture to any significant degree (e.g. more than 10°). The goal was to bend one in a U-shape without fractures, supposedly impossible using physical forces under normal conditions and over a short period of time. One participant did this successfully once. Many people, both participants and non-participants claiming no PK ability, tried to accomplish a similar feat using physical strength and dexterity and the blades were broken in every case without ever having been permanently bent.

A target provided by an outside experimenter was constructed in the following manner. A small aluminum bar 3″ x ½″ x ⅛″ was sprayed with a lacquer and before this dried, small hollow spheres about the size of salt grains were sprinkled over its entire surface. The bar was then sprayed again to adhere the spheres to it as well as possible. The spheres covered about 1/3 of the surface area of the bar and were closely enough spaced that it was impossible to grip the bar without contacting a number of spheres. The spheres were brittle and fragile so that exerting more than a very light force by touch, much less than that required to bend the bar, would crush them. If the bar was bent, examination of the spheres would give evidence of whether normal physical (contact) force was used. This target was placed on a table in front of a participant who was asked to bend it without touching and who then concentrated on it for about 20 minutes. At this point it spontaneously bent near the middle about 30° according to observing participants. Two other participants observed the participant at the time and did not see any contact made with the bar or other movement by the participant before or during the bend. The bend was reported to have taken place smoothly over about a 5-second interval. E and the guest E were nearby and had periodically observed the participant concentrating and had also not observed any contact being made with the bar. Neither was observing when the bar reportedly bent. None of the spheres were found to be crushed. A few were displaced due to handling after the bend, prior to close examination though this was not thought to be related to the prior PK attempt.

Experiments with Pendulum

A pendulum arrangement was constructed that contained two equal length 5″ swinging pendulums in a closed plexiglas cube. One pendulum was selected as target and participants asked to influence it to swing in an indicated direction without touching the cube or what it was positioned on. The second pendulum served as a control against using external force to act on the cube to cause the target to swing, for this would cause the control to swing also. (There still existed the possibility of applying a rotational force to the cube, with an axis co-linear to the control pendulum which would cause the target to swing along a perpendicular to the line between pendulums while the control remained still.) Several participants were able to induce motion in the target pendulum while the control remained stationary without touching either the cube or its mooring. Motion was in the desired direction (not perpendicular to the line between the two pendulums) and resulted in a linear swing of ½″ after a gradual acceleration from rest over about 5 minutes. The mooring and flooring underneath were solid and no motion could be induced by rocking the body back and forth in regular oscillations of various frequencies. Participants were not observed to move their bodies during the attempts except for the hands and arms. There were no earthquakes reported by the news during the times of successful attempts. The occurrence was captured partially once on videotape, showing the acceleration from about ¼″ swing to ½″ swing over a several-minute period in the target pendulum while the control remained motionless. Usually about 5 minutes after the target had begun to swing the second pendulum would begin to swing slightly, probably because it was physically coupled to the target pendulum by being suspended from the same supporting member. In general, trials with pendulums produced successful results when the bobs were plastic or crystal glass faceted spheres about $\frac{1}{2}''$ in diameter but not when they were wood spheres the same size, metal bolts about $\frac{3}{8}''$ wide, or irregularly shaped $\frac{3}{4}''$ chunks of rose quartz stone. It was not clear why some pendulum bobs failed to be influenced. The success ratio for trials on the system seemed to be about one success per 10 minute trial period.

Notable Failures

Notable failures to obtain phenomena indicative of PK occurred when participants were asked to bend-with touching $\frac{1}{8}''$ and $\frac{1}{4}''$ thick plexiglas strips, to bend metal objects sealed in glass flasks, to concentrate at a distance on an ordinary liquid thermometer bulb to heat it, or to concentrate on a sheet of liquid crystal sensitive to temperature to heat it. A number of trials with these targets were attempted over several sessions and no evidence of influence observed though, with the latter targets, temperature variations of under about $\frac{1}{2}°$ would not have been observable.

Generally when two or more participants attempted to influence the same target system at the same time, no enhancement of success seemed to occur. Contrary to this however, was the result that one of the successful pendulum-movers never achieved a successful result when alone outside research sessions, while during sessions he achieved obvious individual success. Other participants noted no pronounced enhancement of their skills when with the group; indeed, some noted better success at home, in private, or when with other persons not involved with the research.

A Case Where PK Ability Increases with Time

Finally, there was one case of apparent steady development of ability in a participant, Dave. At first Dave was capable of only moderately difficult spoon bends with what seemed a fair amount of physical exertion. He could not put any twists in the stem of a spoon, for example, a difficult bending feat. After several months he became able to put a twist, even two, in the axis of a spoon in one or several separate PK efforts. Several months later he could install 3 twists, as well as being able to fold the *bowl* of a silver-plated spoon back on it self in a tight U. About a month later he was able to bend the bowl of a stainless steel spoon in half and back on itself for the first time. During latter sessions of his involvement he became able to exert influences without touching: his was one droop-over while holding a spoon stationary in the hand and the bend on the spoon-with-weight from the next room. Dave's apparent development continued until circumstances forced him to move from the area and discontinue participation and it is possible his ability may have continued to improve had he remained. Only one other participant showed any similar increase in ability, this involving suddenly becoming able to influence the pendulum system after about 8 months of participation in regular research sessions; the ability lasted for the remainder of that participant's involvement with the group.

Discussion

It was the aim of E to determine whether or not participants were exerting macro-PK influences on target systems. Results, while not conclusive, indicate that on some occasions they may have been. However, it is the feeling of E that if PK was exhibited it was only infrequently. Similarly, a conservative estimate is that only 6 of the participants showed results suggestive that something paranormal might have taken place. Among these 6 were both teenagers and adults, males and females; the 6 were a representative sample of the entire group. Hoped-for videotape evidence of demonstrative events never was obtained; at best E has an edited videotape of a few effortless-looking bends and pendulum movements and accelerations.

It should be remarked that E never noticed any of the participants lying about how a particular result was achieved, e.g. by attempting to represent physical maneuvers as purely psychokinetic or by substituting a bent artifact for an unbent target through sleight-of-hand. None were ever observed to produce effects called for in a fraudulent way. Nothing on the video tape records was ever observed that would be incompatible with this assertion.

Generally the research failed to provide evidence for what mental techniques might be optimally related to macro-PK. The majority of apparent PK events observed occurred while a participant seemed to use the "non-method": not concentrating at the time of influence on anything or in any specific way but just vaguely intending PK bending. That the results occurred so often with a lack of conscious technique, and amidst casual conversation does bear similarity to what was noticed about the "Phillip" group's PK effects and the conditions under which they seemed to occur (Owen and Sparrow, 1976).

Future studies with persons claiming weaker forms of macro-PK ability may well benefit from group research sessions. It appeared that maintenance of the light-hearted though serious, casual (yet formal when necessary) atmosphere helped to elicit PK. This is not unlike the findings of other PK researchers (see Batcheldor, 1966). Certainly the social interaction at meetings between persons holding similar beliefs both about the world and about themselves offered a reward that counteracted disappointment at the infrequency of occurrence of strongly evidential phenomena. E was relaxed, casual, friendly and supportive during sessions as well as directive, in a distinct effort to break from the traditional aloofness associated with the role of experimental psychologist. The group developed a cohesiveness of purpose that allowed any individual's success on a task to be defined and felt as a success on the part of the group and this too seemed to help foster a supportive atmosphere for PK.

The provision of a period in each session when bending attempts were not assessed for evidence of PK seemed to build morale and provide a momentum for later PK attempts. Participants could also get the feel of a few physical bends before trying psychokinetic ones if they wished. And once bends of any type began to occur they reported feeling like the ice had been broken, that PK was happening in the room and that it therefore seemed more likely to happen for them soon. This supports the feeling of other experimenters that witnessing an event of apparent PK helps to stimulate later production of genuine PK (Brookes-Smith, 1973).

A final consideration for future research on PK abilities of persons similar to those of this study is the development of a methodologically sound means of testing for PK allowing some touching of the target and application of ordinary physical force to it. If such a design can be found that does not present a task so psychologically formidable that it discourages subjects, then a fair assessment of the presence of "mini" macro-PK ability in the general population might be undertaken. More extensive tests might provide data on whether the ability can be taught or elicited in previously untalented persons; one participant in this research claimed he had "taught" the PK-spoonbending skill to 23 of 25 persons he attempted to teach it to, though no attempt to assess the genuineness of this claim was made. If such a methodology can be found, it would allow the hypothesis to be tested that many persons possess some modicum of macro-PK ability and that it is not just an anomalous skill possessed only by a few in the population.

Mark G. Shafer   August, 1979
School of Social Sciences
Univ. of Calif., Irvine
Irvine, CA 92717

NOTE: Mark Shafer will be joining Prof. Peter Phillip's staff at the McDonnell Laboratory for Psychic Research, Washington University, St. Louis, MO 63130 in September 1980. Persons interested in supporting research in PKMB can contact Shafer at the above address.

References

Batcheldor, K. J. Report on a case of table levitation and associated phenomena. *J.S.P.R.*, 1966, *43*, 339-356.

Brookes-Smith, C. Data-tape recorded experimental PK phenomena. *J.S.P.R.*, 1973, *47*, 69-89.

Hasted, J. B. An experimental study of the validity of metal-bending phenomena. *J.S.P.R.*, 1976, *48*, 365-383.

Owen, I. M. with Sparrow, M. H. *Conjuring Up Phillip: An Adventure in Psychokinesis.* New York: Harper & Row, 1976.

An example of how difficult some scientists find it to reconcile experiences with paranormal phenomena and conventional concepts of physical realities.

'I don't believe in psychics any more' — Prof John Taylor

HAS HE RECANTED GELLER TEST RESULTS?

PN Reporter

IN an incredible about-turn Prof John Taylor, who publicly endorsed Uri Geller's psychic gifts, has virtually recanted his support for the Israeli metal-bender.

He did so in Sunday's "News of the World." His account was headlined, "I don't believe in psychics any more."

Before you read Taylor's remarks, consider the testimonial he signed on King's College notepaper — Taylor works there — in 1974. It was printed on a record sleeve when Geller produced an LP. Taylor affirmed:

❝ I have tested Uri Geller in my laboratory with specially-designed apparatus.

The Geller effect — of metal-bending — is clearly not brought about by fraud. It is so exceptional it presents a crucial challenge to modern science and could even destroy the latter if no explanation became available.

As a scientist I have been investigating some of the dozens of people who appear to have the ability to bend pieces of metal, first demonstrated so efficiently by Uri Geller.

Some I have tested can achieve this without contact, as can Uri. Others only can do this when they hear Geller or see him on TV.

Results have been written up in two scientific papers and two further papers are in preparation, as well as a book. ❞

A year later Taylor's book, "Superminds," called "an inquiry into the paranormal," was released.

In the first chapter Taylor says that on a David Dimbleby TV programme Geller sat between the presenter and himself.

Uri gently stroked one end of a fork, "which resulted in its breaking within a minute or so."

Dimbleby loosely held the other end. Uri, Taylor testifies, did not appear "to be exerting any pressure or force, certainly not enough to break it.

"A startling feature of the demonstration was that the end of the fork just fell off as if the neck had become plastic a moment before."

Taylor states that the variety of metal objects Geller supernormally deformed, "keys, knives, forks, spoons, nails, iron rods and so on, is astounding.

"In my office the evening before the celebrated Dimbleby show he bent the Yale key of a colleague of mine by stroking it gently.

"The total angle was no more than about 30 degrees."

Later Taylor says, "So many cases of bent keys have occurred at demonstrations given by Geller that it is hard to feel any doubt they did actually happen."

The scientist also affirms to having viewed stopped watches supernormally restored by Geller.

"He never touches them, but asks someone else to take them while he holds his hands over theirs.

"This method is not a hundred per cent effective, nor does the watch always keep going . . .

"It is still a remarkable phenomenon, especially when accompanied by the bending of the watch hands inside the glass as occurred on the Dimbleby programme."

Taylor continued that he had investigated Geller "and numbers of children in England and have been convinced that supernormal abilities do actually occur . . .

"In all the total available evidence puts the Geller phenomenon truly into the class of the supernatural."

The same year Taylor was featured in the "Observer Magazine." His astonishingly frank account was titled, "How Geller convinced me."

Taylor said he was invited "to do a hatchet job" on the Dimbleby programme

"Here was I, a trained physicist, a researcher for the past 20 years into the mysteries of matter and mind, witnessing something that I knew I could not explain to myself — let alone to those millions of viewers."

Taylor added, "Someone who has performed in public more than 1,400 times without once being caught cheating has some claim to be taken seriously."

Apart from his powers of telepathy and psychokinesis (supernormal movement of

objects) "even stranger things have gone on around him. One of these is the movement of objects across great distances."

It was then 16 months since he first saw Uri "demonstrating the impossible on the TV programme."

Success achieved

If the Israeli could achieve metal-bending without touch "then the Geller effect would indeed be beyond current scientific understanding." In February 1974 "a successful test of this kind was carried out with Geller by myself."

His powers were tested on pieces of metal (aluminium and copper), strips of various types of plastic, some single crystals of potassium bromide long enough to be stroked like pieces of cutlery, various wire mesh tubes and a sealed glass tube containing a strip of aluminium.

A small but sensitive Geiger counter — to detect radioactivity — was included in the appliances.

The various strips of metal and plastic, and the sealed glass tube, were laid a few inches apart on a metal sheet.

A strip of aluminium, placed inside a wire mesh tube with its end firmly fixed, was also laid out.

The objects had been prepared in the metallurgical department of Taylor's college. There was no chance of Geller having access to them before the experiment.

"Two of my colleagues were also in the room with him acting as observers," Taylor affirmed.

"First of all, Geller tried to bend a metal rod without touching it. He failed.

Done without touch

"It was then observed that one of the aluminium strips lying on the tray was now bent, without, so far as could be seen, having been touched either by him or by anyone else in the room."

To see whether Uri could repeat the metal-bending feat on the TV programme, he was then handed a teaspoon.

"I held the bowl end while he stroked it gently with one hand.

"After about 20 seconds the stem's thinnest part suddenly

became soft for a length of about half a centimetre. Then the spoon broke in two.

"The ends were rapidly hardened up again — in less than a second. There was also, as could be determined by touch, a complete absence of heat at the fracture."

Under laboratory conditions, they had been able to repeat "this remarkable experiment."

The scientist said Geller could simply not have surreptitiously applied enough pressure to have brought this about. The teaspoon could not have been tampered with. It had been in Taylor's possession for a year.

"Then he gently stroked a single crystal of potassium bromide, about two centimetres long. It split into two pieces within ten seconds.

"It was difficult to assess the force that had actually been applied to the crystal. But subsequent tests showed such crystals cannot be broken by gentle stroking alone."

When Geller held his hands over a blue plastic strip this became discoloured. Such discolouration is normal when bending these plastic strips, though he was not able to bend it without touching it.

Sealed strip bends

After this series of tests the objects on the tray were re-examined. It was found that the last five centimetres at one end of the aluminium strip in the closed wire mesh tube was now bent with a radius of curvature of about five centimetres.

"One should bear in mind that Geller was continually under the scrutiny of the two observers. He could not unseen have opened the sealed tube containing the aluminium strip and interfered with it," Taylor stated.

"Indeed he was occupied trying to bend other objects at that time. Further, there was no evidence of any tampering with the tube end."

Taylor's final test was to determine if Geller could produce a deflection on the Geiger counter. This would indicate whether he could induce radioactive radiation.

Sound becomes wail

When it was held near the psychic he registered a zero count on the instrument. He then took the monitor in his hands and tried to influence the counting rate.

"At first nothing happened. But by extreme concentration, and an increase in muscular tension associated with a rising pulse rate, the needle deflected to 50 counts per second for a full two seconds. The drama was

heightened by the sound effects."

A small loudspeaker revealed that each count produced a "pip." Before the young Israeli affected the machine the sound was of a steady "pip . . . pip . . . pip."

"In his hands the sound suddenly rose to become a wail, one which usually indicates dangerous radioactive material nearby. When he stopped concentrating the wail stopped — and the apparent danger with it.

"This wail was repeated twice more. Then when a deflection of 100 counts per second was achieved, the wail rose almost to a scream."

Shown by needle

"Between each of these attempts there was an interval of about a minute."

Taylor said a final attempt made the needle deflect to a reading of one thousand counts per second, again lasting for about two seconds. This was 500 times the background rate. In the process the machine "was emitting a scream."

At the end of the session the Geiger counter was tested to see if its counting rate could be modified by pressure on the monitor to produce the same effect.

Despite the considerable force applied, no change came in the counting rate from that caused by background radiation.

"It therefore seemed unlikely he had achieved this effect by distortion of the monitor head."

Geller returned to Taylor's laboratory. He obtained results that "enormously widened the range of phenomena and gave a very clear demonstration of his ability to distort a wide range of materials."

A balance used to weigh letters and parcels, sensitive enough to measure a quarter of an ounce, was used. A brass strip about 20 centimetres long was taped horizontally to the platform of the balance.

The major portion of the strip extended out from the platform. Geller stroked the top surface of it while Taylor measured, both directly by reading the scale and using an automatic recording device, the pressure he applied.

At the end of the test the strip had acquired a bend of ten degrees. Yet at no time had Geller applied more than half an ounce of pressure.

"It was out of the question that such a small pressure could have produced that deflection. What is more, the actual bending occurred upwards — *against* the pressure of the finger."

During this experiment, "It was a little disconcerting, to say

the least, to have the needle indicating the amount of pressure on the letter balance, also bending as it did through 70 degrees.

"This didn't seem to upset the operation of the balance. But it made reading the scale difficult. However, the more devastating was yet to come."

A pressure-measuring device, a small cylinder embedded in a strip of aluminium, had been used with various subjects. No bending had been achieved.

"In Geller's case the consequences were drastic. While holding the strip in one hand he made it bend in the appropriate region so that the pressure could be measured. But as the bending occurred the mechanism in the cylinder suddenly stopped functioning."

The scientist took the apparatus from him. "To my horror I observed the pressure-sensitive diaphragm began to crumble. A small hole appeared in its centre. It spread across its whole surface until the diaphragm had completely disintegrated.

"The entire process only took about ten seconds. After another three minutes the strip in which the cylinder was embedded had bent a further 30 degrees.

"The Geller effect had been validated. But at the cost of £200 worth of equipment!"

Then Geller held his hands over a plastic container holding a small crystal of lithium fluoride. Within ten seconds the crystal broke into a number of pieces.

"There was absolutely no chance of his having touched the crystal. Throughout the experiment I could see a gap between his hands and the container holding the crystal," Taylor wrote.

"He also buckled a small disc of aluminium, again inside a plastic container, while I held my hands between his and the container to prevent any possibility of his directly manipulating the disc."

Geller then concentrated on a strip of copper on which was glued a thin wire.

Deformed at distance

He tried to bend the copper strip without direct contact. Nothing happened after several minutes.

"We broke off to start measuring his electrical output. Turning round a few moments later I saw the strip had been bent. The thin wire was broken.

"Almost simultaneously I noticed a brass strip on the other side of the laboratory had also become bent. I had placed it there a few minutes before, making sure then it was straight."

The scientist pointed out to him what had happened, "only to hear a metallic crash from the far end of the laboratory 20ft away. There, on the floor by the far door, was the bent piece of brass.

"Again I turned back, whereupon there was another crash. A small piece of copper which had earlier been lying near the bent brass strip on the table had followed its companion to the far door."

Before he knew what had happened "I was struck on the back of the legs by a perspex tube in which had been sealed an iron rod. It had also lain on the table. It was now at my feet with the rod bent as much as the container would allow.

"Pandora's box had certainly opened up! None of the flying objects could have actually been thrown by Geller. He was some distance away. He could not get close to them without being seen."

Taylor made a check under more repeatable conditions. He set a compass on a stable surface. He asked Geller to try to cause the needle to rotate without touching it. This he did by passing his hands over it, turning the needle up to 40 times.

Taylor tried to simulate the feat, keeping ten centimetres from the compass as Geller had.

"It proved impossible, either by imitating his movements or by stamping on the ground. Even rocking or rotating the compass directly had little effect except when an obvious effort was used."

Objects 'fly'

At the end of this session, a loud click was heard at the other side of the laboratory.

"We discovered the small piece of metal, which had flown to the far end of the room, was no longer lying on the floor.

"We searched the laboratory. It was nowhere in sight."

A later search after Geller left revealed the metal under a radiator.

"This left me in a state of even greater mystification than before. Objects had apparently been made to 'fly' through the air. A compass needle had been caused to rotate without the intervention of a visible mechanism.

"These events seemed impossible to comprehend. I should certainly have dismissed reports of them as nonsense if I had not seen them happen for myself."

In Sunday's "News of the World" Taylor said he was "impressed" when he first heard of Geller. However, Taylor has previously maintained he was a sceptic.

To pinpoint answers

After the "stunning TV appearance" Geller made on a Dimbleby programme, Taylor tested him for about 90 minutes in his laboratory.

"But in spite of the friendly and encouraging atmosphere, he didn't succeed in causing any abnormal effects," he told readers.

"I'm sure I could pinpoint many answers for the effects he achieves if I could test him with properly prepared experiments, but he doesn't appear to be willing to be tested under these controlled conditions."

Geller, Taylor added, seemed to turn the scientific world upside down and put his whole faith in science at risk.

The professor's interest in the supernormal was whetted. "I thought there might be something in it, and that we might learn more about the human mind," he said. "But every so-called psychic phenomenon I investigated crumbled before my eyes."

Preview dismissed

Taylor said he attended seances, visited haunted churchyards, studied healing case histories, and watched psychics bend spoons. He checked records of predictions and interviewed prophets and hypnotists.

"Now, after seven years of detailed and exhaustive research into so-called psychic phenomena, I am convinced that no such things exist."

Taylor began by describing a premonition a woman had about the Moorgate Underground station tragedy in which 43 passengers died and 74 were injured.

Though Taylor said that "survivors described precisely the scene the housewife had seen in her dreams," he dismissed her preview as "quite simply an astonishing coincidence"!

In his view it was merely a "mystifying trick of the mind" with nothing supernormal about it.

The professor opined that there are many baffling mysteries not yet explained. "But I am sure that science will eventually find an answer for them all."

It was difficult, he added, "to explain the success" of psychics like Dutch clairvoyant Gerard Croiset.

"I feel sure he is an honest man who is convinced of his own powers," said the scientist.

Taylor described a "well documented" case in which Croiset gave psychic clues that were later confirmed.

The clairvoyant's chances "of accuracy were absolutely minimal. It's unlikely he could have gathered any clues through contacts or accomplices in Britain."

Healers praised but —

Not all of Croiset's attempts had been successful. "Even those which appear so may still be coincidental," Taylor asserted.

He admitted that psychic healing "seems to confound my findings. I have no scientific or logical explanation for some remarkable examples."

Though he conducted laboratory tests between healers and patients, Taylor found no evidence of an energy transfer.

However, PN has printed photos depicting how patients' fingertip auras become enlarged after healing.

The reverse happens with healers; theirs diminish.

Taylor felt that healers "may be among the very few people in the paranormal world who are actually bringing real benefit to those who believe in them."

Whether or not energy was transferred, a healer's "soothing touch seems able to give patients the will to live."

But how does Taylor explain absent healing cases in which the patient does not know treatment had been sought by a third party? How can animals or babies be given the will to live?

No names given

Taylor cited the case of an unnamed American medium who "confessed he was just one of a group of 2,000 other fakes who spread their network across the United States."

Each kept personal information files about sitters, and traded details.

The medium would utilise an accomplice who, dressed in black, crept round seance rooms making objects rise in the air.

"They would even lift their clients off the floor by grabbing the legs of their chairs," Taylor explained. "Not once did anyone catch on.

"I regret," he ended, "that this sort of trickery is widespread in the psychic world."

No supporting evidence was given for this extraordinary statement.

Taylor's latest book, "Science and the Supernatural," appears later this month.

The Committee for the Scientific Investigation of Claims of the Paranormal

The Committee for the Scientific Investigation of Claims of the Paranormal has the following objectives:

- To establish a network of people interested in critically examining claims of the paranormal.
- To prepare bibliographies of published materials that carefully examine such claims.
- To encourage and commission research by objective and impartial inquirers in areas where it is needed.
- To convene conferences and meetings.
- To publish articles, monographs, and books that examine claims of the paranormal.
- To not reject such claims on a priori grounds, antecedent to inquiry, but rather to examine them objectively and carefully.

THE SKEPTICAL INQUIRER (formerly THE ZETETIC) is the official journal of the Committee.

Committee sections have been established in Canada, France, Belgium, Germany, Great Britain, and New Zealand. The Committee also has a UFO subcommittee.

PARANORMAL ACTION ON METAL
AND ITS SURROUNDINGS
J. B. Hasted and D. Robertson

In issues (1, 2, 3, 4) of the *Journal of the Society for Psychical Research* the dynamic strain data obtained without touch or strips of metal suspended in the vicinity of child 'paranormal metal-benders' were reported and analysed. In this contribution we consider not only dynamic strains in the metal but structural, electrical and psychological effects. Most of the data was obtained with Stephen North, now sixteen years of age, as a subject, but new experiments have also been conducted with Willie G, Julie Knowles, and Clifford W, aged eleven.

Recent resistive strain gauge sessions have included investigations of localization, and of surface of action configuration.

Localization

Previous reported investigations[3] of the localization of synchronous dynamic strain signals were conducted with three strain gauges arranged in line along a metal strip. It was found that in general the centre strain gauge signal was the largest of three synchronous signals. It appeared that the strains were centred within a "region of action," of variable position, size and power. Each set of three synchronous signal magnitudes were fitted uniquely to a Gaussian $[I = I_o \exp\{-\alpha(x-x_o)^2\}$ of width $\frac{1}{\alpha}$ and centre $x_o.]$. Thus the variation of α, x and I_o from one synchronous signal triplet to the next could be studied statistically; some consistency was found in the position and size of the region of action. Negative values of α were only found rarely.

In recent sessions we have repeated these experiments with five strain gauges arranged along a metal strip. A dummy strain gauge[4], circuitry and sixth chart recorder channel were included in order to avoid confusing any electrical artifacts with paranormal dynamic strains. Five data points will not in general fit exactly on a Gaussian curve, but we can nevertheless compute the best fit to each signal quintet and the least squares error. The data for session SNHH with Stephen North are analysed in Table 1, and the fitting of signals from a pair of events is illustrated in Figure 1*; one is among the best fits and one among the worst. Thus the generalisation that there is nearly always a bell-shaped pattern of signal magnitudes, or 'region of action', remains valid.

Four further sessions have been devoted to the study of distribution of signal magnitudes along a single metal strip. In each session five strain gauges were used, equidistant and separated from their neighbours by 3.5 cm. The metal strips, typically 20.3 x 1.1 x 0.11 cm. were deployed in one of three orthogonal directions with respect to the subject; the left hand of Stephen North extended to about six inches from the nearest end of the strip. In one session, JJ, a permanent bend was observed, and the disturbance was such that it has not been thought worthwhile to analyze the data. In three other sessions, Gaussians were fitted to the data: in session K, only 10 signal quintets out of a total of 20

---

*Figures 1-5 at end of article.

Table 1

Gaussian parameters for the events of Session SN HH

Before Instruction

Number	I_o (mV)	α	x_o	$E = \sqrt{\sigma/n}$
1	2.5	.030	10.8	.069
2	11.0	.007	2.9	.041
3	34.0	.009	7.6	.050
4	4.8	.038	9.6	.054
5	9.9	.009	0.3	.073
6	26.3	.014	3.5	.06
7	18.9	.046	4.3	.067
8	3.6	.027	7.0	.091
9	2.7	.008	0.9	.110
10	40.5	.016	3.3	.045
11	53.5	.013	3.4	.088
12	33.3	.004	5.2	.014
mean values	20.1	.020	0.58	

After Instruction

Number	I_o (mV)	α	x_o	$E = \sqrt{\sigma/n}$
1	8.1	.016	8.6	.036
2	11.9	.023	14.2	.031
3	4.9	.036	13.2	.045
4	12.5	.005	25.0	.050
5	2.4	.036	11.3	.167
6	8.1	.014	6.8	.090
7	17.5	.019	10.2	.067
8	16.1	.020	9.9	.130
9	10.8	.021	12.2	.104
10	22.8	.007	5.3	.130
11	17.3	.020	11.2	.080
12	11.9	.018	11.4	.191
13	14.1	.005	16.6	.053
mean values	12.2	.018	12.0	

were at all suitable, but in session DD all except one of 14 quintets recorded were readily fitted. In Session HH, 26 quintets were recorded, and only one was entirely unsuitable. After the first 12, Stephen North was asked to concentrate on producing the 'action' in a region further from his outstretched left hand than he had already produced action. It was not possible at this stage to conduct this experiment double-blind. Nevertheless, the chart-recorded data were computer-fitted, the parameters of the Gaussian being reproduced in Table 2. Inspection of the values of x_0 and their mean shows that in fact Stephen was successful in moving the action away from him by 11.4 cm.

The previously defined[3] indecision parameter J for the sessions was recorded to have the following values:

DD   0.18

HH   0.40

JJ   0.30

KK   0.05

There is clearly much irregularity in the spatial variation of signal magnitudes. This may be termed 'localisation of the action'; its lower spatial limits may be investigated by increasing the spatial resolving power of the array of uniformly spaced strain gauges. If y is the separation between neighbouring strain gauges, then analysis by means of a trigonmetric series

$$I(y_n) = a + by + c \sin y + d \sin 2y + e \sin 3y$$

yields a series of parameters a - e specific to each signal quintet. For a simple bell-shaped region of action the parameters c, d, e decrease successively. But when fine structure dominates $e > d > c$. The parameter $L = c/e$ could be regarded as a measure of the localization of each signal quintet.

A feeling for its meaning can be obtained by an inspection of Figure 2; the quantity L has been computed for actual Gaussian curves of widths shown, and a histogram of the L values calculated from signal quintets is plotted on the same scale.

New miniaturized strain gauges have become available, particularly suitable for localization studies. Micro Measurements Type EA-09-031-MF-12 is capable of considerable spatial resolving power, and is illustrated to scale in Figure 2 (inset). The session with Stephen North using this multiple strain gauge resulted in localisation parameters l which are statistically summarized as a histogram in Figure 2. It should be stressed that there is no proof that when the localisation is as small as this, the extent of the region of action is as large as usual (20 cm). It would be necessary to conduct high resolving power and low resolving power observations simultaneously if both upper and lower limits were required.

Synchronous Strains and "Surface of Action" Configuration

In earlier studies with Nicholas Williams using two and three "sensors" (small independent metal specimens each carrying one strain gauge), many synchronous signals were observed with the subject at several metres distant.[2] Most synchronisms were obtained when the sensors lay on a vertical surface stretching radially outwards from the subject (a 'surface of action'); but since a minority of synchronous signals were obtained with the sensors arrayed around the subject and equidistant from him, it was postulated that the surface of action could sometimes display curvature. It was recognised in our discussion of these studies that other interpretations would be consistent with the data, and it was stated that further observations would be made.

We have now extended the observations, with Stephen North as the subject.

Normally five sensors were used simultaneously, the remaining chart recorder channel being used for the dummy strain gauge.

Table 2 summarizes the data analysis for these sessions. We define the synchronism ratio S for an event as the ratio of the number of the synchronous signals to the total number of sensors exposed. The mean value of S, denoted $\bar{S}$, is calculated for a session. We also tabulate a mean value S_w weighted according to signal magnitudes. It is clear from Table 2 that both $\bar{S}$ and $\bar{S}_w$ decrease in the order RV > RH > EV   . This is in accord with the Nicholas Williams sessions[2] from which it was deduced that the surface of action was normally radial (R) and vertical (V).

Table 2

Data analysis summary for surface of action experiments.

Session	Configuration	Number of Sensors	Horizontal or Radial Extent (cm)	Vertical Extent (cm)	Number of Signals	$\bar{S}$	$\bar{S}_w$
EE	RV	5	26	26	}14	0.69	0.90
PP	RV	4	21	13			
GG	RH	5	26	7	}19	0.41	0.49
LL	RH	5	30	8			
FF	EV	6	36	15	}33	0.31	0.29
HH1	EV	4	18	15			

Stephen North behaves differently from Nicholas Williams in sessions in that he cannot rid himself of the idea, which seems to be correct in his case, that metal-bending action usually extends from his hands or arms. Normally he points one hand, or even one finger, in the direction of the sensors. When these are mounted in a radial configuration, it is natural that there are synchronisms on several sensors; the 'surface of action' might be regarded as an invisible extension of the subject's arm. The relevance to 'observational' theories of psychokinesis is obvious.

The occurrence of equidistant (E) sensor synchronisms in Stephen North's sessions was therefore of particular interest. It became apparent to me during my witnessing of them that possibly both hands might be involved. As will be seen from Table 2, the horizontal distances between the synchronous sensors were quite small; although Stephen was asked to produce action on the entire array, he was accustomed to point his left hand at the left-hand sensor; on occasion the right hand would also point as though he felt that this was the natural way to produce a wider action. When both right and left hands were pointed, synchronisms would sometimes occur at the sensor at which they were being pointed. Thus the conception of the surface of action as an extension of the arms is somewhat strengthened and it is possible that more than one surface can be produced by one subject.

A pair of remarkable sessions was held with Stephen North using one sensor strapped to the forearm and one suspended in front of him. The forearm sensor was in the form of a circular disc with a rosette of three strain gauges at the centre; with this equipment the direction of the individual strain vectors can be determined[4]. The disc was mechanically decoupled from the forearm by its being mounted only on its screened leads, so that the disc was raised about 1 cm above the hairs on the forearm. If signals were obtained on this sensor, the experiment would show to what extent the strain vectors were aligned along the forearm. Also there is the question of whether synchronous signals would be observed on forearm sensor and suspended sensor.

The data from these sessions do not support the notion that the forearm sensor strain vectors show any tendency to be aligned along the forearm; the angular distribution appears to be fairly random.

However, the arrangement in time of the dynamic strain signals on the forearm and suspended sensors turns out to have tantalizing features, as will be seen from Figure 3. It appears that each set of signals on the forearm is followed after an interval by a signal on the suspended sensor (indicated by a diagonal broken line). Of course this is only one of several possible interpretations but it is nevertheless worthy of notice. What is surprising is the very long series of times between the corresponding signals. If this interpretation is correct, a very slow speed of the surface of action is indicated.

Touching of the Sensors

It is necessary to devize a policy of protection against touching of the sensor by the subject. We have on four occasions successfully obtained video or moving picture records of strain gauge sessions, including in the field of vision both sensors, the hands and the moving chart pens. It cannot be denied that signals in these sessions were not always plentiful, but at least no evidence of touch was apparent in the records.

Another investigator[5] has reported such evidence to us and noticed that strain gauge signals appeared both when touching was photographed and also when the record showed no touch. The subject was permitted to hold one end of a thick bar in his hand, and the strain gauges were mounted at the other end which was exposed to the action without touch by the other hand. It appeared that the subject regarded the ability to produce manual signals as a sort of insurance against the possibility of his not being able to produce paranormal signals, which he was able to do without great difficulty. As is often the case in psychic research, a mixture of paranormal and natural effects had to be encountered.

With child subjects the tendency to touch is less well developed than with an adult psychic; we have observed very little touch but on one occasion a tendency was observed to snatch at the sensor when the noise of the moving pen on the chart record was heard; thus the hand arrived distinctly late. Nevertheless, this could not be tolerated and, on some excuse, a moving target was substituted which cured the tendency. Partial screening has the same curative effect. Also we installed a highly sensitive electrical 'touch detector' similar in operation to the touch panel switches used in elevators. It seems to have proved its value mostly as a deterrent.

Electrical Effects

During a session with Stephen North using both electrostatic touch detector and resistive strain gauges, a particularly strong permanent deformation signal of a metal disc was recorded whilst a close observation of the hands was being maintained; it was clear beyond doubt that the closest hand (the left) was at least four inches from the metal and was stationary. But Stephen cried out that he felt a prick at the end of his thumb at the moment when the chart-recorder pens were heard to move. Furthermore, the touch detector recorded a signal which must have been caused by the passage of a pulse of electrical current to the metal. I quickly examined Stephen's thumb and a tiny mark could be seen. When the finger was squeezed, a miniscule drop of blood appeared. Moreover, the metal disc showed a deformation through about 20°.

It has been believed for some time that paranormal electrical effects can sometimes take place in physical mediumship. Eusapia Palladino and Stanislava Tomcyzk were able to discharge gold leaf electroscopes by holding the fingers at 5-6 cm distance[12]. This action took place 'suddenly at the end of a certain time; it required 'an effort' of will and was accompanied by tingling at the ends of her fingers'. The similarity to the present observation is striking and significant. Brookes-Smith[6] reported the development of temporary conduction paths on the surface of the table in sitter-group experiments; these were synchronous with mechanical effects. An early experiment[7] conducted with Uri Geller pointed strongly towards the paranormal production of electric current in a stainless steel tube.

In the winter of 1978-9 we decided to search systematically for electric signals at metal electrodes exposed both to Stephen North and to Matthew Manning; for this purpose a sensitive low impedance input operational amplifier was built, the improved circuit being shown in Figure 4. Because of the low input impedance of this instrument, it is insensitive to electrically or magnetically induced artifacts produced without touch of the exposed input electrode. Although actual touch produces electrostatic artifacts, no witness or observer could produce signals when the hands were stationary and separated from the electrode by a few inches. Nevertheless Stephen North was able to produce spontaneous signals, and Matthew Manning was also able on request to produce signals correlated in time with violent circular motions of his arms. Ultimately these were found to be capacitative in origin, there being an unusually high static charge on Matthew Manning's hands. It is therefore of great importance that the hand is not moved violently during the sessions. A motionless hand will not induce dynamic signals, unless considerable electrostatic charge were to move rapidly along the skin—itself an effect which might be accorded the status of paranormality.

The spontaneous dynamic signals produced also in static hand experiments with Julie Knowles could be interpreted as a production of a surplus or deficiency of carriers (electrons) in the metal electrode. Tests were made for atmospheric ionization by means of a four-inch diameter ferrite ring wound with a toroidal coil and connected to a separate amplifier. Placed between the subject's hand and the metal electrode, this will detect, by induction, time variations of atmospheric current. Although dynamic signals were first observed, these disappeared on screening the coil; they appear to have been induced paranormally directly onto the wires of the coil. Thus we have found no evidence for atmospheric currents.

It is apparent from sessions with Stephen North that some electrical signals are synchronous with dynamic strain signals whilst some are not. Two distinctly different types of action are involved. It may be that the electrical detector is as sensitive a detector of psychokinetic action as is a resistive strain gauge. Greater care with electrical screening of strain gauges is necessary than had at first been anticipated. When an unscreened strain gauge on metal faces directly towards the hand of the metal-bender, it is possible that it may receive electrical signals. In our earliest strain gauge experiments[2] the screening was thorough. In some later experiments with incompletely screened strain gauges,[3] these were mounted on the metal face opposite to the metal-bender; and of course with strain gauge insulated from the metal.

Our experiments on electrical effects are as yet under-developed; the most probable interpretation is that short bursts of charge can be controllably produced remotely and paranormally on, or in, remote metal targets. This is in line with the early interpretations of the effects produced by Eusapia Palladino. Both Langevin and Curie believed that no atmospheric ionization was produced[12].

Structural Effects

In the pioneer studies of metal-bender Jean-Pierre Girard by Crussard and Bouvaist[8] three paranormally produced structural effects were reported: anomalous hardening, anomalous softening, conversion of austenite to martensite.

The anomalous hardening was confirmed by the authors[4]; electron microscopic examinations carried out by Crussard and Bouvaist showed that in the region of anomalous hardening a high density of dislocations, especially loop dislocations, were present. There was no permanent deformation of the specimen although a very slight paranormal thinning took place.

The question therefore arose: were the paranormally produced dislocations linked quantitatively to strain gauge signals? We attempted to investigate by arranging that Dr. Bouvaist would monitor the dislocation density on an aluminium alloy specimen before and after its exposure, with resistive strain gauges mounted, to sessions with Stephen North. In three sessions a large number of resistive strain gauge peaks was obtained.

The dimensions of the specimen were 6 x 4 x 0.2 cm, and the six gauges were mounted after the manner of the pips on a playing card, but with three orientated orthogonally to the other three. However, more than ten recorded permanent deformations occurred during the sessions and since the specimen finished up smoothly curved in orthogonal directions, it is difficult to estimate just how much this contributed to the formation of dislocations. The analysis showed a high density of dislocations throughout the specimen but unfortunately the differential between pre-exposure and post-exposure values showed insufficient variations to enable correlations with the strain gauge data to be meaningful. Two subsequent experiments with ultra-pure perfect silicon crystal wafers resulted in multiple fractures. It cannot therefore be claimed that there is quantitative correlation between dislocation density and strain gauge records.

The hardness enhancement when dislocation densities are increased is in line with metallurgical expectations. But an interpretation of the anomalous softening must be sought along different lines. In these cases Crussard and Bouvaist reported the appearance of melting at grain boundaries, seen in low magnification electron micrographs. This behaviour is normally characteristic of quasi-viscous creep, which takes place at temperatures close to the melting point. Thus what is suggested is a localized microscopic action whilst the bulk of the metal hardly changes temperature at all. This action may be related to three previously reported findings.

1) The rare 'plasticization of metal' in which temporary local softening, without heat, is observed[7].

2) The anomalous accelerated bendings of specimens of the triple eutectic alloy of bismuth, tin and cadmium[1] which has been inferred from the absence of hardening enhancement at the deformation to take place by creep.

3) Electron micrographs showing local melting of a fractured gold ring reported by the late Dr Wilbur Franklin[7]. Although these have been criticised because of the possibility that the condition could have been caused by cavitation during brazing in the manufacture, the question must remain open.

The final paranormal structured effect reported by Crussard and Bouvaist[8] has been the conversion of regions of high carbon steel from a metastable state into a stable state: from austenite into martensite. Such conversions can also be brought about by heat (to 600° C) or by violent mechanical action such as shot-peening.

The diagnosis of these regions is carried out by electron micrography but a useful subsidiary technique has also been used, based on the fact that the martensite is ferromagnetic whilst the austenite is not. Ferromagnetic regions are detected by means of the spatial dependence of the relative motions of specimen and permanent magnet in various designs of experiment.

This reported result is consistent with a finding made by the present authors, together with Elizabeth Rauscher, using commercial stainless steel cutlery. Such cutlery is usually slightly ferromagnetic, and if a search is made for poles with a small compass needle, then the normal configuration is with two poles only, one at each end. Such items, after checking for absence of subsidiary poles, are offered to metal-benders. It has been found in eleven cases that cutlery paranormally bent sharply or twisted tightly shows subsidiary poles on each side of the bend or twist. Such poles cannot easily be produced in deformation by mechanical force; violent hammering or heat treatment are found to be necessary.

The subsidiary poles are evidence that there is a region at the bend or twist in which no path of ferromagnetic domains exist between the ends of the specimen; the entire cross-section of the specimen must have passed into the non-ferromagnetic phase.

Although the tests here reported are of a qualitative nature, and have not been performed a large number of times, it is likely that a structural phenomenon is responsible for observations.

The twisted spoons are themselves evidence of some kind of structural change. Figure 5 shows a close-up photography of a witnessed twist brought about in the hands of the sixteen-year-old Japanese metal-bender Masuaki Kiyota. When a similar stainless steel spoon is twisted by the application of torque using tools, fracture will occur before a pitch as tight as that shown in

Figure 5 is reached. This is because the stress-strain curve for all metals, which is linear in the limit of small stress, eventually flattens and passes through a maximum at which point fracture must occur. It follows that at no point on the metal can the strain (relative elongation) exceed a certain experimentally well-known value characteristic of each metal and typically in the region of 0.2. Neglecting hump-back distortion, the strain ϵ_0 at the short surface of a bar of width 2r twisted through pitch p is given by

$$\epsilon_0 + 1 = (p^2 + 4 \pi^2 r^2)^{1/2}/p$$

A pitch as tight as that sometimes found in the teaspoons of Masuaki Kiyota would demand values of E_0 in excess of 2, which would be unobtainable without some temporary change in the stress-strain characteristic, which is of course structure-dependent. Attempts are in progress to monitor permanent structural change on the twisted region by microhardness measurement.

A permanent structural change effect has been observed in the anomalous plane bends produced by Willie G on strips on brass. Such thin strips (7 mm x 0.5 mm) can be bent with a minimum of force but only out of the plane of the flat surface; a anomalous in-plane bend is much more difficult to achieve mechanically and is usually brought about by the use of rollers. Willie G is able to bring about anomalous in-plane bends by stroking. Annealed specimens of α-brass (70% Cu, 30% Zn) were prepared by Mycock and Smith and anomalous plane bends were achieved by Willie G. Etching allows a distinction to be made between regions of α-brass and β-brass (60% Cu, 40% Zn), which appear darker. Inspection of the records shows that the dense β-brass regions appear at the anomalous plane bend. It is not supposed that the stoichometric composition of the alloy changes macroscopically but rather that structural transformation occurs locally, redistributing the regions of different structure. This finding is to be taken as preliminary and further work is in progress.

Psychology and Micro-PK

Previous investigators of psychokinesis have obtained information from which generalizations might be made about the psychological states of the subjects at the moments at which action is recorded.[9] It is apparent that the resistive strain gauge in a suspended piece of metal is a suitable piece of equipment for this type of experimentation. This idea was put forward by Julian Isaacs who has commenced the study of audio records made of conversations taking place during recorded strain gauge sessions[10]. These are somewhat in the tradition of 'sitter-group experiments' in which the expected psycho-kinetic events are paranormal rapping phenomena, similar to 'spirit rapping', and table movements.

Isaacs distinguishes two interpretations: that of Whitton[11], who proposes that the subject's unconscious is triggered by certain background noises of which he possesses hidden fears due to their association in childhood with emotional conflict, and that of Batcheldor[9] who proposes that a sudden distracting stimulus, producing a changed state of consciousness, can be accompanied by a momentary state in which the action can occur. Isaacs finds that[10] the second interpretation is not in implausible agreement with his observations. In the present paper it will be helpful to record the relevance of our own experiences.

A sudden relief of 'concentration' has certainly been found by us to be an effective inducer of signals. Physicist Dr R. B. started training himself in transcendental meditation and became confident that with sufficient practice he would be able to produce signals. After several weeks of solitary practice, we held a session with him. During the meditation period no signals were observed but immediately upon resuming conversation a group of substantial signals appeared.

With Stephen North and his family it was commonplace of the first few sessions that after a period of concentration, a burst of signals would appear when Mrs North suggested a break for tea. As soon as this was recognized by Stephen himself, without help from me, the signals failed to appear on cue.

This example might be interpreted in an alternative way; namely, that Stephen was responding to an offer of a reward. Indeed, eleven-year-old Clifford W. produced his best signals when food was mentioned—'chicken principe' and MacDonald's'. However, these mentions were references to past joys, and may resemble Julian Isaacs record[10] of a signal precisely of the "H" of 'Oh, what a Happy time that was!'

The state of mind of the experimenter also enters into the observations, perhaps directly, or perhaps because visual or auditory evidence is picked up by the subject. A routine or casual approach by the experimenter is not likely to be rewarded with signals. On the other hand, an attitude that is not neutral may perturb the whole psychology of the experiment which should be initiated and governed by the attitudes of the subject, unless a planned intervention is intended. Sometimes a stable routine background is deliberately imposed; for example, a task in model-building for Nicholas Williams, or listening to recorded music. However, it has not been possible to correlate signals with details of this background such as successful achievements in the model-building or climactic moments in the music.

Our instincts as experimenters are to exercise great caution in reaching conclusions on the basis of insufficient experience.

Figures 1, 2, 3, 4 and 5 referred to in article appear on next page.

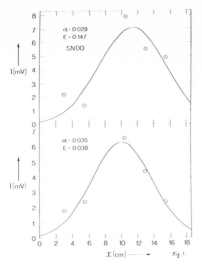

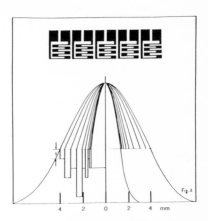

1. The fitting of Gaussian curve to two signal quintets from session DD with Stephen North. The upper curve represents one of the least satisfactorily fitted quintets, the lower curve one of the best fitted sets.

2. Inverted histogram of the number of localization parameters I. calculated for signal events recorded on miniaturized strain gauges shown above (Type EA-06-031MF-120, bisected). The scale I. is taken to be that of the illustrated Gausians whose I. values have been calculated. In this way the effective localization (about 2 mm) obtained during the session SNMM is illustrated.

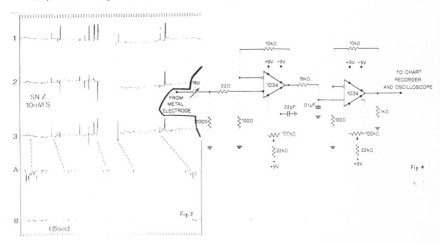

3. Some dynamic strain signals obtained on sensors mounted on Stephen North's forearm and suspended in front of him, in session SNZ.

4. Circuit of improved electrostatic detector used in Stephen North electrical observations.

5. Photograph of stainless steel spoon seen to be twisted, quickly but gently, in the hands of Masuaki Kiyota.

References

1. J. B. Hasted, "An Experimental Study of the Validity of Metal-Bending Phenomena." *Journal of the Society for Psychical Research.* Vol 48, No 770, 1976, pp 365-383.

2. J. B. Hasted, "Physical Aspects of Paranormal Metal-Bending." *Journal of the Society for Psychical Research.* Vol 49, No 773, 1977 pp 583-607.

3. J. B. Hasted, "Paranormal Metal-Bending," In course of publication in *New Horizons* 1979.
    J. B. Hasted, "Merkmale paranormaler Metallbiege-Phaenomene" *Zeitschrift fuer Parapsychologie und Grenzgebiete der Psychologie.* Jg 20, Nr 3, 1978 pp 173-184.

4. J. B. Hasted and D. Robertson, "The Detail of Paranormal Metal-Bending." *Journal of the Society for Psychical Research.* Vol 50, No 779, 1979, pp. 9-20.

5. J. Bouvaist, Pechiney Aluminium, Grenoble, private communication. 1979.

6. C. Brookes-Smith. *Journal of the Society for Psychical Research.* Vol 48, 1975, pp 73-86.

7. J. B. Hasted in "The Geller Papers," Ed. Charles Panati, Houghton-Mifflin Co. Boston 1976, pp 183-196, 197-212.

8. C. M. Crussard and J. Bouvaist. *Memoires Scientifiques Revue Metallurgique.* 1978, February, p. 117.

9. K. J. Batcheldor. "Micro-PK in Group Sittings: Theoretical and Practical Aspects." 1968. Society for Psychical Research Library.

10. J. Isaacs. A preliminary report on some micro-p.k. experiments. Parascience Proceedings (3) 1978. In press.

11. J. L. Whitton. "The Psychodynamics of Poltergeist Activity and Group PK. *New Horizons I,* (5) 1975. pp 202-211.

12. R. Sudre. *Treatise on Parapsychology,* Allen and Unwin, 1960. pp 218-224.

13. J. B. Hasted. *The Physics of Atomic Collisions.* Chapter 10, 2nd Edition. Butterworth's London. 1972.

COSMIC IRRADIATIONS IN (MASS) HEALING PROCESSES: A MANIFESTATION OF MICRO AND MACRO COSMOS UNITY.

By Barbara Ivanova, Moscow, U.S.S.R.

BARBARA IVANOVA has written extensively about her work involving PK, healing, etc. We were first put in contact with her by Dr. Gerda Walther, a German parapsychologist, in 1975. Since then we have received numerous articles about her work. In a recent letter she described a "Round Table" on healing held in the U.S.S.R. in May 1980 in which she, Safanov and other healers participated, the day after "we had official experiments in a hospital and the organizers told about our results. Some professors of physics spoke at this meeting." In that letter she included the summary of a paper she prepared for the International Conference on Psychotronics Research, Sao Paulo, Brazil, in 1979. We present this summary as another example of the activities which are carried on in other parts of the world, and of the concepts which are evolving to explain little understood phenomena which do occur.

This experimental and training work is devoted to the cosmo-bioenergetic healing processes in groups—methods which have been used by the author, who is the first teacher of healing in the U.S.S.R. We consider healing an energy-informational interaction of bio-cosmic influences, selectively resonating to sick organs of the body. Our combined methods include:

a) transference of bio-cosmic energy to a collected group of persons by healer, and

b) "immersions," "mutual healing," and other group techniques.

Psychological, physiological, ethical, and consequently, social results are registered, as well as difference between the two methods: bio- and cosmo-healing.

A. Chizhevsky says:

Organic life is possible only where there is free access of cosmic radiations, because to live means to let pass through the organism, the flow of cosmic energy in its kinetic form.[1]

If access is blocked, as a result of conditions or actions, illness is inevitable. We may, in a general way, consider the body as an auto-regulating and auto-renewing cybernetic system. It cannot function well if one of its feeding-subsystems (the one which gives the energy) cannot operate properly. The irradiations of the healer interact with cosmic irradiation. By means of our volitional-emotional impulses, we transform, accumulate, concentrate and direct the irradiations to the audience (group). The mechanism of the process is connected with the resonance of the bio-system. Experiments in influencing the respiratory system, rate of heart-beat, muscle contractions, etc. under objective control[2] show that impositing changes (i.e. oscillation frequencies) volitionally on the bio-fields of other bio-systems is possible. We cannot exclude the

245

possibility of influencing cosmic irradiations either.

The geologist, V. Neumann, a man of daring thought, says that the meridians of acupuncture are the body's energetical framework—a system analogous to, and connected with the structural energy network of the Cosmos, which extends from galaxies and even to elemental units. On Earth this system is represented by a unified network of force triangles and pentangles. This theory has been developed in the U.S.S.R. by Kislitzyn, Goncharov et al[3] and expanded by V. Neumann.[4] The frequencies of this cosmic network are resonant and achieve a co-resonance with the organisms they influence.[5]

A. Dubrov, a participant in the I, II and III International Congresses on Psychotronic Research (at I in persons, and at the II and III only presenting papers—as all the others of us) has demonstrated that living systems have magnetic fields which interact and are connected with cosmic factors. He suggests that it is reasonable for yogis to believe that they can derive energy from the Cosmos.[5,6] When we utilize cosmic energy in our healing processes, the healing is more thorough than when only our own bio-energy is used. Not only human beings feel the difference. We carried out some official experiments, submitting other living systems to the influence of our methods. Reactions were much more impressive when certain gestures were made, combined with certain concentration-forms, to link these systems with cosmic influences. The difference was distinctly seen and heard via apparatus. However, as the related experiments are unfinished, we have no further data to reveal thus far.

We consider healing as a selective resonance to energy-information influence. It is selective because the irradiations select the sick persons among the participants (audience group, at times hundreds of persons) in the same way as leucocytes. They conform to certain natural laws which are not any the less objective because we ignore them. It is an information process, yielding certain data:

    a) lessening or removal of pain, discomfort, etc. (subjectively)
    b) lessening or removal of bruises, tumors, etc. (objectively)
    c) changes in blood pressure, EEG results, etc. (measurable)

The impulses stimulate the defensive and adaptationable mechanisms of the body, accelerating the energy exchange with the environment, including cosmic influences. The exchange—the "inhalation" and "expiration" of energy—proceeds via active body points with low resistibility, through which the energy balance of the bio-system (or unity of bio-systems) is restored.[7] The body's self-healing processes then may continue. Hence this healing technique is universal.

Our combined methods also include group-"submersions," "mutual harmonization," etc., conditioned by certain exercises which cause the group (audience) to react as one whole, one being. Certain physiological, psychological and social results[8] as well as moral and ethical alternations and developments caused by our Cosmos-contact methods, are registered.

The author considers the role of Man in Cosmic processes as a transducer of cosmic irradiations, generator of bio-cosmic fields, and instrumental in the life-processes of the bio-sphere.

More facts: the cataclymic explosion, known as the "Tunguska Mystery," which was followed by intense radiation, caused insect and plant mutations and other effects pointing to a "residual bio-physical field," says the newspaper, *New York Post* (October 23, 1978). According to the *Tass* report, (October 6, 1973) in the epicenter of the catastrophe, an anomalous increase of vegetation took place, and some other events occurred. "Neither the gravitational nor the electromagnetic field have such characteristics," says Prof. A Zolotov, who led the most recent expedition there. We may draw some conclusions about a type of concentrated cosmic irradiations with beneficial inflence, generated by as yet unknown factors,in positive proportions.

The participation of cosmic irradiations in healing and other beneficient processes is seen by the author as a manifestation of micro and macro Cosmos unity.

References

1. Chizhovsky, A. Terrestial Echo of Solar Storms, Edit, *Myal,* Moscow. 1976. p. 26.
2. Sergeiov, C. Magicial Crystal. *Niodiolia* (Journal). No. 36. Moscow, 1978.
3. Goncharov, N., Morozov, V., Makarov, V. Is the Earth a Huge Crystal? *Khimia y Zhiza* (Journal), No. 3. Moscow, 1974.
4. Neumann, V. Framework of the Universe. *Tekhnika-Molodiozhi* (Journal), No. 9. Moscow, 1973.
5. Ivanova, B. Prof. Dubrov's Theories. *International Journal of Paraphysics,* vol. 12, Nos. 3-4. Downton, England, 1978.
6. Dubrov, A. Geomagnetic Field and Life. *Geomagnetobiology,* Plenum Press, New York, 1978.
7. Ivanova, B. L'azione bioenergetica quale energo-inversione biologica. *Dimensione Psi,* Genoa, July-December 1975.
8. Ivanova, B. Experimental and training work on some group (mass)-harmonizing processes with educating, creativity-heightening, and healing results. *Proceedings of the III Int'l Congress on Psychotronic Research.* Tokyo, June 27-July 2, 1977.

SUGGESTED READING

BANDER, PETER. *Carry On Talking.* Colin Smythe Ltd., England, 1972.

BENDER, HANS. *Telepathie, Hellsehen u. Psychokinese.* R. Piper & Co., Munich. 1972.

BURR, HAROLD S. *The Fields of Life.* Ballentine Books. 1973.

EISENBUD, JULE, M.D. *The World of Ted Serios,* William Morrow & Co.

GELLER, URI. *My Story.* Praeger Publishers. 1975.

GREEN, ELMER & ALYCE. *Beyond Biofeedback.* Delacorte Press. 1977.

GRIS, HENRY & WILLIAM DICK. *The New Soviet Discoveries.* Prentice-Hall. 1978.

*HANSEL, C.E.M. *ESP and Parapsychology: A Critical Evaluation.* Prometheus Books. 1980.

JACOBSON, NILS, M.D. *Life Without Death.* Dell Books. 1974.

KARAGULLA, SHAFICA, M.D. *Breakthrough to Creativity.* DeVorss & Co. 1967.

KRIPPNER, STANLEY (ed.) *Advances in Parapsychological Research: 1 Psychokinesis.* Plenum Press. 1977.

LENS, SIDNEY, *The Day Before Doomsday—An Anatomy of the Nuclear Arms Race.* Doubleday. 1977.

MANNING MATTHEW. *The Link.* Colin Smythe, Ltd., England. 1974.

———— *In the Minds of Millions.* W. H. Allen, London. 1977.

———— *The Strangers.* W. H. Allen, London. 1978.

MISHLOVE, JEFFREY. *Roots of Coincidence.* Random House. 1975.

MITCHELL, EDGAR D. (ed. John White). *Psychic Exploration: A Challenge for Science.* G. P. Putnam & Sons. 1974.

MOSS, THELMA. *The Probability of the Impossible.* Hawthorn Books. 1974.

NAEGELI-OSJORD, HANS, M.D. *Die Logurgie in den Philippinen.* Otto Reichl Verlag. 1977.

*NOLEN, WILLIAM A. M.D., *A Doctor in Search of a Miracle.* Random House. 1974.

PANATI, CHARLES. *Supersenses: Our Potential for Parasensory Experience.* New York Times Book Co. 1974.

PELLETIER, KENNETH R. *Mind as Healer, Mind as Slayer.* Delacorte Press. 1977.

PUHARICH, ANDRIJA. *Uri.* Anchor Press, Doubleday & Co. 1974.

OSTRANDER, SHEILA & LYNN SCHROEDER. *Handbook of PSI Discoveries.* G. P. Putnam & Sons. 1974.

RAUDIVE, KONSTANTIN. *Breakthrough: An Amazing Experiment in Electronic Communication With the Dead.* Colin Smythe Ltd., Gerrards Cross, England and Taplinger, New York. 1971.

RHINE, LOUISA E. *Psi: What Is It?* Harper & Row. 1975.

ROGO, D. SCOTT & RAYMOND BAYLESS. *Phone Calls From the Dead.* Prentice-Hall. 1979.

RUSSELL, EDWARD. *Design for Destiny.* Neville Spearman, London. 1971.

SANDWEIS, SAMUEL. *Sai Baba: The Holy Man and the Psychiatrist.* Birth Day Publishing Co., San Diego, CA. 1975.

SCHRENCK-NOTZING, Dr. Albert v. *Materialisations Phaenomene.* Verlag Ernst Reinhardt, Munich. 1923.

SCHUL, BILL. *The Psychic Frontiers of Medicine.* Fawcett Publications, London. 1971.

SCHWARZ, BERTHOLD E., M.D. *Psychic Nexus: Psychic Phenomena in Psychiatry and Everyday Life.* Van Nostrand Reinhold Co. 1980.

SHERMAN, HAROLD & SIR HUBERT WILKINS. *Thoughts Through Space.* Fawcett Publications. 1973.

SIMONTON, O. CARL., M.D., STEPHANIE MATTHEWS SIMONTON & JAMES CREIGHTON. *Getting Well Again.* J. P. Tarcher. 1978.

STELTER, ALFRED. *PSI Healing.* Bantam Books. 1976.

TARG, RUSSELL & HAROLD PUTHOFF. *Mind Reach: Scientists Look at Psychic Ability.* Delacorte Press. 1977.

TAYLOR, JOHN. *Superminds.* Viking Press. 1975.

TOBIN, BOB. *Space, Time and Beyond: Toward An Explanation of the Unexplainable.* Dutton. 1975.

UPHOFF, WALTER H. & MARY JO. *New Psychic Frontiers: Your Key to New Worlds.* Colin Smythe, Ltd., Gerrards Cross, England. 1974, 1977, 1980.

LYALL WATSON. *Supernature: A Natural History of the Supernatural.* Hodder & Stoughton, London. 1973.

*Authors who maintain they have found no evidence for paranormal phenomena.

Articles and Papers:

COX, WILLIAM E., *Mentalism and Magicians.* Stamford College Press. Singapore.

Journal of the Society of Psychical Research, 1 Adam and Eve Mews, London.
    D. SCOTT ROGO. Theories About PK: A Critical Evaluation. 20 pp. June, 1980.
    J. B. HASTED. An Experimental study of the validity of metal bending phenomena. 19 pp. December 1979.
    WILLIAM BRAUD, GARY DAVIS AND ROBERT WOOD. Experiments with Matthew Manning. 25 pp. December 1979.
    CHARLES TART and ROBERT PALMER. Some PSI experiments with Matthew Manning. 5 pp. December 1979.

PUTHOFF, HAROLD E., RUSSELL TARG and EDWIN C. MAY. *Experimental PSI Research: Implications for Physics.* Stanford Research International. Menlo Park, CA. 30 pp.

TILLER, WILLIAM A. *Creating a New Functional Model of Body Healing Energies.* Department of Material Science, Stanford University, Stanford, CA. 30 pp.

INDEX

Palladino, Eusapia, **238-239**
Panati, Charles, **5, 137, 211**
Paraphysical Laboratory (Down ton), **178**
Parapsychological Association (PA), **102, 107, 148-149, 190, 212, 213, 219**
Pavlita, Robert, **210**
Pentagon (See *Department of Defense)*
Pflasterer, Carolyn, **121**
Philippine Society for Psychical Research, **180 226, 227**
Philippines, **13, 68, 82**
"Phillip" (the imaginary ghost), **226-227**
Piodos, Max, **194**
Planck, Max, **2**
Plasmaphysik Institut, **178**
Plume, Rev. Harold, **194**
Polaroid company, **142, 144, 147**
Poltergeist activity, **157, 168**
Pressman, Maurice, M.D., **127**
Princeton Alumni Weekly, The, **173**
Princeton University, **148**
Psychic News, **193, 228**
Psychical Research Foundation, **180**
Puharich, Andrija, M.D., **20, 167, 187, 194**
Pushkin, V. N., **211**
Puthoff, Harold, **101-103, 129-131, 137, 148, 151, 180, 199, 211, 213**
Psychokinesis (PK), **2-3, 5-6, 10, 21, 58, 68, 114, 122, 128, 146, 151, 153, 170, 181, 219, Chapter XIII**
physical behavior, **154**
psychological behavior, **154-155**

Quirk, Maurice, **41**

Rafone, Kay, **135**
Randi, James, **91-95, 118, 130, 149-150**
Raudive, Konstantin, **190**
Rauscher, Elizabeth, **240**
Reader's Digest, **129, 136-137**
Reynolds, Charles, **130**
Rhine, J. B., **130, 148**
Richards, J. T., **214**
Righ, Rich, **125**
Rindge, Jean, **151**
Robertson, D., **233**

Rockwell, Robert, **138-139**
Rockwell, Theodore, **138-139**
Rockwell, W. Teed, **138-139**
Roll, W. G., **180**
Roman, A. S., **211**
Roy, A. E., **177**
Rutgers University, **132**
Rutz, Dan, **10**

Safanov, Valdimir, **193, 207**
St. Clair, David, **194**
Sandell, David, **115, 117**
Sasaki, Shegemi, **21, 23, 68, 113, 146, 151, 158, 160, 162, 164, 179, 200**
Sauvin, Paul, **182**
Schiebeler, Werner, **151, 178, 189**
Schroeder, Lynn, **202**
Schwarz, Berthold E., M.D., **79-80**
Schindler, John, M.D., **193**
Schmitt, Otto, **83**
Schneider, Alex, **180, 190**
Schwanholz, Willi, **147**
Schweizer Parapsychologische Geselleschaft (Swiss Parapsychological Society), **180, 189**
Schweizerische Vereinigung fuer Parapsychologie, **180**
Science Magazine, **138, 149-150, 198**
Science Digest, **198**
Scott, Christopher, **142-143, 146**
Sergeev, Gennady, **209, 211**
Serios, Ted, **2, 4, 13, 140, 147, 170, 173, 217**
Severson, Roger, **8, 78, 80, 86, 91, 97, 114, 117**
Shafer, Mark G., **68, 172, 190, 219, 227**
Sheboygan Press, The, **120**
Sherman, Harold, **3, 11, 91, 119**
Shevchuk, Elvira, **206**
Shifrin, Avrahan, **209**
Sibley, Marjorie, **83**
Sibley, Mulford Q., **191**
Silicon photo-diode, **16**
Silvio, **2, 133, 169-170**
Simonton, O. Carl, M.D., **70**
Simonton, Stephanie Matthews, **70**
SIMUL, **15**
Sinclair, Upton, **176**
Singer, William, **193**